How Could He Do It?

How Could He Do It?

Emma Charles

preface

Published by Preface 2008

2 4 6 8 10 9 7 5 3 1

This book is a work of non-fiction based on the life, experiences and
recollections of the author. Names and places have been changed
solely to protect the privacy of others. The author has stated to the
publishers that, except in such minor respects not affecting the
substantial accuracy of the work, the contents of this book are true.

First published in Great Britain in 2008 by Preface
1 Queen Anne's Gate
London SW1H 9BU

An imprint of The Random House Group

www.rbooks.co.uk
www.prefacepublishing.co.uk

Addresses for companies within The Random House Group Limited can be found at:
www.randomhouse.co.uk/offices.htm

The Random House Group Limited Reg. No. 954009

A CIP catalogue record for this book is available from the British Library

Hardback ISBN 9781848090019
Trade Paperback ISBN 9781848090699

The Random House Group Limited supports The Forest Stewardship Council (FSC),
the leading international forest certification organisation. All our titles that are printed on
Greenpeace approved FSC certified paper carry the FSC logo. Our paper procurement policy
can be found at www.rbooks.co.uk/environment

Typeset in Spectrum MT by Palimpsest Book Production Limited,
Grangemouth, Stirlingshire
Printed and bound in Great Britain by
Clays Ltd, St Ives plc

To Tamsin and Sam, who make it all worthwhile.

Thanks to the following: to Giles, who battled valiantly for me; to Trevor, who believed in the book; to David, who made it a better book; to the staff and my fellow postgrads at the University of Edinburgh, who gave me sanctuary; and most of all, thanks to Mum and Dad, who are always there.

In many ways we were an ordinary family: mum, dad, two kids, three dogs, one rabbit, two guinea pigs. Mum stayed at home, studying with the Open University, and Dad worked, and the kids went to private schools. We lived in a rather nice semi in a rather nice area of Edinburgh, with a rather nice Volvo in the drive, and took rather nice holidays, wearing rather nice clothes. I loved Daniel deeply and I thought – no, I was sure – he loved me deeply, too. And we both loved our kids deeply (I thought). And that was as it should be. We had it made.

In some ways we weren't a completely ordinary family. There was Daniel, for one; he worked for most of the time we were married as a ship's engineer, and so he was away from home for up to four months and then home on leave for up to two. And his name: Schenker. His father's family came from Switzerland, where Daniel was born, and his father still owned a house and land there, but his parents were now settled in Glasgow. Tamsin, our older daughter, had specific learning difficulties and attended a specialist boarding school, and Claire, our younger daughter, had asthma.

But I'm just ordinary: an unlikely heroine. I am disabled because of back problems, and I use crutches outside the house. I'm pretty fat – I've put on a lot of weight through lack of exercise and, yes, comfort-eating! I've still got acne and I wear glasses. Not the stuff of movies.

But I never for a moment dreamt that my family was all that extraordinary – until that day.

10 December 1996

It started out as a good day, that early December Tuesday. Claire, who had just turned thirteen, was safely installed in her small private school for the day. Tamsin, who was fifteen, had an interview at Glasgow University for a place on an adventure trip to Sinai the following summer. As a treat she was allowed to wear the new clothes which were to be her Christmas present. She looked very smart and grown up in a short tartan kilted skirt and lambswool polo neck, topped by a chocolate wool blazer, and with gleaming brown boots on her feet. Her hair had just been cut to shoulder length and it framed her face in a shining chestnut sheet.

In high spirits we drove through to Glasgow and found the right building (just in time), and I waited in the car while Tamsin went in alone. Half an hour later she emerged beaming all over; it seemed the interview had gone very well. Then we set off to visit Daniel's parents for lunch.

It was always a bit of a strain visiting the in-laws. Mother made no secret of the fact that she wore the trousers, although

3

in the best possible taste, and this was even more evident since Father's stroke a couple of years previously, which had left him with a paralysed arm and leg, and not much short-term memory. I always got the impression Mother was trying to cause rifts between me and Daniel, which secretly amused me. It didn't stop until after Claire was born.

Anyway, it was a pretty average visit. Mother brought up the fact that I hadn't sent her any photographs of the girls for years (in a way that made it obvious that she was hurt, but wasn't going to complain – do mothers-in-law go through a training course in making you feel guilty?) and I promised to send some. I then realised that I had forgotten to bring my late uncle's stamp collection, left to Tamsin, for Father to value. At some point in the conversation, Tamsin called her father 'a silly boy' and was reprimanded by Mother, who made it clear that she thought I should have been doing the reprimanding. But that was a bit diffi-cult, since on that point I agreed with Tamsin.

Finally we were released and, as always when leaving there, the first thing I did while pulling out of the drive was to light a cigarette (Mother is a self-righteous ex-smoker). I was looking forward to spending some time with Tamsin during the Christmas holidays – I missed her during term time. She attended a specialist school for high-ability dyslexics as a weekly boarder (paid for by the local authority, I hasten to add – we have never been that well off), and had a month's holiday at Christmas and Easter because they didn't have any half-term holidays. We chatted as we drove along the motorway about how she would spend her holi-days. That was when the first hint of discord arose.

'Can I phone Jane tonight?' Tamsin asked casually.

'You phoned her last night,' I pointed out. 'We have to think of the phone bill,' for she had been on the phone to Jane for nearly an hour – Jane was a friend from school.

'Well, can I have my own phone for Christmas then?' persisted Tamsin.

'I don't think so!' I replied. 'Who's going to pay the bills?'

'I'll pay them out of my pocket money,' she replied.

'But we give you your pocket money, so we'll still end up paying them,' I explained. I wasn't prepared to give way on this, and began pointing out the sacrifices Daniel and I made for her and Claire. But for once, Tamsin was impervious to reasoned argument.

We arrived home and, feeling somewhat exasperated and ruffled, I went off to fetch Claire from school. She trailed out as usual, carrying her rucksack of books and wearing her version of school uniform. She could not wear tights then without developing eczema on her thighs; so in winter she wore black leggings under her school skirt. The skirt was almost full length, which was just as well as she insisted on wearing jodhpur boots under it. Her light blonde hair was cut in a chin-length bob, and the adult hairstyle and her height made her look much older than she was.

On the way home, Claire asked how the day had gone. I told her about Tamsin's demand for her own phone, and Claire seemed to agree that was somewhat unreasonable. But she could offer no explanation for Tamsin's behaviour.

The argument continued all through the evening. By now I was really puzzled and hurt. Tamsin began making personal attacks on Daniel and me, something she had never done. Again and again I pointed out that she and

Claire had everything we could afford to give them, and we did without things we wanted for their sake.

'So adopt me out!' snapped Tamsin.

I could not believe that this was my Tamsin; she was so unlike her usual self. We squabbled, like all mothers and daughters, but about tidying rooms and picking up mess and cleaning out the rabbit and guinea pigs – we never said hurtful, personal things to each other. At bedtime we did kiss goodnight as usual, but for the first time in Tamsin's life, we parted with an unresolved argument and a coolness between us.

11 December 1996

The next day I woke Claire, we walked our three dogs, and I took her to school as usual. No sound from Tamsin's room. I spent the day writing Christmas cards and pottering around. I heard occasional sounds from Tamsin's room, but she didn't come out. I was still hurt and angry, wondering where the argument had come from and what was the best way to handle it. For once, I decided, I would let Tamsin come to me. Often if we had a disagreement I would make the first move to reconciliation – after all, I was supposed to be an adult, I had to show her how adults resolve their difficulties. But not this time. If she was old enough to demand a phone, she was old enough to explain herself. Doubts crept in through the day – she did have learning difficulties; she'd had a hard time being bullied at her last school. But then I would catch myself softening, and resolve anew that this time it would be different. And so my thoughts see-sawed all day.

In the afternoon I fetched Claire from school.

'Has Tamsin said anything yet?' asked Claire in the car.

'Not a word,' I said grimly. 'I really don't know what's got into her, Claire, she's never behaved like this before.'

At home I decided that enough was enough and went into Tamsin's room, to find that she had actually been asleep most of the day.

'So, have you decided whether you want to be part of our family?' I asked, hating myself.

'Not bothered,' mumbled Tamsin, who had closed herself off from me.

'I don't believe I'm hearing this, Tamsin,' I stuttered, trying not to cry. 'We've done everything we can to make your life as good as possible.'

'You have no idea what I've been through,' she snapped.

'Okay, I know you had a tough time at your last school because of the bullying, but at least your mum and dad have always made sure you know we love you!'

'Maybe you love me too much!'

I recoiled, aghast, and began crying, against all my resolutions. Leaving Tamsin to stew, I wandered around downstairs. Claire was watching TV in the sitting room; I went into the dining room, where I found a pile of Tamsin's possessions lying where she'd dropped them when she came home from school the previous week. In a sudden fury I gathered them together and dumped them in Tamsin's room, saying, 'Well, if you're leaving home, you'll need these!' Then I returned to the sitting room and sat crying. I hated myself for not being able to handle it calmly, but I was also very angry and hurt. Claire was really upset too, and hugged me.

Suddenly, Tamsin burst into the room and flung a piece of paper at me. She called her dog and stormed out of the house while I was still trying to read and absorb the contents of the note.

'Your preshus Daniel has been after my tits and cunt for the last five years. I have to leave or he has to, and you seem to need him. And fuck you, you probly wont beleave me anyway.'

In those few seconds, my whole world came tumbling down. I could almost hear it. Bricks falling into rubble, like you see when a building is blown up. I could almost see the dust, and the dust obscured my vision, and the noise blasted my hearing, so that for a few moments I was blind and deaf.

Claire ran into the room. 'She's gone out and taken Sally, and she's got a bag with her! What's wrong, Mum, what's happening?'

Quickly I folded the note so that Claire couldn't see it. Some part of me was still hoping it was all a misunderstanding.

'It's about Dad. Run after her, I'll follow you in the car,' I cried, struggling to my feet and lifting the car keys. Claire ran out into the early evening gloom, and I climbed into the car. Wiping away more tears in an effort to see clearly, I backed out of the drive and drove around the corner to the main road, where I met Claire returning from the cycle track.

'She's not on the railway path,' she yelled.

Just then a woman whom we often met while walking the dogs, called over from the footpath.

'Are you looking for your daughter? She went down towards the shops.'

'Run after her, Claire,' I shouted, 'get hold of her and don't let go until I come, whatever she does!'

Claire sped down the main road as I turned our big Volvo and drove after her. Parking by the shops, I could see in the street lights that Claire was clinging to Tamsin's coat, while Tamsin tried to swing her off. Sally was barking as her lead became entangled in the girls' legs. I flung myself out of the car towards them.

'Come home and talk about this,' I begged desperately, but Tamsin wouldn't look at me and continued to throw Claire around.

I shouted Tamsin's name, grabbed her by the shoulders and made her face me; she looked up, startled. 'You can't say things like this and then walk away,' I continued more quietly, aware that we now had an audience of interested onlookers. 'Come home and tell me about it.' She had begun to turn away when I added, 'Nobody hurts my kids and gets away with it. Nobody!'

Tamsin looked into my eyes and must have been re-assured by what she saw. Silently she made her way to the car and climbed with Sally and her bag into the back, while Claire and I got in the front. At home I sent Claire up to her room. She was really frightened by now and crying bitterly, but I wanted to protect her if I could. Tamsin and I sat down in the sitting room.

'Well?' I asked in a conciliatory tone. 'Tell me about it.'

'He won't leave me alone,' she cried. 'He's always putting his arms round me and feeling me up. He brushes against my breasts so I know it's not accidental but he could persuade someone else it was.'

Hope blossomed in my mind. Maybe it was just a mis-understanding, an over-tactile father who would have to learn to respect his daughter's personal space.

'Has he ever touched you between your legs?' I asked.

Hope died.

'Last time he was home on leave,' she sobbed, 'I woke up one morning and he was all over me, and he put his fingers inside me!'

'Are you sure?' I pleaded, 'because you'll have to tell police and social services.'

She nodded. Aware that inside me an earthquake was beginning, I looked up the number, phoned social services and asked for a child protection officer. I could speak when spoken to; tears were falling from my eyes, but I couldn't attend to my feelings. I just knew I had to do the right thing, and that you were supposed to report abuse to social services. Eventually I was passed on to the duty child protection officer – a man, of course!

'Where is the child now?' asked the social worker.

'At home with me.'

'Where is the father?'

'He's in the Far East at the moment – he won't be back until January.'

'Oh, that's all right then,' replied the social worker happily. 'We'll send someone to see you tomorrow. Someone will phone you first thing.' As the sounds of my distress penetrated to him, he added in a gentler tone, 'This has obviously come as a shock to you, hasn't it?'

'Yes,' I mumbled through my tears.

'Well, try to get some sleep. We'll talk to you tomorrow. Bye.'

I put the phone down and, of its own volition, my body wracked itself in spasms of tears. Loud wails issued of their own accord from my mouth: I was horrified by the noise but powerless to stop it. I was appalled that Tamsin had been treated so; dimly aware that this spelt the end of my marriage, I was grief-stricken; and I was also very frightened. My whole world had shifted in a monstrous cataclysm, and somewhere inside I knew the shift was irreversible.

'I'm sorry, I'm so sorry!' howled Tamsin as she flung herself into my arms.

'It's NOT YOUR FAULT!' I yelled as loudly as I could. I could hear Claire sobbing in her room, and I said more calmly, 'Go and fetch your sister. Tell her to come down and see me.' I smiled through my tears to convince Tamsin that I was all right. 'Go on.' I nodded, and Tamsin ran upstairs. Claire burst into the sitting room and demanded, 'What's happened? You have to tell me, he's my dad too!'

'He's been touching your sister where he shouldn't,' I replied grimly, and her face blanched.

'He wouldn't do that, it's not true!' she gasped.

'I'm sorry, sweetheart, it is true,' I said, and she started to cry again. We rocked in each other's arms and Tamsin found us like that.

'I'm so sorry, Mum,' she said tremulously, but I began again the litany that I still repeat now.

'It's not your fault!'

'What's going to happen to us?' asked Tamsin anxiously.

'We're going to stick together and we'll be fine,' I said firmly. 'A social worker is coming tomorrow, and we'll work things out from there.'

I made a determined effort to stop crying and went to the kitchen to start dinner, but as soon as I was alone, the tears flowed again. It was as though my whole body had turned to salt water and was flooding out of me. Tamsin came up and gently took away the potatoes and knife.

'Go and sit down, Mum, I'll do it,' she said kindly.

I wandered back to the sitting room and found Claire crying quietly. I lit yet another cigarette and cuddled her. What can you say when your child's heart is breaking and you can't stop the pain or make it go away? Especially when your own heart is lying around in microscopic pieces.

My kids are wonderful. Claire began to comfort me and Tamsin kept popping her head round the door with updates on the fate of our meal.

When it came I tried desperately hard to eat it so as not to hurt Tamsin's feelings, but I couldn't eat much. It was really weird. My mind was working more or less normally but I couldn't stop crying. I lit one cigarette after another. Tamsin kept a constant supply of tea at my elbow.

The girls ate with me, and then went to the kitchen where I could hear them conferring. Tamsin came in.

'Who can we phone for you, Mum?' she asked gently. A part of me was vaguely amazed at the difference in her since she told me about the abuse — it was as if she had suddenly dropped the tons of chains which had been weighing her down for years, as I suppose she had. Suddenly she was an adult and in charge and capable, in a way she never had been before.

I mentioned my friend Jenny and the minister, George. Jenny didn't answer her phone but George did. Tamsin said merely that I was upset and needed to talk, and he offered to visit that evening.

I went to the kitchen for my painkillers, and paused in amazement — all the medicines had vanished from the cupboard.

'Just ask when you need something and I'll get it for you,' said Tamsin, appearing at my side with Claire.

'Where are all the drugs?' I asked in bewilderment.

'We were frightened you would take too many,' quavered Claire with tears in her eyes.

'I wouldn't do that to you,' I cried, the tears falling again. 'How could I leave you now when you need me most?' and I hugged them to me. 'I will never leave you!'

We clung to each other for a few minutes. Tamsin replaced all the drugs and topped up my tea, and I sat down again and lit another cigarette while trying to watch TV and to stop crying. But I couldn't. Claire sat with me while Tamsin washed up, and eventually I managed to dry myself up for a bit.

George arrived about eight o'clock; the girls let him in and then went upstairs. I had talked over problems with George before and knew him as a shy but kind man. I tried to tell him what had happened but couldn't. Mutely I passed him the note that Tamsin had written. He read it and looked at me.

'Do you know this is true?' he asked.

I don't know how I knew, I just did. Tamsin hadn't lied to me about anything since she was about six, and in my mind incongruities were clicking into place, events, incidents which had puzzled me at the time but now made sense. There were to be lots of those.

I can't remember now what George said, but somehow he turned the discussion to practicalities.

'What did the social worker say about telling Daniel that you know?' he asked.

'They didn't really say anything, someone is supposed to be coming tomorrow,' I replied in rising panic. 'I hadn't thought about that. What do I do if he phones?'

'It might be as well not to say anything just now, if you can do it,' he advised. 'It might be a good idea not to say anything to anyone until you have seen the social worker and the police.'

George stayed with me for a couple of hours and then took his leave. The girls came downstairs to see if I was all right, and the routine of bedtime began to unfold. Claire begged to be allowed to stay off school for the next few days and I agreed. The following evening there was to be a Christmas party at the dog-training class which Claire attended with her puppy Lucy, and it was agreed that Tamsin would take Sally and my dog, Fly. Claire insisted on giving me one of her teddy bears to cuddle, and would not be satisfied until I had promised I would cuddle it – she knows I always keep my promises. I sat with her in her room while she cried herself to sleep, and then Tamsin came with me into my room. We often had chats alone after Claire had gone to bed, but that night I was exhausted by the storm of emotion I was undergoing, and we didn't talk for long. I did discover that Tamsin's friend Jane knew about the abuse, and that was why Tamsin had so desperately wanted to talk to her every night. Tamsin fussed around making sure I had everything I needed, and finally took herself off to bed.

As soon as I was alone, the floodgates opened again. My eyes were so sore from crying that I could hardly keep them open, but even with the aid of my usual sleeping pill it was a long time before I slept. I kept going over our lives in my mind, trying to spot where it all began to go wrong, to see if there had been signs I should have picked up.

1977

It began as a holiday romance, but before the week was over I had decided that this was the man I wanted to marry. Ironically I went on holiday to get over the break-up of a long-standing relationship, and meeting someone else was the last thing on my mind. A week's R&R in the country-side, I thought. Just me and my dog, I thought. Wrong.

I arrived at the caravan site in Galloway in mid-afternoon on Easter Saturday and after unloading my van, I took my dog Polly for a walk along the lochside, saying 'Afternoon' to people I met, as you do. I said 'Afternoon' to a man who was fishing, but he didn't reply; so I thought 'Stuff you!' and walked on. The man turned around and said, 'They tell me there are fish in this lake, but I haven't found any!'

Well, of course, being a good Scot, I couldn't allow him to call a loch a lake! We started swapping fishing tales and somehow spent the whole afternoon sitting on the bank, talking. And yes, he did catch a fish, although it was so small he threw it back. We wandered back to the caravan site and made no plans to see each other again, but somehow I knew.

I went for another walk with Polly that evening, telling myself sternly not to be a fool, not to get caught again. Hadn't I just extricated myself from a very difficult relationship? Did I really want to start all that again? Well, yes, actually. He met up with us as we returned to our caravan, and came in for coffee. Of course one thing led to another – but when I wanted to call a halt, he wasn't too hard to dissuade. Golly, I thought, a gentleman to boot!

We had a magical few days, driving around, doing tourist things, having dinner – having dinner! On our first dinner date he split his head open on a low piece of guttering as we ran round the corner of the restaurant, out of the rain. We spent the next hour finding a doctor to stitch his head, but he insisted on going for dinner just the same. I was deeply impressed.

His name was Daniel Schenker and he was a ship's engineer. He was on leave, studying for the Part Two Second Engineer's certificate, and having a few days' holiday over Easter. He was very tall, over six feet three, and very slim. His hair and eyes were exactly the same as mine, a sort of auburn-coloured hair and blue-grey eyes. He had a full beard and moustache – I've never seen him without it. He was gentle, laid-back, easy-going – all the things I wasn't. I was a medical photographer, a job which paid quite well and gave me lots of holidays, but which I wasn't particularly good at. I was too busy trying to look efficient and capable to actually be efficient and capable.

I was thin in those days! My hair was waist length and dead straight, and I was very fit. I had just spent a winter climbing in the Highlands almost every weekend, and I walked Polly every day.

At the end of the week we became lovers before Daniel returned to Glasgow and college, and I to Edinburgh and work. We saw each other every weekend through that magical spring and early summer. We alternated between Glasgow and Edinburgh, and took Polly for many picturesque walks. He passed his exams and was immediately promoted to third engineer, but still had some leave to come.

By this time I was absolutely besotted with Daniel. Having spent most of his childhood in north-east England, he had a faint Geordie burr and, driving the van, working in the darkroom, lying in bed at night, I would find myself silently imitating the way he spoke. I was pretty useless at work, because all my attention was centred on Daniel, but I didn't really care. All I lived for were the weekends. When he touched me, I sort of fizzled inside. I was wildly happy, delirious, ecstatic.

I read recently that this form of extreme attraction is actually a sort of mental illness. I can well believe it. It colours everything you do, everything you say, everything you think, everything you are.

In July we went to Cornwall on holiday, and it was there, in St Ives, that we found the ring, in a little jewellery shop on the picturesque quayside. It was a beautiful diamond solitaire, set in eighteen carat gold, gleaming brightly in the deep shade of the window. Even I had to duck under the low lintel to enter the little shop, and Daniel was almost bent double! We looked at several other rings, but that one called to me. Even though it fitted perfectly, the jeweller was in no hurry to make a sale.

'Go away and think it over,' he advised. So we bought ice creams and sat on the little beach with Polly, and talked it over, and then returned to the shop and bought the ring.

Then we had to come home and face the parents. Mine were all right, they assumed I knew what I was doing, but his mother took some convincing.

'It's all been too fast,' she said, 'like a shipboard romance. You should slow down now. Spend a few years saving and give yourselves a good start.'

I always felt that I would not be Mother's first choice for a daughter-in-law. But we were adults — I was twenty-seven and he a year older. I had been married before, at the age of twenty-one, for a disastrous nine months; he never. I felt we were old enough to know what we wanted.

In August he went back to sea. He joined a ship in Miami: he might as well have dropped off the face of the earth. I wrote every couple of days. I phoned the shipping line once a week — 'Still in port in Miami.' I sank into a deep depression. Had I imagined it? Had it just been a shoreside flutter on his part? Surely not; but why didn't he write? I was even less use at work than before.

At last, after about a month of my increasingly desperate letters, he wrote. His story was that they were at anchor in the harbour, not alongside, and couldn't send mail — I found out later that he couldn't be bothered writing letters. But the good news was that they had a charter and would be in Liverpool in October, and he had been promoted again to second engineer.

Of course I went to Liverpool. I have always loved ships, ever since seeing my aunt off from Leith on a trip to

Aberdeen when I was about eight (they ran ferries in those days). We spent another two wonderful weekends together; although he was working during the day, the evenings and nights were ours. I donned a pair of overalls and went down into the engine room. One of the engines had been opened up, and we could stand together inside one cylinder. I had done some work on my car engine, but this was something else!

I had to return to Edinburgh before the ship sailed, but I had been reassured that the summer had not been a dream, that it was real and permanent. We had sorted out the letters issue (I thought) and had begun making plans for our life together. My short stay on the ship had whetted my appetite, and wives were allowed to travel with their husbands.

A month or so later I had a strange experience. I dreamt one night that there was a fire on board the ship, but that no one was hurt. Unusually I woke up with a very clear recollection of the dream, and wrote to tell Daniel. I was amazed when he replied that there had been a minor fire in the engine room, and no one was hurt. Ever since then, I have never worried about him when he is at sea, because I feel sure I would know if anything was wrong.

This experience just convinced me all the more that ours was a very special romance, a real fairy tale, destined for a happy ending. Life is full of irony.

December 1996

Eventually I slept, and woke the next day with sore eyes. I let Lucy out of Claire's bedroom, where she slept, and the other two out of the dining room, and put them in the garden while I made a cup of tea and had the first cigarette of the day. I felt like a wreck. I had so much to do, but I didn't know where to begin. I didn't really want to begin at all; in some strange way, as long as no one else knew, I could pretend it hadn't happened. I sat at the dining table with my head in my hands, thinking: protect the kids; how can we afford to stay here? do we want to stay here? how do we get another house? I've got no income.

Suddenly I sat bolt upright. My trust! I had to protect that, it was the only asset I really had. Before you go thinking 'rich heiress', let me explain. I used to have an uncle, Uncle Bob — well, he wasn't even a real uncle, he married my grandmother's cousin. Uncle Bob was a Heriot's old boy who had emigrated to Canada as an office boy and ended up as managing director of the company. Apparently when

I was born his first wife had been in Scotland, buying antiques for the American market, and she absolutely fell in love with me. They didn't have any children of their own, and I'm told I was a fetching baby. When Uncle Bob met me as a toddler, he fell in love with me too. I don't remember meeting him until I was about ten, when he appeared bringing the most enormous doll and lots and lots of cuddles. After that, we wrote to each other almost every month, for years and years, and we saw each other whenever he visited the UK.

His first wife died, and he married again quite soon after, but within a year or two he was widowed again. When I was about eighteen, he married a childhood sweetheart − she was the only 'aunt' I ever knew well. They settled in Edinburgh, but were off travelling the world for a good part of the year. He visited Kenya every year because one of his brothers lived there, and he always brought me back a little carved animal. I still have every one, although one of the lion's legs broke, and the rhino's horn. They took many cruises, often on the *Canberra* because they found the *QE2* too stuffy and formal, and sent regular postcards from exotic places. Just after Daniel and I were married, they moved back to Canada for tax reasons, and I saw him only a few more times. He died in 1993, and left an unfillable hole in my life.

A few months after he died, I was contacted by the executor of his will. Uncle Bob had left me thirty per cent of his estate, $75,000. I was absolutely flabbergasted! He had left his step-grandchildren fifteen per cent each, and so he had given me what might be thought of as a daughter's share. I never knew until then just how highly he regarded me. Why are we so reticent? I didn't spend as much time with him as I could have when he was alive, because I didn't want him to think I was pestering him. Now I realise he probably felt I thought he was a boring old duffer, and didn't want to push himself on me. How I wish we had been more open with each other – what a waste!

Anyway, Uncle Bob's estate was to be put in trust for his wife and his surviving brother, who lived in Toronto, and after both of them died, I would receive $75,000. The will had specifically mentioned me, not us as a couple, and I quickly realised I needed to make a new will, so that Daniel couldn't lay claim to the money. But I also needed to find a new lawyer, someone who didn't know Daniel, to protect the trust. I didn't want to pick someone out of the phone book. I decided to phone a friend from church that evening. Her son had recently graduated with a law degree – surely he would know of a good firm.

I called the girls and we had breakfast together. They took the dogs for a walk while I phoned Claire's school. I spoke to the headmistress, Mrs Lucas, whom I knew quite well, and told her what had transpired, somehow managing not to cry – well, only a little! She was predictably horrified, and understood that Claire needed a few days at home, but hoped she would return to school for the final few days of term the following week. Then I asked about the fees. Daniel was due home in January, and I had no idea whether he would go on paying them. She suggested I should write to the governors and ask if Claire could be allowed to stay one term without fees, while we arranged another school. It was just a small school, not rich, and couldn't afford to provide education for anyone without fees.

The next phone call was to the social work department. I needed to know whether I should keep our knowledge secret until Daniel returned; and I desperately needed to know what I was supposed to do next. They were quite vague about telling people, and thought they might be able to arrange an interview for the following day. They didn't want Tamsin to be interviewed more than once, and so they had to wait until a police officer from the Sexual Offences Unit could be present. I came off the phone feeling quite abandoned and bewildered, and crying yet again. I resolved then that until I had spoken to the police, I would tell only those who needed to know. Then I had to dry my tears hastily because I could hear the girls returning with the dogs.

Somehow we got through the day. The girls were cheerful, looking forward to that evening's party at the dog club, and we spent some time making fancy dress for the dogs. I found an old pillowcase and sewed strips of tape on it. Then we drew, coloured and cut out lots of paper watches and stapled them to the pillowcase, which then went on Fly like a horse's blanket. She was going as a 'watch dog'! Tamsin rummaged through the toy box and found the Punch and Judy puppets; I sewed a colourful ruff for Sally, and she went as Punch's dog. Claire found some doll's clothes and an old nappy, and Lucy patiently submitted to being dressed up as a baby.

In the afternoon I had a rest while the girls watched a video. I managed to get some sleep, but it was punctuated by bad dreams. I woke unable to remember any details, just the feeling of foreboding and menace.

Later in the afternoon I spoke to my friend, who rang back shortly after with the name of a law firm recommended by her son. Then after dinner I took the girls and dogs along to the dog-training club, and drove home, intending to phone my friend Jenny. She had been my Open University tutor that year, but we had soon become fast friends.

Imagine my horror when I pulled into the drive and saw Daniel's sister, Susan, standing on the footpath. Her daughter Fiona was at college in Edinburgh, and she had come to collect Fiona's belongings, so that Fiona could travel back to their home in Dundee by train at the end of term. Susan had thought it was a good excuse to drop off our Christmas presents at the same time. Fortunately I had theirs all packed and ready to post.

I don't quite know how I got through the next hour, making tea and chatting about the children. Susan had two children besides Fiona, all younger. Her husband had died a few years before in a car crash.

About half an hour into the visit, I suddenly realised that the note which Tamsin had scribbled the day before was lying casually folded on a coffee table, right next to where Susan was sitting! I didn't dare pick it up – that would just have drawn attention to it. I tried to keep my eyes away from it so that Susan wouldn't see me looking at it. I sat on tenterhooks, trying to be casual; and fortunately she paid it no heed. We're not the tidiest family, and I guess to anyone else it looked like just another piece of clutter.

I never considered telling Susan what had happened. I wasn't yet angry with anyone, and certainly not Daniel's family; if anything, I felt sorry for them, knowing what they were going to have to face.

Finally, at about eight o'clock, Susan left to go to Fiona's. I took a deep breath, lit a cigarette (Daniel's family are all fanatical anti-smokers) and phoned Jenny. I was so relieved when she picked up the phone that I started to cry again as I told her what had happened. She was silent as I told her of Tamsin's dreadful revelations; she asked some pertinent questions.

'I'm so sorry, Emma,' she said at last. 'I thought you were the one person I knew who was happy. You seemed to have your life all sorted out.'

'Tell me about it!' I replied shakily.

'How long has this been going on?' she asked.

'For about five years,' I replied.

'Mmm,' Jenny mused, 'about the same time you became disabled – that'll be his excuse!'

'It's no excuse at all,' I said in amazement. 'We never stopped having a sex life!'

'Oh, I didn't mean it like that,' she said hastily, 'but that's probably what he'll say. If it was only sex he wanted, there are plenty of prostitutes in Edinburgh! Sex abuse is more about power and control than about sex. I just thought maybe you should be prepared for him to say something like that.'

'I think it's more significant that it began just about the time I stopped him from smacking the girls,' I said.

'Oh, yes, that's much more important!' replied Jenny.

'I just don't understand how all this could be going on in the house, and I knew nothing about it!' I burst out. 'How could I be so stupid? People are going to think I knew and just turned a blind eye!'

'But you didn't know, did you?' asked Jenny.

'No, of course not! I'd have sliced him into bits if I'd thought for one moment—'

'People will know that,' Jenny said gently. 'Some women

might put up with it for the sake of keeping their man, but anyone can see that you're not like that.'

We talked on for ages. Jenny was brilliant. She nurtured me, supported me, talked through some of the practical issues and all of the emotional ones. 'You're strong!' she urged. 'You'll get through this! You just have to take one day at a time, and lean on all your friends as much as you need to. I'm always here if you need me.'

After an hour or so, feeling a bit more together, I collected the girls. I looked at Tamsin in surprise. I hadn't seen her so happy for years. Any doubts I might have had dissolved then – it was worth anything to make Tamsin happy again.

Some people have expressed amazement that I just accepted Tamsin's word when she told me her father had been abusing her, without first giving Daniel a chance to have his say. I can't explain it. Partly it was because I knew from reading about the subject in newspapers and magazines that children seldom, if ever, lie about abuse. Partly it was because I knew that Tamsin was a truthful person. Claire still sometimes tried to lie her way out of trouble, but if Tamsin did something wrong, she just owned up and copped what was coming. But mostly it was that somewhere deep inside me, I knew she was telling the truth. Odd bits of behaviour and events began to click into place, a process which went on for a very long time.

Once again, Tamsin went off to bed quite happily, while Claire cried herself to sleep. At last I reached my own bed and in spite of having resolved to blank my mind and go to sleep, I couldn't help crying as I remembered . . .

1978–1980

The four months without Daniel had been like a desert in my life. I lived from one letter to the next, and carried them with me everywhere. There was a rapturous reunion when Daniel came home on leave in January: I couldn't let him out of my sight, and wanted to be touching him every second. I couldn't wait for us to be married so that I would never have to be separated from him again. But there were practical issues to sort out first.

We immediately started house-hunting. Neither of us liked cities, and I wanted to travel with Daniel more than I wanted to continue my career; and so we decided to live in Carlisle, which Daniel already knew and I loved the first time I visited.

Daniel showed me a whole new way of life. We stayed in hotels, which I had never done before; we went out for dinner often, again a new experience for me. I had always just scraped by financially, but Daniel had money and was more than willing to share it. He was well paid and didn't have the same expenses, living on board so much of the time.

We bought a little two-up two-down terraced house in Carlisle. It needed lots of renovation, but we saw it as an adventure. The wedding date was set for August, and we began arranging for a new damp course, woodworm treatment and central heating to be fitted after our honeymoon. We took possession at the beginning of April: I finished work in Edinburgh then, and we moved in together right away. I already had a single bed, but we had arranged to have a king-size bed made that was seven feet long, to accommodate Daniel's legs! It wasn't delivered until a week or so after we moved in, but until then we slept on lilos on the floor. We had bought a king-size duvet, and material to make sheets, covers and pillowcases. I still had quite a lot of household goods from my first marriage, and we bought the essentials, hoping that wedding presents would fill some of the gaps.

Two weeks later Daniel was off to sea again, this time to the Far East. I signed up with a secretarial agency in Carlisle and worked as a temp, spending the time between jobs using the sewing machine Daniel bought me for Christmas to put together a trousseau.

Daniel arrived home a week before the wedding. Everything went to plan – we had a marvellous day, just close family and friends, but it was what we wanted. We drove home that night and, even though we had been lovers for more than a year, that night was truly special! Truly spectacular! The following week we went to Belgium for ten days for our honeymoon. It was the first time I had ever been abroad, and I loved it. I still love travelling.

I loved being Daniel's wife. I loved the fact that now

nothing could separate us. I loved Daniel more than I had ever loved anyone before, and I never got tired of being with him. It didn't matter what we did, so long as we did it together.

We came home from our honeymoon to find that our order for the damp course had gone astray. The firm who were dealing with the woodworm took it over, but couldn't start for six weeks. Daniel and I hacked off all the plaster on the ground floor to shoulder height, and then Daniel left to join a small container ship on a charter between Felixstowe and the Middle East. I couldn't go with him yet: I couldn't leave Polly, and someone had to stay at home and sort out the house. It didn't get any easier, watching Daniel leave. I accompanied him to the station where he was to catch the sleeper to London, but I had to go. Daniel had made it quite clear that he didn't want tearful scenes, and I couldn't stop myself crying.

For the next six weeks I lived in our bedroom, with a camping stove for cooking and a fan-heater for warmth. Despite that, Polly and I were so cosy and happy. Letters were few and far between, but apparently mail from the Middle East was unreliable. Eventually all the work was done, and before Christmas I had decorated the sitting room and reclaimed the kitchen. In December I went to Felixstowe to visit the ship for a weekend and, a month later, joined the ship for the last month of Daniel's trip, putting Polly in kennels.

It was so exciting! We went to Bremerhaven and Amsterdam before setting off for the Mediterranean. We managed to get some time ashore together in the evenings. There was only a single berth in Daniel's cabin, but we didn't mind – we slept so closely together that it didn't make much difference.

It snowed while we were crossing the North Sea: it was so eerie seeing the snowflakes falling on the deck by the light of the masthead lamps, while all around was darkness.

After leaving Amsterdam it took five days to reach the Mediterranean, and as we rounded the Algarve coast one evening we ran into some rough weather. The ship had very flared bows, and we were heading straight into the storm. The bows would rear up violently before cresting the wave and sliding down the other side. Then the ship shuddered to a halt as she hit the bottom of the trough, before beginning the whole cycle again.

The next morning I joined the captain for breakfast in the mess room.

'How are you today?' he asked, looking up brightly and, somehow, expectantly.

'Fine, thanks,' I replied, sitting down and reaching for the menu. The captain's face fell, and he finished his coffee and left the mess. I discovered later that the crew were running a book on how long it would take me to become seasick. Daniel won, because he said never, and he was right!

The weather improved after a couple of days, and we sailed along the Mediterranean to Port Said, and through the Suez Canal. What an experience! I spent all that day on the monkey island – the roof of the bridge – taking photographs with a telephoto lens. Although she was a small ship, I was high enough to be able to see across to the Sweetwater Canal, which contains fresh water (the Suez Canal is salt water). It's a bit like a long, narrow, continuous oasis, populated by Arabs in flowing white robes, camels, dogs, little white brick houses. It was just like a scene from a child's bible.

Late in the afternoon we spent an hour or two in the Bitter Lakes, to allow the northbound convoy to pass us. I suggested a swim, but quickly decided against it when the first mate described the size of the local sharks. We had a slight problem on leaving – when the anchor appeared out of the water, a major power cable was draped over it! After that the first mate was called the 'Big Fisherman'.

We sailed on into the Gulf of Aqaba and up to Aqaba itself. We passed the desert of Sinai, which I viewed with awe, remembering the story of Moses. The first thing I saw in Aqaba was a customs officer walking along the quay, his SLR gun slung over his shoulder. Needless to say I didn't explore much. Daniel was working; as soon as the main engine stopped, the engineers had to pull a piston and clean out the cylinder. This happened every time we were in port overnight, and put a bit of a dampener on trips ashore.

We stayed overnight in Aqaba and next morning I woke as we left the Gulf of Aqaba and sailed on to Jeddah. Here I did go ashore, with the electrician and one of the sailors. We had to leave our passports at the gate for security, but I thought nothing of it as we strolled into the souk. I bought myself a beautiful caftan, and we headed back to the docks. Imagine my panic when I couldn't find my passport. They were left in a box on the counter of the guard hut, and people took their own as they returned. I was beginning to get seriously frightened, and thinking of asking the electrician to go and fetch the captain, when the guard stirred himself from his somnolent slouch in the corner of the hut and emptied out the box. There was my passport — it had slipped down and was lying flat under the others. What a relief!

After Jeddah we sailed south through the Red Sea to Hodeidah, in North Yemen. In the evening I went ashore with the electrician, just to stretch our legs. There was a gunboat at the end of the jetty, with some guards slouched around as usual. We must have crossed an invisible line on the jetty as we strolled towards them, for suddenly they were standing up straight and lifting their rifles. The electrician and I did a smart about turn and strolled back to our ship!

We sailed straight back to Felixstowe from Hodeidah, north through the Red Sea to Suez. I spent an hour sunbathing one day — I hadn't brought any sun protection as I didn't think it would be hot in January. But by evening it became apparent that I was badly burnt all down my back. It was two days before I could sit. Since then I have always been fanatical about sun protection.

Only two things marred the excitement of that trip: the cook and the donkeyman. They shared a crate of beer for breakfast; every morning at eight o'clock you could see the empty crate sailing out of the cook's cabin porthole to splash down in the sea. The food was quite appalling, but there was nothing else to eat. The donkeyman wasn't much use either, and Daniel had tried to have him dismissed before discovering that he and the chief engineer were best mates. So Daniel and the chief were constantly at loggerheads. I was surprised to see what a childish attitude Daniel took. He got very steamed up about petty things, and made a real enemy of the chief; not a wise move.

We returned to Felixstowe, to one of the worst winters for years. Once home, we renovated the kitchen, fitting new units and decorating. We were so pleased with our cosy little house. The only blot on the horizon was the fact that Daniel was demoted to third engineer because of his arguments with the chief.

Polly died while we were home. It was a terrible blow to me, because she was the first dog I had which was mine, not shared. But she'd had a good life, and she died peacefully, and I suppose that's all you can ask. And it did free me to accompany Daniel full-time.

We were together all the time for the next year and a half. We spent one trip on a huge bulk carrier, sailing between Sweden and Canada. There was much more time on shore, and together at that. The trip after that was to the Far East, a dream come true for me. I had heard so much about Hong Kong, Singapore and other ports from Daniel, and was thrilled that at last I was to see them for myself.

There was hardly a cross word between us. We were so much in love, and we faced the world as a team. We had a wonderful life, filled with joy, fun and laughter, and looked forward to more of the same for ever.

December 1996

The next day, the social worker called to set up an appointment with the police and Tamsin for ten o'clock the following Monday. I suppose they weren't in any rush because they knew Tamsin was safe for a few weeks; but it was terribly frustrating for me. Without having heard what Tamsin had to say, the authorities couldn't really give me any advice about what to do next; and I didn't want to question Tamsin, partly because I didn't really want to know any more than I already did, and partly because I had some vague recollections about not coaching witnesses.

I also made an appointment with the solicitor for the following Tuesday, so that I could change my will. The person I spoke to asked if I wanted advice on divorce as well, and although I hadn't given it much thought, I realised that I needed to do something about that, too. I suppose I didn't want to think about divorce – in some strange way, the Daniel who had abused his child had become separated in my mind from the Daniel I thought I knew and loved.

Perhaps it was because he was so far away, and we weren't communicating. And there was a constant, faint air of un-reality about those days.

We spent a fairly normal weekend, doing weekend things like shopping and washing. I had a private home help, a lovely woman called Chris, who came three times a week. I told her what had happened and asked her to keep it quiet. She was very supportive.

I didn't go to church on Sunday. I really couldn't face it – I was still collapsing in tears at frequent intervals, and singing in the choir, as I did, you are on show to the whole congregation. And if I didn't go into the choir, people would want to know why, and I couldn't tell them. While I was having tea in bed that morning, Alison phoned. She was more a friend of my parents than mine, but I usually gave her a lift to and from church as she lived quite close. I told her what had happened, and explained I wouldn't be going. I got the impression that she thought that Tamsin might be exaggerating, but she was very supportive, and offered her help if ever needed. I also called the choirmaster's wife, whom I had known for about thirty years, to explain why I wouldn't be at church for a week or two. She was appalled.

'Stupid man!' she spat. 'How could he be so stupid?'

The most un-normal thing that weekend was that Claire kept disappearing. I found her, time after time, crying on my bed, hugging Lucy and her teddy.

'I want my daddy back!' she would wail. I felt so helpless – it still brings tears to my eyes today to remember how much she was hurting. We cuddled together and cried together: I wanted my 'normal' husband back too, but I knew it couldn't be. Claire had always worshipped her daddy, even though he had never had much time for her, and she was utterly heartbroken. Alison said to me, 'It would have been better if he had died rather than do this!' and I have to agree. Not only had we lost our husband and father; all our memories were now tainted. Even today, Claire doesn't like remembering his cuddles, because she can't be sure whether he was giving her an affectionate hug or himself a cheap thrill.

On Sunday evening Tamsin became quite upset and agitated, as the time for her interview drew closer.

'Have I really done the right thing?' she asked me at bedtime.

'Of course you have!' I exclaimed. 'Nobody has the right to treat you that way. It's not your fault. Even if you danced the dance of the seven veils and begged him to take you, he should not have touched you.'

'But what are we going to do about money?' she quavered with tears in her eyes.

I don't know,' I replied honestly. 'But your dad will have to support us, and he earns plenty, so we should be all right.'

'But what if he won't give us any?'

'He won't have a choice,' I replied darkly. 'If he doesn't do it voluntarily, the Child Support Agency will make him. And in the meantime we'll get income support or something. We'll manage!' I repeated firmly, although inside I was asking myself the same questions, and feeling far from reassured about the future. But I didn't want Tamsin worrying about it. 'The most important thing is to keep you safe from him, and to do that you need to talk to these people tomorrow. And then we'll hear from them what we do next.'

'So I really should talk to these people tomorrow?'

'Tamsin, it's the only way we can protect you. You shouldn't feel guilty about anything – it's not your fault! Dad is the criminal here, and you're the victim!'

Tamsin went up in a sheet of flames. 'I'm not a victim!' she yelled.

This was obviously a very sore point with her. I tried to explain, without actually using the word 'victim', that she shouldn't blame herself for anything. In fact, I wished she had told me years ago. Then I discovered that she had been trying to protect Claire and me. She didn't want to be responsible for breaking up the family.

'You're not responsible!' I repeated over and over. 'It's not your fault, none of it is your fault, it's Dad who is to blame for everything!'

Eventually she was reassured and went off to bed. I went in to see Claire, because a horrible thought had just occurred to me. I sat on her bed and stroked her golden hair. As gently as I could, I asked her if her dad had ever touched her.

'He used to come and give me back rubs,' she replied. 'But I liked that.'

'Nothing else?' I asked.

'He asked me to take off my tee shirt, but I just said no. And once he tried to give me a tummy rub, but I wouldn't let him,' she replied.

'That's fine,' I said. 'I just wondered.' I stayed with her until she fell asleep, then after checking that Tamsin was asleep too, I went to bed. It was becoming clearer now. Claire has always been an up-front, in-your-face kind of kid. Whenever anything was worrying her, she would come

1980–1984

Before I met Daniel I quite definitely did not want children. It was he who felt that we wouldn't be a 'proper family' without them. He loved spending time with other people's children. (It's only as I write this that the significance hits me!) I was never any good with children, I never knew what to say to them. But Daniel was happy to talk and play, and I felt that he would be a good dad. What an irony – he was the only man I ever met whom I trusted enough to be the father of my children.

He was the eldest son of the eldest son back to about 1750, and I suppose he felt it incumbent upon him to produce a family heir. He never really explained why he wanted children; I loved him so much that if he wanted a child, that was fine by me, I would give him a child.

I fell pregnant two years into our marriage, while we were holidaying with Daniel's grandmother on the family farm in Switzerland. We had been 'trying' for a baby for almost a year, without success. Every month when my period came,

I was devastated. Another of life's little ironies: I thought back over all the times in my life when my period had been late and I had worried myself sick in case I was pregnant. It never occurs to you when you're young that you might not be able to have children. So when it finally happened, we were both thrilled to bits.

We immediately began to look for a 'proper' house with a garden, and found it in a little village east of Carlisle. I moved in February 1981 while seven months pregnant. Daniel was in Venezuela, but my parents and sister helped, and soon I was happily buying and painting nursery furniture, and knitting little garments.

We were joined by a new dog, a working sheepdog called Penny. I had done a bit of obedience training with my first dog, but not very much, and I was keen to have a dog I could compete with. She was lovely! I discovered that you get a mind-link with Border collies and working sheepdogs which you just don't get with other breeds. By the time she was six months old, Penny was already showing a great deal of promise.

I didn't have an easy pregnancy. When I was about four months pregnant I contracted a kidney infection, which made me feel very rough. Then just after we moved, my blood pressure shot up and protein was found in my urine. I had pre-eclampsia and had to go into hospital for a week's bed rest. That was a very lonely week, with no Daniel around, although my parents visited most days. Once home, I had to rest most of the time.

The pre-eclampsia was kept under control until the baby was due. Daniel came home about a week before, so that when it was decided that the birth should be induced, he was there by my side. I had been to the hospital classes and felt quite confident of managing the birth; but induced births are notoriously hard, because the labour proceeds much more quickly than in a natural birth. I couldn't understand what I was doing wrong. The midwife repeatedly said how good I was at relaxing, but if that were so, why did it hurt so much?

Late in the afternoon, one of the midwifery sisters popped her head around the door. 'Look at her!' she snorted. 'She thinks she's having a hard time, and she's having a perfectly normal labour!'

Well, that did wonders for my self-esteem, already at rock bottom! I felt as if it was never going to end. I wanted to go home and come back another day. I was tired and hungry, but not allowed to eat in case anything went wrong and I needed an anaesthetic. I was also full of pethidine – it's not a very effective painkiller, I found, but it removed all my self-control. When Tamsin was finally born, all I felt was relief. I was more concerned about whether I would need stitches than whether the baby was all right.

It never occurred to either of us that we wouldn't have a boy. All our plans were centred around a boy, and when Tamsin was born I was bitterly disappointed, and afraid that Daniel would leave us because of it. Such are the rationalities of pregnancy.

Tamsin was born at five to six in the evening and, after checking that we were both all right, Daniel rushed off to phone his mother. He came back mumbling something about her not speaking to him. I was exhausted, both physically and emotionally, and so doped up that I didn't really take in what he was saying. I wanted him to say that it was all right having a daughter, that he loved us, that everything would be fine. But he didn't. He sloped off home because he was exhausted, too. All that night I worried that he would leave. He felt under so much pressure to produce a son – would he now find another wife who would give him a son? I knew, of course, that the sex of a baby is determined by the male, but I wasn't thinking very clearly.

Of course he didn't leave, and it took only a very short time before I loved Tamsin more than I had ever loved anything or anyone. You would have thought we were the only mother and baby ever to have lived. All my life revolved around Tamsin, and I expected everyone else to feel the same as I did. I must have been hell to live with.

I loved being a mother. I loved bathing and feeding Tamsin; I loved doing the washing and hanging the nappies out in the garden. I loved taking her for walks in the pram through the village. I expected Daniel to love the same things. He bathed her, fed her, walked the floor with her when she had colic, but only if he felt like it. His needs always came first. Maybe that was the first sign of trouble. Maybe he felt neglected. I know lots of men do, but I'm afraid I find it exasperating. Men are supposed to be adults, to be able to take care of themselves. Babies manifestly can't, and there is so much work involved in looking after a tiny baby that most women don't have the time or the energy to pamper their men. Why should the man be pampered? He isn't even doing most of the work.

The situation wasn't helped by the fact that Daniel was made redundant just after Tamsin's christening. It wasn't too bad at first. He qualified for a sort of unemployment benefit from the merchant navy which was enough to pay the mortgage and the bills. Daniel decided to take the opportunity to do Part Two of the Chief Engineer's certificate – he had done Part One while I was pregnant and passed with flying colours. It wasn't the same for Part Two – he failed all but one exam.

In the meantime, I had been persuaded against my will to allow Tamsin to be inoculated against whooping cough. There had been a lot of publicity about the risks involved, and I had a very strong gut feeling that Tamsin shouldn't have it. But everyone else – Daniel, parents, friends – thought that I was making a fuss about nothing (as usual), and so I agreed. The first injection caused no trouble, but the day after the second, Tamsin's temperature shot up. She stopped eating and sleeping, and for the next three and a half years had constant ear and throat infections – not serious in themselves, but the accumulated effects were.

I was frantic. Tamsin could throw a temperature of 102 degrees just from being overtired, and I seemed to spend an awful lot of my life at the surgery. I felt I had made a terrible mistake, and wanted someone to take, or at least share, the responsibility for my poor damaged child. Eventually I learnt to cope, and that I really was the best person to care for Tamsin. That was to stand me in good stead later.

When Tamsin was approaching her first birthday, Daniel finally found a job. He had been pretty down about failing his exams, but I was too busy looking after Tamsin to spare much time for him. He began working on oil rig supply ships in the North Sea, first as third engineer, then as second. Gradually I learnt to cope with Tamsin, and our lives began to get back on an even keel.

Daniel's attitude to Tamsin changed as she grew from a baby into a toddler. He had been very good with her as a baby — when he wanted to! — but once she became a toddler, he began to treat her as if she were some strange species of creature which had to be watched constantly if some catastrophe were not to occur. His idea of looking after Tamsin was to shut himself in the sitting room with her and sit and watch as she played. He didn't seem to know how to interact with her. I repeatedly tried to encourage him to build a relationship with her while she was small. It was almost as if he was waiting for her to become a human, and then he would have a relationship with her. But it doesn't work like that. You have to start building the parent-child relationship from the day the child is born, and it's a continuing process. In some ways I suppose it was difficult as he was away from home for six weeks at a time; but then, he had six weeks' leave to do nothing but be at home and spend time with us. In many ways he had more free time than most fathers.

At that time Daniel was still very much the person I had married. I used to get frantic when Tamsin was ill, and I was constantly tired because I was awake half the night with her. He was the one who would calm things down, and take Tamsin for a walk when I got too fraught to deal with her. In spite of his difficulty in relating to Tamsin as a person, I never had any doubt that he was a good father. He just needed time to learn how to relate.

And I never had any doubts about our relationship. Daniel was the first person in my life who always made it clear that he loved me, even if he was fed up with my behaviour. It was his steadfast love which gave me the courage and confidence to grow personally, and I will always owe him a debt for that. Even in the thick of our difficulties, our love for each other never wavered. When I behaved like a spoilt, petulant child, he was calm and loving, taking Tamsin for a walk with Penny when I needed a break, listening to my ranting and raving about the unfairness of life, steadying me when I was worried about Tamsin.

By the time Tamsin was eighteen months old, we were beginning to think about another child. We were financially stable again, our relationship seemed secure, and we really wanted another baby. I was afraid that Daniel might rest all his hopes on a boy, and was determined not to go through that trauma again. We talked it over repeatedly, with me arguing that we had to want another child, not just a son, and I believed that Daniel had agreed.

When Tamsin was two and a half, Claire was born. I had a much easier pregnancy, although I felt sick all the time. Having felt disappointed with the hospital antenatal classes, this time I booked myself in for National Childbirth Trust classes, which turned out to be infinitely superior. The birth began naturally and, although the labour was much longer, I felt in control nearly all the time. I didn't have any pethidine, just gas and air for the final half-hour. When Claire was born, she was put straight into my arms. I saw her first breath; I saw her skin change from blue to pink; I saw her open her eyes to the world for the first time. I loved her deeply from the moment of her birth.

I was delighted to have another daughter, but I think that Daniel was really disappointed. I had made it clear before becoming pregnant that I wasn't going to have a third child; I felt that two were enough to cope with alone, and I thought that Daniel had agreed. He never said anything about wanting a boy instead, or another child, and I thought he had accepted that our family was to consist of two girls.

Claire was given all the 'girly' things that Tamsin hadn't had. She was dressed in frilly pink outfits where Tamsin had worn blue dungarees, and she revelled in it. I had spent a lot of time talking to Tamsin about her new brother or sister. I had explained that he or she would be quite boring for a while, but then would be more fun, and in the meantime we could play while the baby slept. Tamsin showed very few signs of jealousy; she seemed to enjoy helping to bath her sister, and I used to read a story to Tamsin while I fed Claire. I was really pleased that we seemed to have escaped sibling rivalry, until Claire was old enough to make her feelings known. Strangely enough, she was far more jealous of Tamsin than Tamsin was of her. By the time she was six months old she was trying to kick Tamsin off my lap!

As Claire grew, Tamsin became quite a little mother to her. By the time Claire was approaching her first birthday, she wouldn't let me feed her because she wanted to do it herself, but she would let Tamsin feed her.

It was while Claire was a baby that I first realised what a worrier Tamsin was. The three months after her third birthday were a nightmare. Tamsin was naughty, disobedient, cheeky, defiant, all the things she was supposed to be at two and wasn't. One day things came to a head. I had sent her to her room yet again for teasing Claire, and was trying to wash up when I realised that Tamsin was sobbing her heart out upstairs. Being sent to her room was more a 'time out' than a punishment, and usually she was quite happy to entertain herself for a while. I went up and said, 'What's wrong, Tamsin? What's the matter?'

'I don't want you to go away,' she sobbed.

'I'm not going away!' I replied, taking her on my lap for

a hug and stroking her chestnut plaits. 'However did you get that idea?'

'Granny said.'

'When?'

'At Easter.'

Then it dawned on me. If Tamsin was annoyed with someone, she would tell them to 'Go 'way!' During a visit she had said this to my mother, who had replied, 'Very well, we'll all go away!' Poor Tamsin had been fretting for three months, thinking she was to be abandoned. I had to phone my mother and ask her to tell Tamsin we weren't going away before she would believe me.

I discovered another fear of Tamsin's when Claire had an ear infection, just after Daniel came home on leave. Claire cried for half the night and woke Tamsin, who also began to cry. Leaving Claire with Daniel, I went to comfort Tamsin.

'What's wrong, sweetheart?' I asked her. 'Why are you crying?'

'Because if Claire cries all night, Daddy will get fed up with us and go away again,' she sobbed. I stared at her in amazement. It had never occurred to me that Tamsin might think her dad got fed up with us. We had told her that he went to work on a ship, but then I realised that she had never seen a real ship: all she knew was that sometimes her daddy went away, and sometimes he came home. She always cried when he went away, and she was ill more often when he was at sea, but I hadn't made any connection between her illness and Daniel's absence.

Soon after that, Daniel was sent to a ship in the Irish Sea, and when he came into dock in Barrow-in-Furness, I drove the girls down for a visit. Claire was only about eighteen months old and too young to appreciate it, but Tamsin at four was fascinated. She saw all over the ship, including the engine room. After that, she was much more content and secure in her dad's love. But if he had made the effort to build a relationship with Tamsin, and to write to her or phone her while he was away, she might never have been so insecure. Who can tell?

December 1996

Claire had decided to go back to school for the final three days of term, and so on Monday we were up at the usual time and walked the dogs before school. I returned home about nine thirty and tried to wake Tamsin.

'It's half past nine, Tamsin,' I gently urged, 'and the police and social worker are coming at ten.'

She grunted and rolled over, just as the phone began to ring. I went through to my bedroom to answer it. It was the social worker: there would be a delay in getting a police-woman, and they would not arrive until about eleven thirty – unless it would be all right to bring a policeman? I didn't think that was a good idea and assured her that the delay was no problem. I wasn't looking forward to the interview – in fact, I felt really nervous about it, but I knew it had to be done.

Leaving Tamsin to sleep a bit longer, I tidied up the break-fast dishes and the sitting room. I had told my home help not to come that day, so that I had the whole day free. An hour later I tried again to wake Tamsin, this time with a bit more success. I shepherded her into the shower and left her to it. Just as I got back downstairs, the phone rang again. It was the social worker again — it would now be about two o'clock before they arrived. 'Fine,' I assured her. More delay! But events were really out of my control, and I had to be content with that.

Tamsin wandered downstairs for some breakfast, slim in her dressing gown and with her wet hair in a tangle, and I told her of the delay.

'It's okay, Mum,' she said. 'I'll just read.'

She collected some cereal and a drink and returned to her bedroom. She seemed reasonably calm and relaxed. I made a sandwich for myself, collapsed on the settee in front of the TV and tried, without much success, to relax. At least I hadn't had a call from school to collect Claire — she must be coping with her day.

No one arrived at two o'clock. No one arrived at two thirty. At a quarter to three, a small car drew up and a slim, attractive young woman came to the door.

'Hi,' she said, digging in her bag and producing a warrant card. 'I'm DC Barbara White, from the Sexual Offences Unit.'

'Come in, I've been expecting you,' I said as I ushered her into the sitting room.

'I'm so sorry you've had to wait so long,' she apologised. 'We've had problems co-ordinating with the social services. Has the social worker arrived yet?'

'That's probably her now,' I replied, as I spied another small car disgorging its female occupant on to the footpath outside the house. And it was. Her name was Liz Jenkins; she was about my age and looked kind and motherly. As I greeted her at the door, I called Tamsin, who came reluct-antly downstairs.

'There's a slight problem,' I said to the three of them, 'I have to go and collect Claire from school now.'

'That's fine, don't worry about it,' said Barbara as she smiled at Tamsin. 'We'll just have a chat and get acquainted.'

Tamsin seemed quite relaxed, and so I collected my car keys and went to fetch Claire. On the way home I explained about the delays and told her she would have to stay upstairs while the interview went on.

'Can I watch TV in your room?' she asked.

'Of course you can,' I replied with a smile. I asked her about her day: she seemed to have had a good time, and it was certainly much better for her to be at school than moping around at home.

When we returned Claire took all the dogs upstairs with her and I went into the sitting room and offered tea or coffee all round. Once that was settled, I sat down beside Tamsin. We had already discussed what would happen and I had told her I would stay or go as she wanted. I didn't know whether she would find it too difficult to talk in front of me, but that didn't seem to bother her at all. She sat beside me on the settee, hugging her knees under her chin, and tried to answer all the questions truthfully and straightforwardly.

I'm not going to describe Tamsin's statement in any detail. Listening to her engraved pictures on my mind which I still have trouble banishing today. She described her difficult relationship with her father. She could describe the events leading up to an incident of abuse, but then seemed to have a blank in her memory. She did describe the assault she had told me of the previous week, which had occurred the last time Daniel was at home. She told them what he had said and I winced inwardly – I could just hear him saying that. Any lingering doubts I might have had about the truth of her accusations vanished like smoke.

Tamsin also said that she had told two of her friends at school a couple of years ago. They had been playing 'Truth or Dare', and someone had asked what her deepest, darkest secret was. I was to find out later that quite a few people at school knew, including Mrs Jameson, the head of pastoral care and the headmaster's wife, who had been urging Tamsin to tell me for the last month or two.

One thing we had to establish as near as possible was the date of the assault the previous September. Tamsin was sure it had been a Saturday morning. I thought it must have been the 21st, when I went to Stirling for a study day with the Open University; but Tamsin was adamant that it had been the 28th. That meant that Daniel had assaulted his daughter while I was sitting in the dining room, eating breakfast. I shook my head in disbelief. How could he be so stupid? Surely he knew by now what my views were on child abusers!

Throughout the interview it was Barbara, the police-woman, who did all of the questioning, and she was very good at it, too. Liz, the social worker, sat quietly, taking copious notes. When Barbara was finished, she asked Liz if she had any further questions.

'I've none for Tamsin,' she said, 'but some for you, Mrs Schenker. When do you expect your husband to return?'

'Sometime around the sixth of January,' I replied. 'We never really know until he phones me from the airport.'

'That's fine,' she replied. 'I'll have to go back to the office and talk it over with my senior, but we may want to hold a Child Protection Case Conference. I also have to notify the reporter to the Children's Panel.'

'That's okay,' I replied. 'I just want my kids protected.'

'Can I take it that the marriage is over now?' she asked.

'It certainly is!' I snorted.

'This will now be the subject of a full police inquiry,' said Barbara. 'We'll want to interview these two friends at school. When does the new term start?'

'Boarders return on the first Sunday in January,' I replied.

'That's fine.' Barbara smiled. 'The other thing I think we'll do is arrange for a police medical. Often there's no evidence, but we might just be able to get some here, and the more evidence we have, the better. Is that all right with you, Tamsin?'

'Yes,' she agreed blankly.

'We'll also want to interview you separately,' Barbara told me, and we arranged that for the following afternoon.

'What about your other daughter, Claire, is it? Has she been abused?'

'I don't think so,' I replied, and I explained that Claire always came and told me immediately if anything was upsetting her. 'I think he was smart enough to know that if he persisted with her, she would tell me.'

'We still need to take a statement from her,' and we arranged that for Thursday afternoon, after school had finished. 'In the meantime it would be best, if you can manage it, to let as few people as possible know,' said Barbara. 'I know that's going to be hard, but it's not for long. You can just let us know when he comes home, and we'll come and pick him up.'

'I don't think so!' I burst out. 'If he comes back to this house, I can't guarantee his safety!' I had already been aware, through my hurt, of a slow-burning anger against Daniel, but now, after hearing what Tamsin had said, it had erupted into a full-blown firestorm. 'I will let you know which flight he will be on, and you can meet him at the airport.'

'Do you always know when he's coming home?' she asked.

'Yes,' I replied, 'because it's so uncertain, he always phones from the airport before he boards the flight home. I don't usually take a note of the flight numbers, but the last time he came home, I got the flights from London mixed up, so that will give me a good excuse to note them this time.'

'All right,' agreed Barbara. 'If you can do that, we'll make sure we collect him from the airport.'

Barbara and Liz took their departure, and Tamsin ran upstairs to see Claire while I started dinner. Tamsin seemed none the worse for having given her statement, although I felt totally drained. Sitting through that interview with Tamsin is probably the hardest thing I have ever done in my life. I was unspeakably angry with Daniel, hearing what he had done to his own child. But I still loved him, too – I couldn't (I suspect no one can) change in an instant how I felt about someone I had spent half of my life with, and trusted, and relied on, and expected to live with until death.

But I was also determined, now, to provide as much evidence as I could to make sure that Daniel paid for what he had done. I wasn't looking forward to having to talk to him on the phone. I didn't want him to know what was happening, because I had a gut feeling that if he found out, he would just disappear into the Far East. But there was one thing I could do about that. Leaving dinner to cook itself, I went into the dining room and booted up the computer.

The ship was equipped with satellite fax and phone links, but because the phone cost £5 a minute, we tended to reserve that for emergencies and special days – like Christmas. 'I've just got the phone bill and it's horrendous,' I typed. 'I suggest we just use the fax until you get home – it's still expensive to call but it's only for a couple of minutes.' I added some inconsequential chatter and then sent it. It went through first time, and I relaxed a bit. The ship was working off Irian Jaya – yes, I had to look it up on the map too! It's the other half of Papua New Guinea. The crew rarely made it ashore, and when they did telephone communications were a bit primitive. I didn't think I'd have to speak to Daniel more than once or twice.

We spent a normal family evening at home – well, as normal as possible. Claire seemed to have got over her first heartbreak – the arrival that day of the new bicycle which was her Christmas present helped! – and was more like her usual noisy and boisterous self. She and Tamsin spent some time discussing what they should buy me for Christmas. Claire and I had seen a beautiful teddy bear in the local toyshop window, and they decided that would be the perfect present. I had kept my promise to Claire, and cuddled her teddy bear every night, and I was amazed at how comforting it was! I would not have believed that you could gain so much solace from hugging some fur fabric filled with stuffing. I keep threatening to write a paper on the thera-peutic benefits of cuddling teddies.

Now that the interview was over and things were out of my hands, I was feeling a bit more together. The shock and disbelief were beginning to wear off, and I had accepted that our future would be very different. Claire seemed to be feeling better, too, and it was Tamsin who now needed support.

I constantly reassured her that she had done the right thing by talking to the police. It must have seemed like a betrayal to her – after all, this was her daddy! It might seem strange to people who have not experienced it, but abused kids still love the abusive parent. It just makes it that much harder to deal with. How could my dad hurt me like this if he loves me? is the biggest question, and I can't answer it. All I could say was that maybe he didn't know how to express his love properly; but that was small comfort. Eventually I settled both girls and collapsed into bed myself. I cried myself to sleep almost every night that month.

1985–1987

Tamsin's health began to improve when she was four, after a particularly difficult winter when she was ill more often than not. We had built a good life for ourselves in the village. I was busy with Mums and Toddlers and the National Childbirth Trust group; Tamsin went to playschool and ballet lessons, and Claire had grown into an enchanting, contented toddler. Penny was doing really well in dog shows, which I enjoyed tremendously. Daniel had a steady routine of work and home, and our own relationship seemed to grow stronger with every passing year. As far as I knew, he was as contented as I was. We even had some money left over at the end of each month and were able to start saving for the first time in years.

Then it happened again. Without warning Daniel was made redundant. He had no history of trouble in this company, unlike the last time, and the engineering supervisor said the company was mad to get rid of him. But it happened, and we had to deal with it.

It didn't seem too bad at first. Within a month Daniel was offered another job on a seismic survey ship. He did one three-month trip and came home disgusted because he was expected to wear uniform. A few weeks later he was told he was not required again. Still we felt that he would not be out of work for long. It was the mid-Eighties, business was booming, surely good engineers were hard to come by. But apparently not. Daniel struggled gamely on, I typed more CVs and letters than I ever want to see again, but nothing. Not even a sniff of a job.

Money got tighter and tighter. We began to sell things to keep going. My parents helped, but they were not well off themselves. His parents did nothing.

It was at this time that relations between Daniel and his children really soured. It was understandable that he felt pretty bad, but he began to take out his anger and frustration on the girls. I could not leave them alone for even an hour without having to sort out some dispute on my return. Usually the girls had done nothing wrong, but Daniel had no idea what behaviour was reasonable to expect from a five-year-old and a two-year-old, and expected far too much. I tried talking to him. I tried to persuade him to read some books and magazines about young children. He refused point blank to listen. He could not or would not see that he had a problem, and things just got worse.

It came to a head when my mother took the girls shopping on Christmas Eve. She phoned that evening and said that Tamsin had not wanted to buy a present for her dad, because he was too rough with her. It had taken quite a lot of cajoling on my mother's part to talk Tamsin round.

After the girls were in bed, I sat Daniel down and told

him what had happened. I said I understood his frustration, but it was totally inappropriate for him to smack his children or handle them roughly. I hated to do it, but I made it quite clear that either he recognised he had a problem and dealt with it, or he had to leave. Maybe he felt I should have chosen him over the children. I don't know. The children were too small to stand up for themselves, and I had to do it for them.

For the first time he seemed to appreciate the seriousness of what he was doing to his family. He apologised profusely and said that he would sort it out. Christmas came and went, and I could see he was making an effort to be more patient, although he seemed to think that the girls ought to change their attitude towards him immediately.

After the holidays he went to the NSPCC for help, and a counsellor came to the house. We talked the problem through as we saw it. I said I believed that Daniel had no idea how to relate to his children and wasn't prepared to make any sort of effort to find out. Daniel really had nothing to say for himself. The counsellor tried very hard to be neutral. She said there were other ways of learning besides books. She began to visit once a week, trying to get Daniel to open up about his own childhood. I didn't tell her I had tried that already.

His parents had been very authoritarian and controlling, to the extent that they even arranged his first job for him. We talked about how that had made him feel, and also how there were better ways of disciplining his children, and how he couldn't really discipline them until he recognised what was and was not reasonable behaviour for their age. The counsellor left papers for him to read, and exercises for us to do together, but unless I nagged him, he never made any effort. One week I told the counsellor that it seemed that I was doing all the hard work, and that Daniel had to be nagged into co-operating. She forbade me to remind him for a week, and he did — nothing. The next week she said there wasn't much point in her coming any more if Daniel wasn't prepared to try, and I had to agree. Nevertheless, he did improve a bit.

After Christmas our finances were in a parlous state, and I decided I would have to work. Tamsin was at school, so that we needed childcare only for Claire. Daniel was at home every morning — he went to a Job Club in the afternoons — and I parcelled Claire out between friends for the afternoons to start with.

I got the first job I applied for, working in administration in the local health authority. I was almost afraid to tell Daniel, I thought it would only make him feel worse, but he said it was a relief. He said it took the pressure off him, and meant he could concentrate on getting a job himself without worrying about money. And sure enough, he did, only a few weeks later. He began working as a boiler house supervisor in a textile-printing factory.

That summer we hardly saw him. He was working from seven in the morning until four in the afternoon, and so was home in time for tea and bath and bedtime; but he also worked every Saturday morning and most Sunday mornings. Things seemed to be better between him and the girls, but maybe that was only because they spent so little time together.

Although I wasn't aware of it at the time, it was during this time that our 'honeymoon' period really ended. I guess we were lucky it had lasted so long. I gradually became aware that Daniel's outlook on life was very different from mine. It was nothing spectacular, just an accumulation of minor incidents. For example, we had been in the habit of making tea by the mugful; when money became tight, we began to use one tea bag for two mugs. When I made the tea, I always made Daniel's first and then my own, assuming that he would put me first in turn; but then I discovered that he always made his own first. Not much in itself, but symptomatic of Daniel's automatic assumption that his needs came first.

At that time we owned a tiny touring caravan, and often had weekends away in Galloway. After a year or two, I noticed that whenever we prepared to leave, I always ended up carrying boxes of food and bags of clothes out to the caravan, while Daniel cleaned the car windows and checked the oil and water. Given that my back was not very strong, that seemed the wrong way round to me, but Daniel point-blank refused to change anything. Maybe I should have paid more attention to that character trait.

That summer I hired a lovely student to look after the girls during the school holidays. Steffie was studying to be a special needs teacher, and she was very good with the girls, taking them out and playing with them in the garden and at the local playing field. We put the caravan on a site a couple of hours' drive away for the whole summer, and had many weekends there, as well as the second two weeks of August. Once again, the problems between Daniel and the girls resurfaced, but mostly I managed to laugh them out of confrontations.

After the holidays Claire began attending playschool three

December 1996

On Tuesday morning I took Claire to school and then went into town to meet the solicitor. I had brought my copy of Uncle Bob's will, and my own will, and it was a simple matter to alter my will. The solicitor reassured me that the money in the trust fund was mine rather than ours, and promised to draw up the new will quickly. The old will had named Claire's godparents in Carlisle, Maria and Tom, and Daniel's sister, Susan, as guardians. I left Maria and Tom as guardians, but added my parents' names instead of Susan. I had no idea what Daniel's family's reaction would be, but I suspected that they would choose to support Daniel rather than me, and I wanted to be sure that everything to do with the girls was secure.

Then I was introduced to the solicitor, Kim Anderson. She was small and dark and slim, and experienced in divorce law. When I told her what had happened, she said, 'He'll go to prison for what he's done!' I stared at her in dismay. I didn't want Daniel in jail — I wanted him out at sea, earning loads of money so that he could keep us. But if that was the price of safeguarding the girls, then so be it.

There wasn't much Kim and I could do at this stage. I promised to bring in Daniel's pension file, and a host of other papers which she wanted, and then headed home. Tamsin was just waking as I arrived, and we had lunch together before Barbara arrived at two o'clock. Tamsin went off to her room to read, and Barbara and I sat down and talked and talked. I told her of Daniel's attitude towards the girls, of his unreasonable attitude and unnecessary use of physical chastisement. I told her that a few years earlier I had stopped him from going into their rooms at night in his pyjamas. I couldn't tell her why – I had just felt it was inappropriate. Maybe deep down I suspected, but it never reached consciousness. It wasn't even a case of suspecting but refusing to believe – I would never for a minute have tolerated his presence in the house if I thought he was abusing either of the girls.

I began to gain some insight into how Tamsin must have felt the day before. I felt disloyal, treacherous, and had to keep reminding myself that the initial treachery had been Daniel's, and that I had to do this to protect the girls. It felt wrong to be laying open our private lives to a stranger like this; but at the same time, I wanted Daniel to be punished, if only to reassure Tamsin that she had done the right thing. Again, I somehow managed to separate the Daniel I loved from the Daniel who had abused Tamsin.

When we had finished, Barbara said, 'I'm not sure yet what he'll be charged with, either sexual assault or incest. It's hard to know exactly what went on, but maybe the medical will throw more light on it.' We checked the arrangements for interviewing Claire in two days' time, and she told me the medical was to be at five o'clock the following day, at the children's hospital.

When she had gone, I collected Claire from school. It was her last full day – term ended at lunchtime the following day. She came out of school with handfuls of cards and little gifts from classmates, having taken in her cards and gifts that morning. Tamsin was watching TV when we returned, and I left them to it while I cooked dinner. They both seemed all right, although Tamsin was very quiet.

Later that evening, after Claire had gone to bed, I phoned Alison and asked if she could look after Claire for me the following evening. I wanted to be able to concentrate all my help on Tamsin – I had a feeling she was going to need it. Alison agreed to take Claire, of whom she was very fond, and to feed Tamsin and me on our return. Then I phoned Jenny for another chat. I had spoken to her almost every day, and she was a tower of strength. What a cliché! But it's hard to put into words how valuable she was to me. She had had a violent husband and had been divorced twice, and so she had personal experience as well as professional help to offer. I don't think I would have survived without her.

While we were talking, I became aware of an odd thumping noise and Tamsin's voice muttering in the kitchen. 'I think I'd better go and see what's happening,' I told Jenny, and rang off. I found Tamsin walking up and down the kitchen, throwing herself against the back door, and muttering, with a weird scowl on her face.

'What's the matter?' I asked her, but she ignored me. I shepherded her into the corner, talking to her all the time, and she sort of peered at me, as if through a mist.

'Is that you, Mum?' she asked, as she began to shiver violently. 'Oh, don't leave me, don't leave me!' she wailed. I hugged her as tightly as I could and assured her I was not going anywhere. She continued to shiver as I gently asked her what was wrong.

'I made a sandwich, and then I didn't want it, and Claire doesn't want it, and now it's going to be wasted!' she cried.

'Is that all?' I smiled. 'It doesn't matter, we'll give it to the dogs.'

'But we can't afford to waste food!'

'We're not that poor yet!' I laughed gently. 'Come on, come and sit down and calm down,' and we two-stepped through to the sitting room, for Tamsin was holding me fiercely. She continued to shiver violently, and I became really concerned. I decided to call the doctor for advice, and as soon as I explained the circumstances, the duty GP came round immediately. She dispensed some diazepam, and gave me some more for the next day when I explained about the police medical.

Gradually Tamsin stopped shaking and calmed down a little, but she still wouldn't let go of me, and so we slept together. I had been surprised and a little frightened by her behaviour, but I put it down to pre-medical nerves. After all it wasn't a very nice thing to have to undergo. Little did I know that this was to be just the beginning.

1987–1989

In November 1987, I had to take some time off work because of back pain. I have had a 'bad back' since I was twenty, but so long as I took care not to lift heavy objects, it was mostly fine. Now, however, it began to play up in a big way. I couldn't think of anything I had done to upset it, it just got more and more painful over a period of weeks until I couldn't go on working any longer.

I tried bed rest for a few weeks, I tried physiotherapy, I tried everything I could think of, but it refused to get better. I saw a surgeon at the local hospital, who recommended a corset and exercises. That didn't work. After five months' sick leave, I lost my job. It wasn't a financial blow; with both of us working, we had quickly got back on our feet. And Daniel's parents had sold a piece of land in Switzerland – his grandmother had died some years ago – and shared the proceeds with their children. But I didn't want to spend the rest of my life as an invalid unless I had to, and so I asked my GP for a second opinion. He sent me to see a surgeon in Leeds, who felt I should be admitted for tests. We agreed to wait until Claire had started school in September and settled in, which she did with no traumas. In October 1988 I went off to Leeds.

The CAT scan showed a prolapsed disc, and I had surgery. I was in hospital for three weeks. During the week my parents looked after the girls, and Daniel brought them to see me at the weekends. Tamsin, who was seven, couldn't bear to leave me on Sundays and had to be dragged out, while poor Claire quietly acquiesced to everything. I thought Tamsin was just being clingy. I thought that she and Daniel had sorted out most of their problems and, while he was still too quick to anger, things were much better than they had been. Maybe I should have taken more notice then, but it's pretty hard when you're recuperating from major surgery.

We arranged for friends to walk the girls to and from school, and I spent a quiet few months recuperating. Daniel worked as long hours as ever, but he did the shopping, and I was allocated a home help for three months. Six months after the surgery, although I was very much better, it became clear that I would never be a hundred per cent fit, and I gladly returned to being a full-time mum. I began to enter my handicrafts – sewing, knitting, dressmaking – in the local agricultural shows, with quite a lot of success. Life seemed to have settled down to an even tenor, except for the inevitable explosions when we went on holiday and Daniel was forced to spend time with his children.

I really don't understand what the problem was. They were (and are) lovely girls. They have always been well behaved; I got up to far worse mischief when I was a child than they ever did. Over and over I talked with Daniel about what it was reasonable to expect from their age group. Over and over he agreed with me, apologised, made an effort for a day or two. But when the girls didn't respond immediately, he went back to his old ways.

We talked endlessly about our own childhood experiences and how they had shaped our expectations. My family was not demonstrative; my parents were strict, and I spent a lot of my childhood feeling unloved and unwanted. I know now that that wasn't true, that I was and am very much loved and wanted; but it taught me how important overt affection is to children, and how easily they can pick up the wrong impression. Daniel wanted their affection, he almost craved it. But he was not prepared to expend the time and effort to build the sort of relationship with his children which would have led easily to affection. After all, you can't blame a kid for refusing to cuddle a man who has just hit her, can you?

I sometimes felt that Daniel would have been a very happy Victorian father, with his children shut away in the nursery and inflicted on him for only half an hour a day. He wanted immediate obedience and respect from them, but he didn't behave in ways that inspire obedience and respect. He behaved more like a spoilt child: if they didn't do as he said immediately, he threw a tantrum. Why couldn't Daniel understand that he needed to contribute to the relationship for it to work?

One holiday in particular stands out. We went to Spain in June 1989, staying in a hotel for two weeks; because we travelled by coach, it wasn't too expensive. One day we went on an excursion to a theme park with performing dolphins. We loved the show! We were having a really happy day, until I took the girls to the toilet before lunch. Claire leant forward to wash her hands at the basin. Her dress sleeve rode up, and there was clear 'fingertip' bruising on her arm.

I was so shocked! Daniel must have grabbed her really hard to bruise her arm like that. I was frightened too: I was afraid that if a doctor or nurse or teacher saw bruising like that, social services would be called, and we could lose the children.

I really went for Daniel. I pointed out to him the risk of losing custody. I threatened again to kick him out if he couldn't get his temper under control. There was no need for this sort of behaviour; we had enough money to live on, Daniel's job was secure, why couldn't he just relax and enjoy his children? At first he was angry with me for taking him to task; but when he realised I was serious, he backed down and apologised again. But once again, his efforts to improve didn't last long.

Why did I stay with him if things were so bad? Well, they weren't bad all the time, really just during school holidays when Daniel and the girls had to spend time with each other. Mostly, I thought we had a good family life. I still loved Daniel and I thought he loved me. And there were good family occasions, too, when we enjoyed each other's company. I knew the harm that divorce causes to children. I thought with enough love and patience we could make it work. The incurable optimist, huh?

December 1996

The next morning Tamsin was still fast asleep when I took Claire to school. She slept all morning, and woke at lunchtime, in time to come with me to collect Claire from the church where her school had its carol service. By the time we returned home, she was becoming quite agitated again; I gave her some more diazepam, and she seemed to settle down after that. We had afternoon tea with some sandwiches, and diazepam for Tamsin, and then it was time to set off for the medical. I dropped Claire at Alison's house and took Tamsin on up to the hospital. The outpatient department was empty, and it was quite eerie sitting there alone. I don't know how Tamsin was feeling, but I was certainly pretty apprehensive, suspecting what might be in store for my child.

We were not kept waiting for long. Soon a woman came out and introduced herself as Dr Ling. She ushered us into a consulting room, where a female social worker, a different policewoman and another doctor — unfortunately, a male doctor — were waiting. We went through the usual preamble of history taking, and Tamsin seemed quite relaxed. She undressed behind screens and donned a hospital gown for the examination. Both doctors came into the cubicle, and Tamsin seemed to accept them, until it came to the internal examination.

'I'm not having him in here!' she yelled, pointing at the male doctor, Dr Harrison. Dr Ling explained that there had to be two doctors present, and although they had tried to find another female doctor, it hadn't been possible. But Tamsin was having none of it, and I certainly could sympathise. Eventually a compromise was reached. Dr Harrison was to stand by Tamsin's head, hold the stretcher rail and look at her face all the time, and he was to be 'fined' £10 for every millimetre his hands or eyes moved away from her head. This was only possible because video equipment had been installed, so that he could review the findings afterwards with Dr Ling. Tamsin agreed to this, but as soon as Dr Ling approached her, she began to cry out again.

In desperation, I said to her, 'What was that truly awful joke you told me the other day?' Tamsin switched her attention to me, and Dr Harrison caught on immediately, and for the next ten minutes the three of us competed to tell the most awful jokes we had ever heard. At last it was over, and Tamsin could get dressed again. We were asked to wait outside while they looked at the videotapes.

I sat and hugged Tamsin while we waited. She seemed to have relaxed again — no doubt helped by the diazepam. After about half an hour we were invited back into the consulting room.

'The first thing I want to tell you,' said Dr Ling once we

were settled, 'is that everything is completely normal down there. Often girls and their mums are afraid that they will somehow be changed, but everything is fine. We did find a little scar on your hymen, Tamsin,' she continued. 'It would never be noticed by anyone else, it's just that we know exactly what to look for, and it is consistent with what you have told us.' Dr Ling continued to talk to Tamsin, while the policewoman caught my eye.

'It is consistent with what she's said,' she told me, 'but we see it more often in other cases. It might well be that more has happened than she has said – do you understand?'

I wished I could have the chance to speak to her alone – was she telling me that Daniel might have raped Tamsin? I think she was; but there was never an opportunity to expand on it.

Taking Tamsin for the medical was almost like allowing her to be abused all over again. Knowing what I know now, I'm sure it wasn't the best thing for Tamsin. But at the time, we had no idea whether Daniel would admit to anything, and it seemed important to collect as much evidence as possible. But it was still a rotten thing to have to go through.

Soon we were allowed to leave and return to Alison's. While Tamsin ate, Alison quizzed me about the medical and, despite the mounting evidence, she still had doubts about the truth of Tamsin's story. But she never allowed her doubts to affect her support for us.

That night Tamsin had another of the strange attacks, which she came to call freakies. As she was going to bed, she just sort of – went away. It's very difficult to describe. Her body was there, but the thinking rational person that was Tamsin had disappeared. Instead there was a frightened, insensate creature which threw itself at walls and on the floor, and scratched itself incessantly. I was to spend many evenings holding on to her hands desperately, to stop her scratching out her eyes, until the diazepam could take effect.

The next day Barbara and Liz returned to talk to Claire. She described how Daniel had, a couple of years ago, begun to come into her room at night to give her a 'back rub'.

'And how did it make you feel?' asked Liz.

'Happy and relaxed,' replied Claire. Liz and Barbara continued to question her for a bit longer, but it became apparent that although Daniel had begun the early stages, Claire had felt able to set limits, and he had not persisted – although it's impossible to say what might have happened, had Tamsin not told me when she did.

I don't remember too many details about the next couple of weeks. I remember driving to the solicitor's office to sign my new will, listening to the radio. They began to play Berlioz' 'The Shepherd's Farewell', a carol I had sung many times with the choir. I began singing along, enjoying the music, until it came to the line 'Loving father'. Suddenly my eyes were streaming with tears! I had to pull over, switch off the radio and calm myself down. I still don't like singing that carol.

I also made a start on finding a new school for Claire. If Daniel were to be jailed, school fees would be impossible. Tamsin's school had recently been approved for assisted places funding, and so I phoned the headmaster, Mr Jameson, and told him what Tamsin had disclosed. He was horrified.

'This is appalling! Absolutely appalling!' he stuttered, almost lost for words.

'Yes, it is,' I agreed. 'I'm sorry, I know it's a terrible shock, and people need time to take it in. But what I really need to talk to you about is Claire. We won't be able to keep her where she is, and I wondered if you had any assisted places available.'

'I'm sorry,' he replied, collecting his thoughts, 'we've been approved but we won't be awarded funding until after the next election. But I'm sure the local authority will pay her fees, the same as Tamsin. If there's going to be a trial, it would be much better for both girls to be out of Edinburgh.'

'That's a good point,' I admitted, 'I hadn't thought it through as far as that yet. I'll mention it to the social work department, and contact the educational psychologist.'

We chatted for a few more minutes and then rang off. I talked to the social worker the next time she came, but she was more interested in finding out details for the Child Protection Case Conference. I tried to speak to the educational psychologist, Mr Nathan, but he was on holiday. It would just have to wait until next term.

I discovered how deeply hurt Claire was when she asked if she could change her name. Daniel had named her when she was born, and I had told her that one day years ago, when Daniel had been unkind, to make her feel special. Now she wanted to stop being Claire and use her middle name of Samantha, preferably shortened to Sam. She confided that she had always wanted a name that could be shortened to a boy's name! It took us a while to get used to, and for a while she was called 'Cla-Sam', but now it's hard to think of her as Claire.

Cla— oops, Sam also asked Tamsin and I not to say

nasty things about her father in front of her. She could understand how hurt and angry we were, but he was still her daddy, and she didn't want to hear us saying bad things about him. After that, Tamsin and I tried to be more sensitive.

Over the next few days, Sam talked to me a lot about what Daniel had done to Tamsin, and to her. At first, she had not wanted to know any details of what Daniel had done to Tamsin, but after a few days she demanded to know. I told her as gently as I could, and she sat back on my bed, thinking.

'It's not as bad as I thought,' she said eventually. 'I had been imagining all sorts of things – but still, bad enough!' She also talked through what Daniel had done to her, and began to realise that he had been working up to abuse her, too. Eventually she asked to see the police again. Barbara returned and took another statement; but although Sam was now trying less to protect her father than when she gave her original statement, there wasn't enough to charge Daniel with any crime.

We missed church again the Sunday before Christmas. Tamsin was still having freakies every day or two, and still taking diazepam. I had taken her to see our GP, and to see a social worker who specialised in child abuse, and back to our GP. Finally he said I should take her home and just love her. 'She's seen too many people in too short a time,' he advised. 'What she really needs is some TLC, and you're the best person to give her that.' I flashed back to when she had been an ill toddler – yes, I was the best person. I needed to have confidence in my own abilities.

The Monday before Christmas Day, Sam bought the giant

teddy bear from the local toyshop. I remember Tamsin sitting on the floor, in a diazepam haze, trying to wrap him up. She was having trouble coping with anything then, and it took her about two hours to wrap him successfully, but it occupied her morning happily.

Both girls discovered a new form of 'therapy' which kept them busy them all through the holidays – cross-stitching! I love cross stitch and have completed many pictures. I had quite a lot of Aida cloth, which is specially woven for cross stitch, and lots of coloured silks. I also had a book of designs for illustrated mottoes, such as 'I may not be perfect, but parts of me are excellent!' Although Tamsin had never been noted for her patience, she threw herself into stitching with great enthusiasm, and produced some fine work. But as soon as one picture was completed, she had to begin another immediately. Sam enjoyed it, too, although she didn't seem to have the same need for diversion as Tamsin. From being the strongest of the three of us, Tamsin had come to be the weakest. Both Sam and I were feeling better able to cope.

I did have one piece of good news on Christmas Eve – my Open University exam results arrived. Jenny had been teasing me with hints of how good my marks were; but when they arrived, I was astonished. I had scored 88 for continuous assessment, and 94 in the exam! I couldn't believe it – I had thought I'd made a mess of the second exam essay, but when I spoke to Jenny she confirmed it.

'You were the top student in Scotland and third in the UK,' she told me. 'I've really enjoyed boasting about my students this year!'

The three of us discussed what we should eat for Christmas dinner, and I told Tamsin she wouldn't be able to drink alcohol if she was still taking diazepam. That did it. She got through Christmas Eve with no diazepam and no freakies! We went to the Christmas Eve service at the church – always a special occasion with lots of carols. Tamsin refused to sit with Sam, which was a bit of a worry. She went off and sat with some of the other young people. But I could see her from the choir stalls, and she seemed to be fine.

She was fine on Christmas Day. I had cooked the turkey the night before, and we had a magnificent meal at lunchtime, which included a bottle of Asti Gancia. Sam had a glass diluted with lemonade, and I had a glass, and Tamsin had a glass. After dinner we went through to the sitting room to watch the afternoon film on TV. As usual I fell asleep, and while I was sleeping, Tamsin polished off the rest of the bottle!

Tamsin was much better for the rest of the holidays. She stopped taking diazepam and had no more freakies. We did all the usual Christmas holiday things, like shopping in the sales. My solicitor had advised me to use our credit card to buy everything we were likely to need for the next few months, and we had a ball!

I told a few close friends what had happened: Maria and Tom, Sam's godparents, and one or two people in the church. But I was very conscious of the need for secrecy, because it's amazing how people find things out. I remembered that when Tamsin was a baby, we had spent a week in Edinburgh with my parents, without telling Daniel's parents or visiting them. But somehow they found out.

I had to speak to my in-laws, of course. When we had visited them on 10 December, I had promised to take both girls to see them during the Christmas holidays. But I couldn't face that now; I phoned and said I had hurt my back and couldn't drive.

I had to speak to Daniel too. He called a couple of times over the holidays. Neither girl wanted to speak to their father, and so we arranged between ourselves that I would always answer the phone, and they would keep completely silent until we knew who was calling. I always had an excuse in my head, ready to explain why they were not available, but he never once asked to speak to them.

For me it was almost like being two people. I could slip back into my 'pre-knowing' persona while I was talking to him or his family, and then shed it as I put down the phone. I didn't like it; it made me feel dirty, but it had to be done. Perhaps it mirrored the way I could split off my feelings about Daniel the child abuser from Daniel my husband. I knew Daniel had always had trouble facing up to things he had done wrong, and I also knew that he was very much at home in South East Asia. As I mentioned I was afraid that if he knew Tamsin had talked, he would just disappear into the Far East.

I also felt it was extremely important for Tamsin's sake that Daniel should return to face the music; both so that the girls could be given legal protection, and so that Tamsin could see that society does not condone child sex abuse. I thought that perhaps if she saw Daniel punished for what he had done, it would help to remove the guilt she was feeling. She felt guilty about her father being in trouble; she felt guilty about breaking up our marriage; she felt guilty for inflicting hurt on Sam and me. None of this guilt was in any way justified, but I knew it was going to be the hardest aspect for her to deal with, and anything which could help that was worth doing.

I was fuelled largely by anger. Anger kept me going through the days. And compassion, for both girls, but especially Tamsin. I looked back on Tamsin's life: the whooping cough inoculation reaction, the illness, the trouble with Daniel, the bullying at school – and now this. Really, if you set out to mess up a kid's life, you couldn't do a much better job than we had! I never really thought, then, about what the consequences were going to be for me personally. Perhaps because I couldn't really discuss it with anyone except Jenny, it didn't seem very real, or very important. I certainly felt that what Daniel had done to me paled into insignificance beside what he had done to Tamsin, and Sam, too.

Towards the end of December, a bombshell fell. Daniel phoned to say that he had been asked to stay on for an extra six weeks, to fill in while another Chief Engineer went on leave. That was so hard to deal with! On the one hand, I wanted our 'phoney' life to end, so that we could get on with dealing with the aftermath. But I had to be very careful not to alert Daniel that there was anything wrong. He pointed out that the extra leave would come at the right time for him to accompany me to Summer School the next year, and that it would also mean extra money. Eventually I left the decision to him. I said it was all right with me, but he was the one who had to do the extra work, and so he should decide.

He called back a couple of days later to say that he had agreed to do the extra time. That meant he would now be due home in the middle of February. Somehow I managed to keep up a normal conversation, and when it was over I called the police to let them know. Now we were committed to another two months of limbo.

1990–92

In 1990 we moved back to Scotland, to a small town just outside Edinburgh. I sometimes think that was the worst move we ever made, but at the time it felt right. The textile factory was about to close and Daniel was going back to working on oil rig supply ships, sailing out of Aberdeen. It made sense to live closer to Aberdeen, and I had family and friends in Edinburgh.

Penny had died the previous autumn after a long battle with cancer. I was absolutely devastated. The girls wanted a new dog right away, but I couldn't look at another collie; so we went to the local animal shelter and got a little black terrier crossbreed of about eight months. We called her Sally. I don't think she had ever been in a house before. She certainly had never seen a television or a telephone, and to this day she still attacks the hoover. But after three weeks I just had to get another collie. I wanted to continue with obedience training and competitions and, while Sally was charming and cheeky, she wasn't a collie.

I found Fly on a farm in West Cumbria. She was the last remaining bitch in the litter, bred from working stock. She had the classic black and white collie markings – she looked as though she were a white dog, wearing a black Babygro, with her paws and the tip of her tail sticking out. The farmer's wife lifted her out of the kennel and into my arms, and she nestled her head under my chin and snuggled up. Well, I couldn't put her down after that, could I? We brought her home, and while I cooked dinner, she lay at my feet and snapped at Sally. She made it quite clear from day one who her owner was. I started training her for obedience and she proved to have a lot of talent.

We bought a lovely detached house in a new development. It was bigger and had a much bigger garden than our old house, and we thought it was wonderful. There was an excellent local primary school, we had been assured, and so we moved.

The girls seemed to settle down quickly, and Claire brought home a succession of new 'friends', while Tamsin met one or two – she was always more shy than Claire and didn't make friends easily.

Not long after we moved, my back pain suddenly re-appeared with a vengeance, and within a year I was forced to begin using a wheelchair. Not unnaturally, I was pretty depressed about this. There had been doubts about whether surgery was the right option, and when it worked so well, it felt like a private miracle. Now that the pain had returned, it was like God saying, 'Think you're important enough for a miracle, do you? I'll show you!'

I was very angry with God and that was frightening! I could not understand why my life had to be curtailed like this. I did the round of hospitals and specialists again, for quite some years, but eventually I had to accept that this was how I was going to be. It was a huge loss. I had been such an active person, enjoying hill-walking, horse riding, working Fly and playing with the girls. Fortunately Fly is a very laid-back character, unusual in a collie, and she is quite happy to be a family pet.

I was so wrapped up in my own pain and grief for a while that I didn't really see what was happening in my family. It just seemed to me that the girls had become naughty, and needed to be punished far more than previously. But soon I realised that they were worried about me, and frightened, too, and thankfully I saw before too long that the change was in me, not them. I had never really lost my good relationship with them, and soon we were back to normal.

Daniel's attitude to helping in the house and garden became much more obvious now. He would come home on leave saying that now I could have a rest, he would take over. But all he wanted to do were the chores that I could do myself, like washing up. What I really needed him to do were the heavy jobs that I couldn't physically cope with, like weeding the garden and cutting the grass. But he made it quite plain that he was prepared to do only what he wanted to do. I eventually hired a gardener, because it was the only way to keep the garden tidy.

One leave I decided out of curiosity not to ask Daniel to do anything. The garden needed tidying (this was before the days of the gardener); the car had quite a few rust spots which needed treatment now before they grew too big; and there were other chores that I felt should be his responsibility. He did – nothing! He walked the dogs while he took the girls to school, then he would come home and sit down with a cup of coffee and the paper, which occupied him until lunchtime. I needed to have a rest at lunchtimes; Daniel seemed to believe that if I was doing nothing, he should also do nothing. He slept most days until it was time to collect the girls from school. The man who lived next door was a merchant navy officer, too, and he used to spend his leave in the pub or lazing around. Daniel used to criticise him fiercely — he never saw that he wasn't so different.

In 1992 I began studying with the Open University for a degree in psychology. My mother had just begun her third year of an arts degree and was very encouraging, and I felt that this was something I could do regardless of how inconvenient my body was. It was an inspired choice. It gave me back self-respect and a reason for living, which had sometimes been hard to find.

When Tamsin was about nine or ten, she began to have difficulty sleeping. That was usually a sign that something was troubling her, but this time, no matter how I begged and pleaded, she couldn't or wouldn't tell me what it was. She did say that she couldn't keep up with the work at school. I had a word with her teacher, who seemed to think there was nothing wrong. Yes, Tamsin's spelling and maths were not good, and she never wrote very much, but the teacher saw no incongruity. It bothered me, though. I knew that Tamsin was bright and I felt she should be producing more and better work.

At the local primary school, each class had a different teacher every year. After the summer holidays, I had a long chat with Tamsin's new teacher. We discovered together that Tamsin's main problem was in organising her day. In her previous school the teacher had structured the day for the children, but here they were given a list of tasks at the beginning of the day and left to organise themselves. Tamsin tended to stick at the first task for most of the day, because she wanted it to be perfect, and then to have no time left for the other tasks. It took the teacher a week to show Tamsin how to allocate her time, and after that she was much happier about school.

She still wasn't sleeping, though. Daniel and I had always gone into her room in the evening to tuck her in and say goodnight. It was about this time that Daniel began to give Tamsin neck rubs, to help her to relax. He had given me massages, and was very good at it. I hoped it was the first sign that they were beginning to develop a proper relationship. I never had any suspicions.

The following year Tamsin moved to secondary school, and had her hair cut for the very first time! It had been waist length, a sheet of shining chestnut, but now it was shoulder length. It suited her well; she probably felt it was time to rid herself of plaits, now that she was at secondary school.

A few weeks after term began, Tamsin came out of school one afternoon with obvious scratch marks down her face. Daniel had accompanied me to collect her, and when he heard that one of the boys had scratched her face, he went straight in to see the headmaster. The culprit was found and admonished, and that seemed to be the end of the bullying for Tamsin. She still wasn't sleeping, though.

Meanwhile a pattern was emerging in Claire's school life. In the autumn term she had lots of friends, right up until her birthday in December, and as soon as the birthday party was over, all the friends stopped being friendly. This happened every year, and gradually the time when Claire had friends grew shorter and shorter. It was obvious, too, from her behaviour that all was not well, because she gradually changed from being relaxed and easy-going to being tense and short-tempered. I had many conversations with Claire's various teachers over the years. One teacher felt that Claire was reporting being bullied to seek attention, and refused to listen to complaints, which left poor Claire with no protection whatsoever. The following year Claire's teacher was much more sympathetic, and she told me in confidence that there was a nasty clique of girls who ruled the whole class. Claire had been 'sent to Coventry' for being English, and anyone who was friends with Claire was also 'sent to Coventry'. Most of the staff at the primary school tried very hard, but they had no support from the parents of the perpetrators – children learn their attitudes at home, after all.

January 1997

Life returned to some sort of normality after the New Year. Outside the house we kept up the pretence; inside we looked after each other. I returned to my usual routine of choir practice and church; only a few people knew what had happened, and we spoke about it only by phone.

Tamsin returned to school and seemed to be coping well. We had arranged for her to see a clinical psychologist at Dumfries hospital, and she was to be transported by Mrs Jameson. These arrangements had been discussed the previous November, when a Future Needs Assessment had been held. The subject of Tamsin's self-esteem had come up, and I had expressed my concerns. Tamsin had won a prize for art the previous year but, far from being pleased, she was acutely embarrassed. It wasn't just false modesty, she truly believed she did not deserve a prize. We had decided then that Tamsin should be referred for some therapy to improve her self-esteem. Now, of course, her problems with self-esteem were much easier to understand.

Tamsin received a letter about the trip to Sinai: she had not been accepted, because of her lack of experience in camping. But the writer was most encouraging, and urged her to reapply in future years. It was probably for the best: she would have had to raise over £1,000 in sponsorship, which would have been difficult at the best of times, and I had no idea then how ill she was going to be.

Sam also returned to school, but without Tamsin's enthusiasm. She had had asthma when I was working in 1987, but it had disappeared when I lost my job. It had reappeared when she was being bullied at school but, after she moved to her Edinburgh school, it had disappeared again. Now it returned with a vengeance. She had one chest infection after another, and missed a lot of school. She doesn't complain about things which upset her, apart from letting me know about them, and I guess it was just the stress showing through.

I began to look forward to my final year of Open University. Some friends had suggested I might need to defer, because I would have so much else to cope with. But I felt I was going to need something completely separate in which to lose myself when the going got tough, and so it proved. I also began to make enquiries about what I was going to do after graduation. I had a feeling I would need to think about earning my own living, if Daniel was going to be in prison.

But my work options were severely limited by my physical condition. A degree in psychology really only qualifies you to go on to postgraduate training, and at my age and with my disability, the chances of getting a place in post-grad school were not high, to say the least. But I had been thinking for the previous six months about moving into philosophy. I had been introduced to it in 1996, when studying social psychology. I began to study it only to boost my marks – I had no interest in philosophy as such then. But it wasn't long before I was hooked. There is something immensely satisfying about struggling for understanding and then finally achieving it. Edinburgh University offered a one-year taught MSc course, which could act as a sort of 'conversion' course; but to reach that I needed my degree, and first class honours if possible. I decided to go ahead with my final year, and I have never regretted it.

I was also working on Sam's schooling. When Tamsin was sent to her school, funding decisions were made by the educational psychologist; but now the social work department had at least as much say in the decision as the educational psychologist.

We had now been allocated a social worker, Tina Thomson. She seemed very young to me – she was in her mid-twenties. It was probably unkind of me, but I couldn't help noticing the influence of the three months or so of psychology she would have done as part of her training. Whenever the girls or I told her something, she would ask earnestly, 'And how do you feel about that?' I never actually did it, but I was always tempted to reply, 'How I feel about it is something I will discuss with my friends!' To be fair, she was trying to help us; but her idea of what we needed and mine were worlds apart.

We discussed Sam's schooling at some length. I was most reluctant for Sam to return to state schooling. She had such horrendous experiences before, and she still found it very hard to trust people of her own age enough to make real friends. Sam had let me know that she was not as happy at her private school as I had thought. She wasn't being bullied at all; but she had been so defensive when she started there that the other kids had given up trying to be friends. It had been all right so long as she had a happy home; but now that home had gone pear-shaped, school was becoming almost unbearable.

Tina was not very encouraging about Sam's chances of being funded at Tamsin's school. As far as we knew, Sam did not have the specific learning difficulties which Tamsin did; although Sam had similar difficulties with writing and spelling to Tamsin's, she was regarded as something of a maths genius, and was extremely well co-ordinated phys-ically, unlike Tamsin. However, Mr Nathan agreed to do some testing with Sam, as that is the only way to reach a clear diagnosis of specific learning difficulties. Tina visited us every week or two, assessing how we were coping with life. Her main criterion for sending Sam to Tamsin's school was Sam's home situation; no matter how often I tried to explain, she could not or would not concentrate on the educational opportunities offered uniquely by Tamsin's school, but repeated that she could see no reason for Sam to be away from home. I tried talking about the bad effects a public trial could have on Sam's self-esteem, but Tina seemed to think we were just spoilt. Tina was supposed to be a support to us, but in many ways she was more of an ordeal.

I didn't speak to Daniel very often that month, but I did quite a lot of business for him. During his previous leave last September and October, he had contacted many ship-ping companies with a view to changing employers. One of those was a new company, Jepson's Shipping, based in Aberdeen. They had ordered a fleet of new ships, and were looking for chief engineers who would be able to take delivery of a new ship, complete her trials and sail her to her destination. The personnel manager, Jim Morris, was very keen for Daniel to join the company; they were offering in excess of £30,000 a year, and Daniel could choose his work pattern. The only snag was that the first ship was not due for delivery until January 1997; so Daniel had returned to his present employer for one last trip.

Now Jim Morris began phoning me every week or two, to see whether Daniel had returned. He certainly was very keen to have Daniel working for him. Here, too, I had to pretend that all was normal, and I promised to let him know as soon as Daniel returned.

I didn't have much time that month to think about how I felt. Sam needed a lot of nursing, and Tamsin had a week off school with flu at the same time as Sam was ill. I had very little contact with Kim, the solicitor, as there was nothing we could do until Daniel came home. We did discuss the possibility of my using the Power of Attorney to buy a new house and move; but Kim felt that would be seen as misuse. And of course, we would have lost touch with Daniel; not only would he have been alerted to the trouble he faced, we would not have known when he was returning, if at all. I was pretty naive then – I thought Daniel would be obliged to provide housing for us, and I also thought he would be so overcome with shame and remorse that he would do everything in his power to help us. Like I said, pretty naive.

1993–1995

By the time Claire was ten, she was beginning to refuse to go to school, and I felt that the only option was to move her to another school. It seemed that she would meet with the same if not worse anti-English discrimination at other schools in that town, and the only solution was to send her to a private school. Daniel was inclined to feel that Claire was just 'being a nuisance' and took some persuading. But even he had to admit that Claire was obviously very unhappy, and finally he agreed. Claire was moved to a small private school in Edinburgh, with fees that we could afford, and seemed to settle in quickly and feel much happier.

As far as Tamsin was concerned, her problems with school-work seemed to go from bad to worse. It was clear to me that she was a bright child, even allowing for parental pride. She was continually surprising me with the breadth of her knowledge about animals; I thought I knew a lot about animals, but Tamsin at ten could explain the difference in coat pattern between a jaguar and a leopard. I arranged for her to have extra lessons in maths, with a very sympathetic maths teacher, but he seemed to think she had a real difficulty. In contrast, other subject teachers judged Tamsin's ability at the level of her written work, which was pretty awful.

I had pestered both her primary school headmistress and secondary school headmaster to refer Tamsin for testing, as I thought it possible that she did have some sort of specific problem, as opposed to being not very bright, but so far without success. My patience finally ran out at the beginning of her second year of secondary school, and I wrote to the director of education asking why it should take years of irreplaceable schooling for a child to be assessed. I threatened to write to the newspapers, and suddenly, surprise, surprise — the educational psychologist had time to see Tamsin!

It took until the spring term for the testing to be completed, and then it was shown that Tamsin did indeed have specific learning difficulties. I discovered later that it was likely that this was a result of her reaction to the whooping cough vaccine and subsequent illnesses. While the testing was going on, I made contact with a school which specialises in high-ability children with specific learning difficulties. The headmaster was most encouraging, and felt he could offer exactly what Tamsin needed. The only problem was that we could never have afforded the fees. However, the headmaster put me in touch with a parents' support group, who told me that Tamsin needed a Record of Needs; if we could obtain that, the education authority would pay her fees.

Tamsin's educational psychologist was most supportive,

and it is largely thanks to her that we completed Tamsin's Record of Needs in two months, rather than the more usual two years. It took many phone calls – basically I just made a complete nuisance of myself with the education authority! – but at last they agreed, and Tamsin was sent to boarding school at the age of thirteen, coming home at weekends.

It was only after Tamsin left the local school that I discovered just how much bullying she had endured. Even today I still don't know the whole picture; as far as I can make out, after the boy who had scratched Tamsin's face was disciplined, Tamsin was beaten up for 'telling'. Over the course of the next two years, she seemed to have been beaten up on a regular basis. She often came out of school with bruises, but she has never been well co-ordinated, and she always had a convincing reason for the bruising.

Tamsin was also very badly affected by the attitude of her teachers, who seemed to believe she was either lazy or stupid, or both. Despite being encouraged by us to believe in herself, Tamsin rated her abilities at the same level as her teachers and believed that she was indeed stupid. But I felt that once she moved to her new school, and discovered that there were other children like her, who were bright but unable to express themselves on paper, her self-esteem should rocket. She certainly seemed much happier and more settled at the new school, although there were signs in her artwork of how badly damaged she had been. All her paintings at that time were mostly black and dark grey, and cemeteries and gravestones were a frequent theme. She also began reading almost exclusively horror books, and quickly became a great fan of Stephen King. But I felt that with time and understanding from her new teachers, she would recover.

In 1988 my brother and his wife had migrated to Australia. It was a country I had never been much interested in — we had thought about moving to Canada, having been there and liked it, but Australia seemed so far away. My parents had been to visit my brother, and raved about it, but all I could think about was all those poisonous spiders.

One of the consequences of my back pain was that I had to spend an hour or two lying down at lunchtime. Just for something to do, and also because there were many days when the only adult voice I heard was on TV, I began watching Neighbours and Home and Away. One winter day I was lying shivering on the settee, wrapped in blankets, watching all that glorious sunshine and all those beautiful beaches, and I thought, 'This is stupid! If I have to spend most of the rest of my life lying down, it might as well be somewhere warm.' I sounded Daniel out the next time he phoned, and to my surprise he was full of enthusiasm. We spoke to my brother about sponsorship, and he was also very keen. So gradually we began to collect together all the pieces of paper we needed.

The most important factor was for Daniel to finish his Chief Engineer's certificate; so he spent the spring of 1993 travelling through to the Nautical College in Glasgow every day, mostly by bus. And this time, finally, he passed the exam! At last!

In December 1993, my parents were going back out to Sydney to visit my brother for a couple of months. We held a family gathering for them a few days before they were due to go away, and my mother begged us to go too, just for a visit, so that we could see for ourselves what it was like. We looked at each other and wondered. 'Well, we've paid off the car loan, we can afford it now,' I said tentatively.

'Let's investigate!' said Daniel eagerly.

We phoned my brother that night to see if he would have room for us as well as my parents, and he was thrilled to bits with the idea. By four o'clock the next afternoon I had arranged a bank loan, sorted the flights and car hire and booked the kennels for the dogs.

I didn't want to leave for Australia before Christmas, because Claire at ten still believed in Santa Claus. I thought it was probably the last year that would be the case, couldn't see how we could transport all the 'Santa' toys to Australia without her knowing, and didn't want to spoil the magic. So we were to leave from Manchester at midnight on Boxing Day, returning two weeks later. We were so excited!

In some ways that holiday was a dream. Australia was everything I had imagined and much, much more. Television scenes really don't do justice to the beauty of Sydney's beaches and harbours. The weather was hot and sunny, my brother and his family were so welcoming, everything was wonderful – except that the old problem reared its ugly head with a vengeance!

We arrived in Sydney in late morning. We had been advised that the best way to avoid jet lag was to stick to local time from when we arrived. We had a late lunch and sat around talking in the afternoon. My brother had a swimming pool in the garden, which the girls wasted no time in trying out.

We managed to stay awake all day, but then Daniel began

dozing off at about eight o'clock. Tamsin was feeling sleepy too, and I suggested she should go and tug the hairs on her dad's legs for a joke, to wake him up. Tamsin got up off my knee, took a couple of steps towards Daniel, and then collapsed in his lap, whereupon he awoke violently and slapped her repeatedly. I was utterly horrified, but I couldn't say much as my brother and parents were there. Daniel tried to apologise to Tamsin, but she would have none of it. That set the tone for us as a family for the two weeks. Daniel was defensive and I watched him like a hawk. Tamsin was wary of being left alone with her dad. Claire just had a good time. We had fun, but there was a constant undercurrent of mistrust which coloured everything.

During the second week, the great fires in Sydney erupted. We spent three days on evacuation alert, with fire on three sides and the sea on the fourth, but we were never in real danger. It made a spectacular sideshow, but that was tempered by the knowledge of the damage being done. It also severely curtailed our activities. Another consequence was to prove more serious.

The girls had been sleeping in a glassed-off veranda at the back of the house, nearest the fires, while we had a bedroom at the front. Because of people going in and out of the back door, the veranda became quite smoky, and as Claire suffered from asthma, we decided to put the girls to bed in our room and sleep on the veranda ourselves. In the morning I woke up covered in mosquito bites, which quickly turned septic. Despite antibiotics my right foot was swollen to twice its size in a couple of days.

We had one lovely day, the day before we left. We went down into the city, to Darling Harbour. There is a funfair on the quayside, and Claire tried out all the adventurous rides with her dad, but Tamsin stuck close to me. We spent the last of our dollars on yet more tee shirts – when I had travelled with Daniel, I used to collect tourist tee shirts everywhere we went. We took boat rides all round the harbour. We took photographs of the bridge and the Opera House. We just were tourists and for once, Daniel seemed to enjoy the company of his girls.

The next day we flew home, a twenty-four-hour journey. My right foot was still too swollen to put to the ground, and my left leg doesn't work very well because of the nerve damage in my spine. I was allowed to stay on board during refuelling stops, and spent much of the flight on a crew seat with my foot up on the opposite seat. We arrived in Manchester on a cold, wintry morning and spent most of the day driving home. During the night I rose to go to the toilet and searing pain shot through my right calf. It turned out that the combination of the long flight and the infection in my foot had caused a deep vein thrombosis – a clot in my leg. I was stuck in hospital for three days on a heparin drip.

As if that weren't bad enough, Daniel had to leave. He had been offered a trip as acting chief engineer, to pick up a ship in Egypt and sail her out to the Far East. The company had been trying for some time to persuade him to work overseas, but we weren't keen, because it meant three-month trips, instead of two months. But Daniel decided to accept this, without committing himself to anything (he said). He left the day before I got out of hospital, after arranging for our home help to stay with Claire that night. Tamsin had already returned to school – the local authority provided transport — and Claire was still at the local primary school then. Even though I knew Daniel had to go, I still felt completely abandoned.

The next morning the dreadful drip was taken out of my hand. Why do they hurt so much? When I woke up after the surgery on my back, my hand hurt more than my back! I took a taxi home to an empty house, which was very strange. My leg was still very painful, and I was taking large doses of warfarin, which does terrible things to your mind. It was another four or five weeks before my leg stopped hurting and I could drive, and my home help had to do the shopping and take a taxi to the house. But we managed.

Daniel wrote after he had been gone a month. He had signed an overseas contract, committing himself to working in the Far East, on three-month trips. No consultation — apparently I wasn't to have any say. I was mad! I was having trouble sleeping anyway, because of the pain in my leg, and now this! I wrote furious letters to Daniel. I expressed my anger at the way he made unilateral decisions about things that affected all of us. I also — again — tried to point out how he was damaging his children. As usual he wrote back saying he was sorry, he'd try harder, etc., etc.

When he returned after that trip, we had a serious talk. I felt that if we were going to stay together as a family, whether we went to Australia or not, we had to sort this out once and for all. We went over all the same ground we had covered before: how he had felt when he was a child; how there were better ways of raising children; how I felt about being excluded from major decisions. Once again he said he understood, he was sorry, he could see my point, he wouldn't give up after a day or two. But nothing really changed, except maybe that I was more vigilant, and left him alone with the girls less often. I trusted him less, without being able to put my finger on what I distrusted. I can see now that that slowly had a corrosive effect on our relationship.

But we went ahead with our application to emigrate. At the same time as Tamsin was having her psychological assessment, and Claire was starting her new school in Edinburgh, we were collecting all the data we needed. By August of that year it was time for our medical examinations. That was the real crunch point. I can't walk at all without a stick, and not very far with one. We had discussed all this with my brother in Australia. 'Walk into the medical, without your stick,' he had urged. But I couldn't – I had felt much better in the heat of Australia, but I really can't walk far here. My left leg just stops working, and my balance isn't very good either. However, my GP provided a letter outlining what the problem was, and being very positive about what I could do. I was in my third year of Open University and doing well, and I had my photographic qualifications as well. The medical seemed to go off all right, and we waited with crossed fingers.

Alas, it was not to be. We were told in October that our application had been refused, because of my health – or lack thereof. My brother appealed, but to no avail. He advised us to wait a year or so and then try again, but to employ an advisor next time. We were pretty disappointed. Daniel didn't say much – he seemed to be quite philosophical about it. Maybe he wasn't. Maybe he was really angry and upset with me, for scuppering his chances. I don't know, because he never said.

We decided to move into Edinburgh. The girls were so fed up with being bullied because they were English, something which didn't seem so prevalent in Edinburgh, according to English friends there. The anti-English prejudice in West Lothian is really quite stunning. I used to meet a regular group of people when I took the dogs out – I have an electric buggy, and there were lots of footpaths away from the road, so it was a wonderful place for dogs. On a sunny Friday one woman confided, 'I hope we don't get rain tomorrow and the south gets sun, or my life won't be worth living.' It turned out that if the south of England had sunshine at the weekend, while we had rain, her husband used to yell at the TV forecaster about 'they English stealin' our sun!' Unbelievable!

The other reason for moving into Edinburgh was to make Claire's journey to school a bit easier. She had been in hospital three times the previous year with unexplained hip pain, and finally we discovered that her right leg was ten millimetres shorter than her left. Having a raise fitted to her right shoe helped a lot, but she had a twenty-minute walk from the station in Edinburgh to her school, which she found quite hard. I wasn't able to drive her to and from school every day because it caused too much back pain. The most sensible thing to do seemed to be to move nearer her school.

So we sold our dream house. We were quite shocked, because prices had stagnated since we bought it, and we actually lost money on it. But Daniel had been confirmed as chief engineer, and was making good money. We bought a large semi-detached house in a fashionable suburb in West Edinburgh, just up the hill from where my parents had lived when I first met Daniel. He was away all the time the buying and selling was going on, but I had a power of attorney and could do everything myself, and we discussed everything by phone and letter. We were all looking forward to the move with eager anticipation.

February 1997

Suddenly Tamsin wasn't coping at school. One morning I had a phone call from Mrs Jameson, the headmaster's wife who was also head of pastoral care. When Tamsin first told me that Mrs Jameson had known about the abuse for a few months, I had initially been very angry that she hadn't immediately passed it on to me. However, after some thought I realised that whatever the girls told Mrs Jameson in confidence had to be respected; otherwise, no one would ever tell her anything. We had talked it over during the Christmas holidays, and I had thanked her for taking care of Tamsin, and for urging her to tell me.

Mrs Jameson was calling to say that Tamsin had had a major freakie overnight. The local GP had called and given her diazepam, and she was now fine. However, Mrs Jameson called again the next day: Tamsin had had another freakie, and the doctor felt she might be happier at home for a few days. I set off on the two-hour drive immediately, arriving at lunchtime to find Tamsin sleepy but lucid. I brought her home, little realising it would be months before she returned to school.

Even at home, Tamsin continued to have fairly regular freakies. She wouldn't talk to the doctor herself, but I called our GP for advice every few days. She was taking diazepam again, and I wasn't keen for her to go on like that indefinitely. Eventually my GP contacted the Adolescent Unit at the local psychiatric hospital, and the doctors there suggested trying her on betablockers, to reduce the physical effects of her anxiety. They seemed to help, but Tamsin was still a bit of a wreck.

Daniel's return was postponed again and again. All through February, he faxed to say it had been put off for another week, and another. I spoke to him on the phone a couple of times, and also spoke regularly to his mother. Despite the rocky start to our relationship, she seemed to have grown to like and respect me. I was fairly sure that that would end abruptly once she knew what had happened; I thought she would find a way of making it my fault, and I wasn't keen to find out what would happen then.

I told my own parents in February. They had moved to Australia by then, and I had spoken to them every week or two, but hadn't said anything about Tamsin's disclosure. But gradually it became intolerable to keep deceiving them; so one day I asked, 'Does Daniel ever phone you when he's abroad?' I was pretty sure that if they knew, and Daniel phoned them, they would not be able to avoid saying anything.

'No,' replied Mum.

'Well, brace yourself for a shock,' I said. 'We're splitting up, although he doesn't know about it yet.'

'Oh, dear,' Mum said blankly.

'Tamsin told me about a month ago that he's been abusing her for the last five years,' I said as gently as I could.

'Oh, no!' wailed Mum. 'Oh, this is awful!'

We must have talked for about an hour. I had been reluctant to tell them, partly in case Daniel phoned them, but also because I was discovering just how much of a shock it was for people to find out. I hated inflicting pain on friends and family by telling them; I began to understand dimly just how hard it had been for Tamsin to tell me. None of this was my responsibility, or Tamsin's; yet we both felt responsible for inflicting pain on others when we told them.

The girls bought me a present for Mother's Day, to replace Daniel, they said. It was a female dwarf rabbit! She had a mottled brown and white coat, and enormous hind feet, and I called her Porridge. I couldn't help laughing! What a fitting replacement for their father — at least Porridge wouldn't hurt them.

During that month we packed up all of Daniel's belongings. Sam, who doesn't at all mind heights, went up into the attic, and we went through the contents of every box — and there were a lot! Everything was repacked and marked as Daniel's or mine. We packed his clothes, too; mostly into suitcases, and then boxes when we ran out. I wasn't prepared to give him all of our suitcases; we would need some in the future too. We went through all the photographs. The girls did not want to keep any of their father, and neither did I; but I thought perhaps that might change in the future, and so I kept one wedding photograph and one of us as a family.

It was a very difficult task, and I was reminded of the friend who believed it would have been better if Daniel had died. It was hard going through all our souvenirs: little bits and pieces that I had collected while we were travelling; lace tablecloths and napkins and skin rugs which we had bought on our honeymoon; wedding presents. I left all the wedding presents together, apart of course from the items which we used every day, because I thought Daniel would probably want some of those. I had read of women unpicking the stitching in their husbands' clothes, or even cutting them up, but I was never tempted. Partly it was because I try to live so that I will have no regrets; but partly also it was because I still loved Daniel.

My attitude towards Daniel was quite ambivalent at this time. I can't shut off feelings all at once, and we had loved each other for almost twenty years. But I was blazingly angry about what he had done to Tamsin, and to Sam, too. What he had done to me was something I never really thought about. I didn't feel particularly betrayed. I certainly never felt any animosity towards Tamsin, and I never saw her as any sort of rival. It is very frightening to realise that you have been living with someone for almost twenty years, and have spent hundreds of hours talking things through with him, and yet there is a whole large part of his life that you don't know anything about at all. It makes me wonder how much any of us can ever know about someone else. I had always been totally honest with Daniel, and I assumed he had always been totally honest with me. That manifestly was not the case, yet it has taken years for me to understand this, and to question what he says.

It was a very strange period. To all outward appearances nothing had changed, except for Tamsin's and Sam's illness. It was normal for there to be just the three of us; we did the shopping as normal, with the normal amount of money; we lived in the same house; we drove around in the same car. I spoke to Daniel and his family as usual. But at the same time everything had changed. Tamsin was so ill and confused; Sam was so hurt and confused. I was just confused! I didn't know what would become of us. Daniel's family were extremely wealthy and could buy us a little house and give us an allowance to live on, out of their small change. But if they took his side and cut us off, as I suspected might happen, what would become of us?

I kept having visions – no, nightmares! – of being stuck in a tiny council flat seven floors up with no lifts, surrounded by drunks and drug addicts. And would we be allowed to keep the dogs? We stood to lose everything else – I couldn't bear the thought that we might lose our beloved dogs as well. What if we could only keep one? Or two? How could we choose? Lucy was the youngest and the most likely to settle happily in another home, but she was Sam's mainstay – Sam had lost her beloved daddy, how could I deprive her of Lucy as well?

It might seem as though I was coping extremely well, all calm and unruffled. I tried to be that way during the day for the girls' sake, but once they were asleep at night, or out of the house, round and round my mind would go in circles. Many bitter tears were shed. 'This is too hard!' I would cry, 'I can't do this!' And yet I did do it, day after day. What choice did I have?

1995–96

Daniel arrived home on a Saturday in July 1995, four days before we were due to move and a week before we were going to summer school in York. I had booked Pickfords for the removal and they were doing most of the packing, because I could never be sure just when Daniel would be home, and I couldn't do the packing myself because of my back. He was naturally curious to see our new home, but we just drove past the outside, rather than disturb the present occupiers. He knew what the inside layout was – he had been in my parents' house often enough.

The moving went smoothly. The men from Pickfords turned up on Tuesday and packed all the breakables in lovely white paper, which meant they wouldn't need washing when they were unpacked. Tamsin, by now fourteen, flirted with the removal men, and Claire as usual got in the way, but we were happy and excited. We had so much room in the new house. It had the same number of rooms, but they were all bigger, and the sitting room and dining room were completely separate – I had plans for a study area in the dining room. We had arranged for a stairlift to be installed, but that was not going to happen until we got back from York, and so I had to struggle up and down the stairs for the first few days.

The girls were having a week's residential riding holiday in the Yorkshire Dales while Daniel and I were at summer school. We set off on Friday afternoon and stayed overnight with Claire's godparents in Carlisle. Early on Saturday we drove across the Pennines, and found the stables without much trouble. We dropped the girls and their luggage off and headed down the motorway to York. We enjoyed ourselves when we were alone, because the main, really the only, source of disagreement between us was the girls. Without them around, Daniel was more relaxed and more like the man I had married. Sometimes I felt a bit resentful towards them, but only fleetingly – after all, they were children, while Daniel was supposed to be an adult. I felt he should take at least half of the responsibility for their relationship.

We thoroughly enjoyed our week in York. As always, the work was very demanding, but also fascinating, and there was lots of good company. We phoned the girls every night. Daniel phoned on Sunday, because I was involved in a quiz night, and came back grinning. 'How are they?' I asked.

'They're fine – now!' he replied.

'What's happened?' I demanded with a mixture of alarm and resignation. It turned out that they had gone up to the field to collect the ponies that morning. One of those being left in the field had whirled round and kicked out, and caught Claire on the elbow and shoulder blade. She had been X-rayed at the local hospital – no fracture – and been given a sling, returning to the stables by late morning. After lunch, she threw the sling away and just had a good time – typical Claire!

Summer school finished on Friday afternoon, but the girls' holiday continued until Saturday, and so Daniel and I had the whole night to ourselves. We checked into a large hotel at Scotch Corner for a luxurious evening alone, after a week in separate bedrooms in the student residence. The following morning we set off on a leisurely drive to the stables, stopping whenever anything took our interest.

When we arrived at the stables, there was no one there – they had gone for a final ride. They had each been given a pony to look after for the week, and of course had fallen in love with them. Claire left quite happily, but Tamsin had tears in her eyes as she bade 'her' pony farewell.

We enjoyed our journey home, winding through the Dales and along the A68 – an old Roman road which goes straight as an arrow for miles, but up and down like a roller coaster. Once home we began the process of settling in and unpacking. The house was in pretty good condition but we wanted to redecorate – at least the girls and I did, and Daniel said he did, but that didn't seem to extend to actually doing something about it. He had been horrified by the state of the fuse box when we moved in, but somehow never got around to doing anything about it that leave. We did have a lot of unpacking to do. We had boxes of breakables which had not been unpacked for about three house moves.

Soon it was time for Daniel to return to sea, and for the girls to go back to school. Tamsin's school had moved at the same time as us, from Peebles to the depths of

Dumfriesshire. They now had much more room, better classrooms and thirty acres of grounds including a small loch. We drove Tamsin down for the first time. The girls were housed in a cottage in the grounds, which had been freshly decorated for them. Tamsin shared a room on the ground floor, which looked across a couple of acres of lawn to the main school, an old baronial mansion where the boys' bedrooms, the classrooms and the offices were. It was beautiful, and everyone was very excited about the new school.

Daniel flew off a couple of days later, and Claire and I settled into a new routine. Tamsin travelled down to school on Sunday evening and home on Friday afternoon on a minibus service provided by the school. Claire had been catching the 8.10 a.m. train to Edinburgh; but her school day started at 9.15 a.m., and so now we had time to exercise the dogs together before I drove her to school. There was a cycle track near the house, where the old railway line had been covered in tarmac, and that made a splendid dog walk. I spent my day studying and collected her from school in the afternoon.

Our dog population now totalled three – Claire had been given her own puppy, Lucy, that summer. That had caused a bit of grief! We had discussed it at the beginning of the year. Sally was really Tamsin's dog, and Fly was definitely mine, and I felt that now that Claire was eleven, she was old enough to look after her own dog. Daniel and I discussed it on our own and with the girls, and had decided that if we went to Australia, Claire would be given a dog there, and if not, she would be given one here. But when the time came, Daniel denied ever having talked about it. He was vehemently opposed to the very idea – quite unreasonably,

I felt, especially in view of the fact that we had spent so much time talking about it the previous winter. But eventually he gave in with bad grace.

We found Lucy at the local animal shelter. Originally we had wanted a young dog of about a year old, so that we didn't have to go through the whole house-training bit. However, the youngest 'adult' dog was two, and nipped, whereas there was a litter of beautiful puppies, just about ready to leave. Claire fell in love with Lucy the moment she saw her. She was a scrap of honey-coloured fur, with a black tip to her tail and black edgings round her ears and lips. She had dainty little feet, and I thought she probably wouldn't grow too big.

When we brought Lucy home, the other two weren't quite sure what to make of her. Sally was very bossy, leaving Lucy in no doubt about who was in charge, while Fly was terrified of her to begin with. However, by the end of the first week, Fly had discovered that Lucy would play 'hide and seek' around the garden shed with her, and from that moment, Fly and Lucy have been the best of friends. Fly was nearly six when Lucy came, and behaved as though she were semi-retired; but Lucy gave her a new lease of life, and she still behaves more like a two-year-old than the ten-year-old she now is.

You know the saying about looking at a puppy's paws to gauge how big it will grow? Forget it! Lucy had tiny feet, but they grew faster than any other part of her. She grew, and grew, and grew! She's now about the size of a Labrador, but with a longer muzzle and tail and a tucked-up tummy; we think she's a Labrador-greyhound cross. But she's the best thing that ever happened to Claire. She and Lucy are inseparable, and Lucy has been Claire's best friend ever since she arrived.

That autumn something happened which changed life for the three of us. We were offered the chance of free screening at a chiropractic clinic, and because I felt that Claire was at risk of back problems because of her 'odd' legs, I took them both at half-term. I was astonished when the chiropractor diagnosed Claire's asthma from looking at her thoracic vertebrae. I was flabbergasted when he diagnosed Tamsin's recurrent tonsillitis from looking at her neck. Both girls began regular treatments immediately. Then after my exam was over, I began to have treatment myself. The chiropractor made no promises, but felt he could certainly make a difference. And so it proved. I never regained the full use of my legs, but my pain levels stabilised and then fell. The best aspect was that it took all the fear away. If I had a fall at home – not unusual – it could take weeks to recover; but now all I had to do was trot along to the clinic, and I'd be feeling better in days. Claire found she had much less hip pain, and threw herself into hockey with enormous enthusiasm. Even Tamsin seemed to feel a bit better, although she still wasn't sleeping.

That Christmas Daniel was home. We decorated the sitting room, and Daniel replaced the fuse box. We bought a new bed. We threw a party. We went out without the girls. Life seemed to be settling down again. I thought we had it made. We had the big semi in leafy suburbia. We had a Volvo at the door. Both girls seemed to be settled well in school.

But Tamsin still wasn't sleeping. She didn't like her father being around her, but I thought that was just the same awkwardness I had felt with my father at her age. And she was ill. She had come home from school with tonsillitis. She had another dose of tonsillitis just after Christmas, and a third in the New Year, and finally was diagnosed as having glandular fever. She missed the whole spring term. She had been due to sit nine Standard Grades in May, but all that had to be put on hold for a year.

Daniel went back to sea at the end of January, and I began my fifth year of Open University. This was my first honours year, social psychology. The course was new – in its first year of presentation. The work looked more interesting than I had expected. Coming as I did from a scientific background, I had felt completely at home with the more 'scientific' aspects of psychology. I had just done a year of neurobiology, and loved it. But I had to complete this year to obtain a degree profile acceptable to the British Psychological Society, and by now I had accumulated three distinctions from four years' study. I was beginning to have academic ambitions, and trying for first class honours so that I could continue with postgraduate work. So I determined that I was just going to work hard, even if I found it a bit boring.

But I didn't. My tutor was an Irishwoman called Jenny, and we seemed to 'click' from the first time we spoke on the phone. We spent hours chatting after tutorials on Saturday mornings. As Jenny lived quite near us, I used to give her a lift home, and soon she was coming back for lunch, meeting Daniel and the girls, becoming a family friend. She was a single parent with one son still at home and an older, married stepson, and she was a staff tutor for the Open University. Having helped to develop the course, she was very interested in feedback from students, and seemed to value my opinions.

Because it was a third-level course, there was a lot of reading to do, and that and looking after the girls filled my days. Claire began taking Lucy to obedience training classes and seemed to be doing well with her. Tamsin returned to school after Easter, just about the time her father came home. When I look back on it now, every weekend that leave she seemed to have a friend to stay, or went to stay with a friend. Claire had arranged to go to a dog show in Glasgow on the final weekend of Daniel's leave, and then Tamsin phoned from school to ask if she could stay with a friend in Glasgow that weekend. I reminded her that it was her father's last weekend, and she said she would probably meet us at the dog show – but she didn't. But I didn't think much about it at the time. I thought it was a normal part of growing up, spending less time with her family and more time with her friends.

We didn't have a holiday that summer. Daniel was away for the whole of the school holidays, and so we had day outings instead. We had become members at the zoo, and I now had a trailer to carry my electric buggy around, and so we went there often. Tamsin had ambitions to be a primatologist, and Jenny had done some research with chimps, so they had lots to talk about.

Just before Daniel came home in September, the girls and I bought wallpaper and paint for their bedrooms. They had previously been occupied by boys and were rather stark and uninviting. Tamsin had wanted to paint and rag-roll her room, but I thought the plaster probably wouldn't be good enough; but we managed to find some paper that had the same effect. Claire bought paper with cute puppies and a matching border.

Daniel didn't seem very pleased to find that he was expected to come home and decorate. When we first married, he had been very keen on DIY, but as time went on he became less and less keen to do anything in the house. Now I wonder if it was because he didn't choose that house himself; but we had discussed it on the phone and he agreed with the location, and had seemed very happy with it. I couldn't work out what was wrong with him. All he seemed to want to do was play solitaire on our lovely new computer. We had spent £1,600 just for him to play a card game!

The rooms were decorated, but grudgingly.

Tamsin followed the same pattern as the previous leave, trying to have friends to stay or go to visit friends. But still I didn't twig that she was trying to avoid her father. I spent one Saturday at Stirling University at a study day, leaving early in the morning and not returning until mid-evening. By now I was completely hooked, both on social psychology and on the philosophical issues it raised. I had met philosophy before, and been bored by it. But I realised quite early in the course that the road to high marks was to deal with the philosophical issues as well as the psychology, and so I began studying it for the sake of my marks. However, soon it began to exercise a fascination of its own, which it still has today. It wasn't easy – I had to read some passages over and over until I finally extracted the meaning. But that was so satisfying: to struggle for understanding, and then achieve it. I thoroughly enjoyed the study day, and returned in mid-evening to find, for once, a scene of calm and a meal all ready.

Daniel went back to sea in early October, and I worked relentlessly until my exam at the end of the month. Then it was relaxing time! Tamsin had chosen curtains with an

March 1997

February had come and gone, and still Daniel didn't come home. Jim Morris phoned every few days, despite my assurances that I would call him as soon as Daniel returned.

Tamsin was a little better on her betablockers. She was having fewer freakies, but she still couldn't face going back to school, and she still needed a lot of care and attention and reassurance. Sam was just Sam. She carried on with her normal routine; she walked the dogs with me; she did the shopping with me; she carried the washing out to the drier in the garage and back again; she looked after the rabbits and guinea pigs. She was so worried about what would happen with her schooling, but she kept cheerful most of the time. Having Lucy helped a lot.

We were still waiting for the Child Protection Case Conference to take place, and after that there would be an Inter-Agency Assessment to decide whether the local authority would fund Sam at Tamsin's school. In the meantime, as Daniel's salary was still coming into the bank every month, her school fees were still being paid. It must have been a very anxious time for Sam, but she coped magnificently.

I had a lot of nightmares at this time. I kept dreaming that Daniel had come home and the police had missed him at the airport, and I couldn't find, or remember, the number of the police station. Once I dreamt that he had raped me and was trying to get to Sam, and I was dancing naked on the lawn, screaming for help. Another time I dreamt that he was home, and Tamsin was safe, but Sam was dead. Once I woke up screaming, 'Get out of my head!' I was very aware of the almost telepathic link I had had with him, and was desperately afraid that somehow he would pick up on our distress.

Sam and I talked about what we would do if Daniel came home without warning, or if the police missed him at the airport; I didn't dare discuss it in front of Tamsin.

'We could send him upstairs for a shower while we call the police,' I suggested.

'But Mum,' gasped Sam, 'he would see all his clothes were packed!'

'So he would, I never thought of that! Well, we can't unpack everything!'

We wracked our brains and eventually decided that once we knew Daniel was on his way, we would leave the house and not return until we knew he was in custody. Because he was flying from the Far East, he would call from the airport in Jakarta the day before he arrived home, and we usually met him at Edinburgh Airport the following morning.

I was in close touch with the police, as the time drew

nearer for Daniel's return. We had discussed the possibility that Daniel might leave the country given the chance, but the police did not have the power to remove his passport. However, they had assured me that they would make vigorous representations in court for it to be confiscated.

Daniel's homecoming had been 'next week' since the middle of February, but at last it seemed it really would be next week. The date was set for the first Tuesday in March. I told Barbara and she arranged to be on duty that day, and awaited my call with the flight details.

On Monday, I took Sam to school and then sat waiting by the phone. When no call had come by two o'clock, I phoned the ship.

'Sorry, love,' said Daniel, 'the chief's not back yet. He's coming tomorrow.'

On Tuesday, I took Sam to school and then sat waiting by the phone. When no call had come by two o'clock, I phoned the ship.

'Sorry, love,' said Daniel, 'the chief's not back yet. He's coming tomorrow.'

On Wednesday, I took Sam to school and then sat waiting by the phone. When no call had come by two o'clock, I phoned the ship.

'Sorry, love,' said Daniel, 'the chief's not back yet. He's coming tomorrow.'

'When on earth is he actually going to get there?' I exploded. I was still conscious of playing a role, but even in my former life, I would have been exasperated by the continual delays, especially when Daniel had been gone so long. And the tension now was almost unbearable. I couldn't concentrate on anything. I couldn't read, and I was snappy with the girls, who were also feeling the strain. All I could do was sit and smoke and watch the clock.

'He's in the hotel tonight,' replied Daniel, 'and he'll definitely be aboard in the morning.'

On Thursday, I took Sam to school and then sat by the phone. At lunchtime it rang – at last! Daniel was off the ship and at the airport. I made sure I got the flight numbers, because of the mix-up the last time, I said, and rang off. It had been a difficult conversation. Daniel was elated at finally coming home, and full of protestations of love. Normally I would have reciprocated, and I did, but it was extremely difficult to force any enthusiasm into my voice.

I called Barbara immediately and assured her that this time it was definitely on. I also called Sam's school and told them she would be absent the next day, for family reasons. Then I called Lisa, our account manager at the bank, and told her what had happened.

'Oh, Mrs Schenker! How awful for you!' she gasped. 'Oh, Mrs Schenker! I can't believe it. Oh, Mrs Schenker!'

Perhaps unfairly, I was by now becoming rather impatient with the length of time it took for people to grasp what I was telling them and move on to business. However, eventually Lisa took hold of herself.

'What we normally do with a marriage break-up is to freeze the joint account,' she said. 'Have you got enough money for now?' I assured her we had enough to last until the following week, which was the earliest I could come to see her.

'I want you to cancel the Visa card immediately,' I said. 'If Daniel has the opportunity, I think he might just buy himself a ticket to Singapore and disappear. The police can't remove his passport and there's no guarantee that the court will, especially if he denies it.'

'We can certainly do that,' she replied.

I also called Jim Morris. Now that Daniel was in the air, no one could warn him not to come home; but I was still cautious. I told Jim Morris merely that we were splitting up, but not the reason. I gave him Daniel's mother's phone number, and said he would probably be able to reach Daniel there the following Monday.

I arranged for the choir members to be told that evening, and did not attend myself. I called a few who I felt were friends, rather than acquaintances, so that they could hear the news from me. All were sympathetic, but some found it hard to say anything at all.

Somehow we got through the rest of the day. Tamsin found it hard to settle, and needed a lot of reassurance that, yes, she had done the right thing, and no, it wasn't her fault, and yes, we would be well away from the house before Daniel's flight landed at Edinburgh.

That evening I phoned Daniel's mother, ostensibly to let her know that Daniel was on his way. But really I wanted to talk to her 'normally' for just one last time. Something told me that we would probably never speak again once she knew what Daniel had done. I felt desperately sorry for Daniel's parents, knowing what they were going to have to face in the next few weeks. It was really difficult not to say anything about it, but I felt that Daniel should tell them, not me.

We had decided to spend the morning at The Gyle, an edge-of-town shopping centre. The police had my mobile number and would call as soon as Daniel was in custody.

In the meantime, as an antidote to the fear, I had withdrawn all the money I could before the credit card was cancelled, and we were going to have some retail therapy!

For once, Tamsin got up immediately she was called, and we swiftly walked the dogs and were on the road by eight thirty. As soon as we arrived at the shopping centre, I went straight to the nearest jeweller to have my wedding ring cut off. I was torn between tears at losing something that had once been so precious to me, and relief that I no longer wore any sign of being attached to Daniel. I sold it for scrap – it was worth only £8, but I felt it was a symbolic act.

We wandered around the shopping centre, which is only a couple of miles from the airport. Daniel's flight was due to land at nine thirty. We went upstairs to the cafe. Was that his flight passing overhead?

Time wore on and my mobile didn't ring. At ten thirty we bought drinks and went outside. It was a lovely, warm, sunny spring morning, and as we sat by the fountain, I called the police station.

'Sorry,' said the desk sergeant, 'we haven't heard anything yet. We'll call as soon as we do.'

Tamsin asked if she could have £5, but wouldn't say for what. I gave her the money and as I watched her sprinting back inside the mall, closely followed by Sam, it dawned on me what she was doing. She had been nagging me for the past couple of years to have her ears pierced, and now she was doing it! Oh, well, she had been warned – I don't do teeth, and I don't do sick, and I don't do ears. If anything went wrong, she would have to deal with it herself.

Ten minutes later they emerged, Tamsin proudly sporting gold studs. She was so pleased with herself that I couldn't be angry, and after all as she pointed out, it was her body, she was nearly sixteen, she would look after them. And it took everyone's mind off the wait. What on earth was the delay?

We went back inside and wandered around again. The minutes crawled by, and still the mobile didn't ring. I imagined all sorts of scenarios: Daniel had missed the flight; the police hadn't found him and he was on his way home by taxi; the police had found him, but he had escaped. We bought some clothes, and some computer games, and some magazines, and after another interminable hour, I called the police station.

'We've just heard they've got him,' replied the desk sergeant. 'The flight was delayed, but they're on their way back to the station now.'

I rang off and told the girls – I think we were all mightily relieved. We went home and played our new computer games, but all the time my imagination was running riot. At half past four Barbara called me.

'He's admitted everything,' she told me. 'We've got his confession on audio and videotape, and he's added some details to what Tamsin told us about last September, which makes it a very credible confession. He wants me to tell you that he's never raped Tamsin, and he's never been unfaithful to you with anyone else.'

'Did everything go all right at the airport?' I asked.

'Yes, the first thing he asked was if you had had an accident, but once we told him what it was about, he came quietly. He refused to talk about it there – he wanted to wait until we got to the station. He nearly talked my ears off on the way into town! All about his flight, and his trip, and what he had been doing.'

'Yes, that's Daniel,' I said sadly. 'What happens now?'

'It's too late for him to go to court today, so he'll be kept in the cells until Monday and then go to court. I'll come round and see you in the morning, and give you more news then.'

I put the phone down, put my head in my arms, and cried my eyes out. Even though I was convinced Tamsin had been telling the truth, still a tiny part of me had hoped it was all a mistake, it wasn't true, it wasn't happening, we could work it out. Now it was all gone.

I called Sam's godmother, Maria, and told her what had happened. I couldn't help crying.

'You're feeling sorry for him!' she gasped in disbelief, and it was true. All day I had been imagining him, expecting to come home to a joyful reunion, and instead being met by the police and carted off to be charged with assault. I had thought of him sitting in the interview room; sitting in a cell; hearing the doors clang shut; knowing they closed off all access to his family and to the life he had known, as well as to the exit.

Maria couldn't believe I could still feel sorry for him, after seeing Tamsin so ill, but I still loved him.

I called Jenny, and met much the same response. My friends were puzzled that I could still have feelings for Daniel. But you can't suddenly stop loving someone you've loved for twenty years. It took a long time and a lot of unpleasantness to kill my love for Daniel.

Barbara arrived mid-morning the next day. Daniel had asked for his suit and a decent shirt and tie for his court appearance, and for a warm sweater. He always felt the cold when he came home. Sam and I rushed around, unpacking his clothes and repacking what he would need. It was almost as though he were in hospital, rather than in a police cell. We still felt so much love for him, and wanted to make him as comfortable as possible. Tamsin kept out of the way.

Barbara said that Daniel was just lying in his cell, thinking. He didn't want newspapers or books, just tea and lots of it. He had been seen crying, which made me feel awful. I had never known Daniel to cry, not even when his beloved grandmother died.

In some ways the balance between us had shifted over the years. At first I loved Daniel desperately. I would have done anything for him. I was fairly sure he loved me, but I wasn't so sure that he needed me as much as I needed him. But as time went on, I became much more independent. Partly it was due to Daniel's unwavering love in our first few years together. Having sole responsibility for both girls for much of the time probably had a lot to do with it. I had fought many battles over the years, such as for Tamsin's Record of Needs and funding for her school, which had given me a lot of confidence in myself. In more recent times I had learnt through bitter experience that Daniel couldn't be relied on for help, except with what he himself wanted to do, and had become much more self-reliant. I had also grown a great deal through my studies.

Daniel, on the other hand, seemed to have stood still. For the last few years he had seemed to rely on me much more than I did on him, and I was fearful of what the break between us would do to him. I imagined him heartbroken at losing me and the girls, and filled with shame at having committed such a horrific crime.

These thoughts preoccupied me all weekend. Once again

I cried myself to sleep every night. Once again my dreams were filled with menace and foreboding.

Barbara phoned on Monday afternoon. Daniel had been bailed, with strict conditions not to approach either Tamsin or me, and his passport had been confiscated. The custody sergeant had refused to allow him to have any of the clothes we had provided for him, and I felt so sorry for him having to appear in court in the same clothes that he had left Jakarta airport in, four days previously.

The Child Protection Case Conference had been called for the following day, and was held in the local social work centre. I brought Tamsin and Sam with me, because Tamsin was pretty ill and Sam wasn't old enough to take responsibility for her, and one of the social workers looked after them while the meeting went on. Mr and Mrs Jameson from Tamsin's school were there, and also Sam's headmistress, Mrs Lucas. Barbara was there, and Tina, and a senior social worker.

Barbara explained about the conditions of bail. Daniel had been bailed to a hotel — really a posh word for a bail hostel — which, we realised with horror, was only five minutes' walk from Sam's school. Worse still, because Sam was not to be a Crown witness, her name did not appear on the exclusion order which protected Tamsin and me. But there was nothing we could do about it, except to be vigilant.

Mr Jameson explained that all the senior members of staff were aware of the circumstances. The only way to get to the school was by car, and all visitors were expected to report to the office. Arrangements had already been made that if Daniel were to turn up there, he would be detained in the office and the police called. Mrs Lucas said she would institute the same arrangements at Sam's school the following day.

Tina then gave her report. She felt that both girls had a warm relationship with me, and the fact that I had reported the abuse immediately gave her confidence that I would not allow Daniel to see them. She felt there was no need to take the girls into care, or even to place their names on the 'At Risk' register. It became blindingly obvious that if I had not taken the steps I had, I could have lost custody of the girls, and I was more glad than ever that I had reported the abuse promptly.

Sam's future schooling was briefly discussed, but this was not the correct meeting to make decisions about funding. The senior social worker pronounced herself satisfied that all appropriate measures had been taken in the meantime, and the meeting closed.

The following day I went out to the bank. When we moved to Edinburgh, we had left our joint account at the branch in West Lothian, because we had telephone banking set up and because we knew our account manager, Lisa. The first shock was when Lisa told me that Daniel had been to the bank the previous day. He had opened a new account for himself and had arranged for £2,000 to be transferred to it as soon as his salary was paid in at the end of the month. We discussed the best way forward for me and the girls, and Lisa advised me to open a new account in my name only. She wrote a note for me to sign, authorising her to transfer the remaining funds from the joint account into my new account as soon as the salary arrived, and then removing my name from the joint account. That way I would not be left to pay the household bills with no income.

On my return home, another shock awaited. A letter had arrived from the Edinburgh store where we had an account, demanding the return of my card. Shortly afterwards, a bailiff appeared with a legal document, cancelling the power of attorney which I held. I had to hand over the power of attorney and sign the document. I began to feel a bit like a criminal myself. I had imagined that Daniel would be feeling crushed, humiliated and placatory. I was soon to discover how little I actually knew him.

Tamsin was still unwell. She had been having quite a few freakies, despite the betablockers, and was having to take diazepam again. She had enormous difficulty in sleeping at night, sometimes lying awake until almost daylight and then sleeping most of the day. Sometimes she had night-mares and woke me with her screaming.

About a week after Daniel's return, she burst into my bedroom at 2 a.m. and announced, 'I'm sick of not being able to sleep, so I've taken five of your sleeping pills!' And with that, she collapsed on my bed and fell asleep. I phoned the emergency doctor, who advised that she was unlikely to come to any harm, but that I should watch her all night in case she rolled over and suffocated. What a long night that was! It really brought home to me how much damage Daniel had done to her.

In the morning, I called Tamsin's clinical psychologist in Dumfries and told her what had happened. She seemed to feel that this was more of a cry for help than a serious suicide attempt. 'Ask her why she couldn't wake you before she took the pills,' she suggested. 'Sometimes kids have a serious self and a wild self, and the serious self can be horrified by what the wild self does, but unable to stop it. You need to work out a plan so that the next time she feels desperate, she already knows what to do.'

That sounded to me like good advice. Tamsin slept nearly all day, and wasn't really awake enough to talk until after tea. When Sam went to her room to do her homework, I asked Tamsin what she thought we could do to make her safe.

'I need locking up,' she said sadly. 'I couldn't stay at school because there was no one around at night to keep me safe, and even you can't protect me during the night.'

I was horrified by what she said. We discussed what had happened the previous night, and it turned out that Tamsin had emptied all of the drugs we possessed out of their bottles, and lined them up on the kitchen worktop, while she decided what to do. It seemed we were fortunate that she had taken only five sleepers. Now I realised that the person Tamsin was most frightened of was not Daniel, but Tamsin. I felt that this was way too much for me to deal with alone; so while I hugged Tamsin, I called the emergency doctor again. We discussed the matter briefly and he felt he needed to talk to Tamsin himself.

We went along to the local hospital where the emergency doctors are based. Poor Sam was beginning to get used to being dragged all over the place! She sat quietly in the waiting room while Tamsin and I spoke to the doctor.

'What you really want me to do is to tell you whether Tamsin is safe at home with you,' he said.

'Well, that's the immediate issue,' I agreed.

'I have to say I don't think admission to a psychiatric hospital is the best option,' he said. 'I do understand that you don't feel qualified to make the assessment alone, and that you want to share the responsibility. I will give you some sleeping pills for Tamsin for tonight, but you'll have to contact your GP in the morning for a proper assessment.'

So that was what we did. Tamsin slept well that night, and in the morning I spoke to our GP, Dr Mackenzie. He already knew about the overdose, and agreed to phone the psychiatric hospital. He rang back an hour or so later to say that the registrar would see Tamsin at the Adolescent Unit at five o'clock that day. I didn't want to drag Sam along yet again, and so I phoned friends from the choir who lived near the hospital. Lorna agreed at once to take care of Sam.

Five o'clock found Tamsin and me sitting in the waiting room. The psychiatric registrar came along and took Tamsin away to speak to her alone. They were gone for about an hour, and then the doctor asked to see me alone.

'What's been happening?' she asked. 'There don't seem to be any major problems, but Tamsin said you would fill me in on the background.'

'You mean she hasn't told you?' I asked, amazed. 'She disclosed just before Christmas that her father has abused her for the past five years.'

The doctor's face was a picture. 'Oh!' she said. 'Well, that certainly puts a very different perspective on it!'

We discussed the situation for some time. The doctor felt that in view of the fact that Tamsin had said nothing to her about the abuse, she probably wasn't ready for counselling; but the doctor felt that it would be helpful for their counsellor to see Tamsin for the next few weeks. She felt that continued use of diazepam was justified in the short term, and she prescribed some stronger sleeping pills for the next couple of weeks.

After that, Tamsin seemed to improve quite a lot. I had no idea what she and Sheila, the counsellor, discussed, but it seemed to help, and a few nights of sleeping well made a huge difference. The freakies stopped, and Tamsin began to return to her old, bubbly, cheerful self, full of fun and jokes. She was still pretty volatile, but she had had a volatile temperament ever since the whooping cough inoculation reaction, and this I felt I could deal with.

The following week I had a phone call from my solicitor, Kim. Daniel had turned up at the office, screaming and shouting in reception that no passport equalled no job, and he wanted the house put on the market immediately. Kim advised against that, but warned that we would probably be forced to sell it soon.

'But I can't get a mortgage,' I told her. 'I don't have any income and I can't use my trust fund as security, because the money is abroad. Surely Daniel has to provide housing for us?'

'He has no legal obligation,' Kim said. 'This is something you will have to take responsibility for. If you can't get a mortgage, you'll have to rent something, but that won't be easy because of the dogs.'

I was horror-struck. I looked at some advertisements for private rented property, but even a small flat would cost at least £400 a month, which we didn't have. I didn't know anything about housing benefit, but I thought we couldn't afford a bungalow, and we couldn't put a stair lift into a rented house. It felt like my nightmares about council housing might actually become reality. It felt like another hundred-ton weight had just been deposited on my shoulders.

In the middle of the month, Kim passed on letters which she had received from Daniel, which confirmed that, far from being contrite, he was blazing mad! He provided a list of items which he regarded as his sole property, and demanded that I should pack them ready for someone else to collect. He also demanded photocopies of all our financial papers, and asked for explanations about the mortgage and insurance policies. I had carefully gone over all of this with him in 1995, when we had bought the house, but obviously it had gone in one ear and out the other.

I was absolutely stunned by Daniel's reaction! I had expected him to feel guilty about what he was putting us through, and to want to take care of us as best he could. Instead, it seemed that now that he was cut off from us, Daniel would do what Daniel wanted to do, and that certainly did not include helping us. After all, we were the ones who had got him into trouble. We could whistle for support!

April 1997

In many ways April was a better month, but then it wouldn't be hard to better March. I had managed to secrete the princely sum of £654 out of the joint account before my name was removed, and although that was all the money we had, we also didn't have to pay the household bills for the moment, as they were still coming out of what had been the joint account. I had my disability benefits and child benefit, and I applied for income support, which was granted immediately. So we had enough to live on for the next few weeks.

Tamsin was much better, and returned to school for the summer term. She had two weeks of school before sitting six Standard Grades – Mr Jameson had decided that she had missed so much school that she should defer English, maths and computing, all subjects with which she had extra difficulty. But she went cheerfully off to school each Sunday evening, and returned equally cheerfully on Friday afternoon. She had stopped taking diazepam and sleeping pills, but was still on the betablockers. But they were handed over to the matron, as I felt it was safer to keep Tamsin and drugs apart for a while.

Daniel had a job! I think George, the minister, had a hand in it, because he felt that would be the best way to occupy Daniel's time while he waited for the court case, and now Daniel was working offshore in the North Sea. Kim immediately submitted a claim for £1,500 per month in interim aliment; the mortgage and household bills totalled £1,200 per month, and that was the least I felt we could manage on. Daniel's lawyer wrote back with a copy of a wage slip from Highland Offshore, showing that Daniel was receiving only £1,200 per month, and offering £750 per month. That caused a serious rethink. I knew I wouldn't get away with not paying bills for very long; we had to reduce our outgoings drastically.

The house had to go. The mortgage was over £600 a month, and there was a life assurance policy costing £80 a month as well. The first step was to reduce these payments as much as possible; I contacted the building society to arrange to pay interest only, which cut the mortgage to under £500, and I arranged to cancel the insurance policy.

Next the car. We were paying nearly £200 a month for the loan, £40 a month for insurance and £20 a week for petrol. I loved my big Volvo, but it had to go. I had been entitled to a Motability car for several years, but had preferred to take the benefit in cash. Now I began to investigate contract leasing seriously, and found it was a really good deal. My benefit paid for the leasing, the insurance, repairs and servicing, and AA membership. All I would have to pay for was petrol.

I spent an interesting couple of weeks looking at different makes of car. I couldn't afford to pay a deposit, which limited us to small hatchbacks. And there had to be enough room in the back for my wheelchair and the electric hoist which lifts it in and out of the car. I needed an automatic with power steering and brakes. I tried out a Corsa and a small Peugeot, but I fell in love with the Citroen Saxo; not least because it came with a sunroof. But it also had a 1.6 litre fuel injection engine, and front-wheel drive; my first car was a Mini, and I have many happy memories of driving fast around the twisting Highland roads. Lisa at the bank had said there was about £4,000 left to repay on the car loan; the dealer offered me that for the Volvo, and so we were all set. Delivery would be at the beginning of July. I was so excited! My first ever brand new car!

We had a memorable moment at the car dealership. I was completing the endless forms with the agent, Greg, with Sam sitting beside me. Meanwhile Tamsin was sitting inside a Saxo in the showroom, playing with the controls.

'How do I adjust the seat?' she called across the show-room.

'There's a bar under the seat – lift it up and the seat will slide,' advised Greg.

There was silence for a few moments before Tamsin again interrupted.

'I can't find it,' she called.

I was exasperated by her constant interruptions. 'Just fiddle about a bit between your legs!' I called – and suddenly realised what I had said! Greg's face turned bright red, as the showroom erupted in laughter.

We needed the lighter moments in life, as financial reality impacted on me with a vengeance. I added up all the household bills, mortgage, etc., after these reductions had been made. It still came to nearly £800 per month, and we also needed money for food. My benefits would help but they weren't enough to live on, and my income support would stop, of course. Daniel didn't have any overheads on board ship — no food or heating or lighting to pay for — so Kim wrote and said I would accept £850 per month. But the most Daniel would go to was £775. Kim pointed out that he could make life very difficult for us by refusing to pay our household bills, and it seemed that I had no choice but to accept. Eventually I agreed to accept £775 per month, but we did manage to delay it until the beginning of July.

In April we had the Inter-Agency meeting to decide Sam's future education. Tina had written to me to say she could not support the request for Sam to go to Tamsin's school. She felt that Sam was well looked after at home, and that the relationship between us was strong and supportive, and therefore there was no need for her to attend a residential school. Tina had obviously felt that she could not risk telling me face to face, and I felt a bit let down by that, and very let down by her decision, although not terribly surprised.

It was a difficult meeting. Sam had made it plain she did not want to continue at her school. She understood now why she had found it difficult to make friends, but felt it was too late to change anything, and wanted a fresh start. Mr Nathan, the educational psychologist, was quite keen for Sam to go to Tamsin's school, but the decision was no longer his to take – most of the power rested with the social work department, and they were most reluctant to pay fees for Sam. They suggested that she be placed in a state school with lots of support, and couldn't quite see why I felt that being the centre of attention in this way would only make life more difficult for Sam.

I left the meeting in despair. It was clear that the social work department were not going to pay for Sam. My only hope was that the Conservatives could win the election on 1 May; if that happened, Tamsin's school would be given funding for assisted places, and Sam could go after all.

One thing I had to deal with immediately was to submit a claim on Tamsin's behalf for criminal injuries compensation as Tamsin didn't want any involvement in it. This had to be done before the end of April when Tamsin turned sixteen, the age of legal capability in Scotland. I filled out the forms with the help of my solicitor and sent them off. Tamsin was quite excited to see that she might be awarded some thousands of pounds, depending on how long it took her to recover mentally.

'Don't get too excited,' I warned her. 'The solicitor thinks it will probably be about two years before you actually get any money.'

We couldn't afford a holiday over Easter, but we went out for day trips. One trip was to Deep Sea World, just over the Forth Road Bridge in Rosyth. Because I use a wheelchair, I do not have to pay admission, and I am allowed one helper at half price. We also had a coupon for a free child's entry from a newspaper. It was a super day – the whole building is wheelchair accessible, and there is so much to see. We had another day at the zoo, as our membership had been paid for that year.

That month I wrote to Daniel's mother. I didn't know how Daniel's family would react, and had even bought an answering machine so that I could screen calls if necessary, but there had been nothing but an ominous silence. Then Jenny suggested that maybe Mrs Schenker was afraid that I would be abusive towards her. 'After all,' she said, 'if it was my son, I would expect his wife to come after the whole family with a sawn-off shotgun!' That was a thought that had not occurred to me. I talked it over with George, our minister, and then wrote Mrs Schenker a short letter. I simply said I was sorry I had not been able to tell her myself what had happened. I wanted to thank her for the kindness she had shown me in the past years, and to reassure her that I blamed no one but Daniel. I understood if it was too painful for her to talk to me just now, but if ever she wanted to contact me in the future, she should not hesitate.

I needn't have bothered. George came round one day to collect the rest of Daniel's belongings, and brought a letter from Daniel – breaking his bail conditions, I might add – which went some way towards explaining his attitude. 'Mum is quite bitter it couldn't have been dealt with in the family,' he wrote. So that was it. I was to be blamed for reporting the abuse. It was made quite clear that if I hadn't gone to the police, 'the family' would have seen we didn't suffer.

I have to say it never entered my head not to report the abuse. Strictly speaking, it was social services who involved the police, but yes, I had co-operated fully. It had been made quite clear to me from the start that if I didn't co-operate, the social workers would have looked very hard at whether I should be allowed to keep the girls. If they had been taken into care, Tamsin would have returned quite quickly, because she was sixteen that month, but Sam was only thirteen. They needed one parent who was prepared to put their needs first.

The facts of the abuse would have come out whether I reported it or not. Tamsin had been so ill, and for her to receive appropriate treatment it was essential that the doctors knew what they were dealing with. Doctors have a duty of disclosure if they think a child is at risk, and the girls would have ended up in care.

And anyway, who is protected by dealing with such matters 'in the family'? Only the abuser. If we had quietly divorced, Daniel would have had unrestricted access to the girls, and I was not prepared to risk their security. Not reporting it might have left other children at risk, too; there is evidence to suggest that men who are prevented from abusing their own children might turn to other children. I had no idea at this stage whether Daniel was a threat to other children, but I had to do everything in my power to protect ours. And Tamsin needed the reassurance that society does not tolerate abuse, which only Daniel's punishment could secure.

No, I had no regrets, but I was at first puzzled, and then shocked by Daniel's apparent inability to acknowledge the implications and horror of his particular crime. This was my first experience of the denial which abusers and their families use to protect themselves from acknowledging the harm they have caused. I searched the library for books on the subject. There wasn't much available, but I came to see that this denial is what allows child sex abuse to continue. Abusers – the only person a paedophile loves is himself, and I won't use the term – abusers tell each other that the children are harmed by the fuss their parents make when they find out. They believe that the child enjoys the experience, and comes to no harm. And this denial is total and almost impenetrable.

In Daniel's case, it seemed to me that he felt he was being unfairly victimised by a vindictive, jealous wife who felt spurned. If only he knew! I had spent the last couple of years working hard to try and keep our marriage together. I had kept reminding myself of why I had first fallen in love with Daniel, because the Daniel I was married to then didn't seem to want to take part in any sort of family life. I had told myself that it was I who had changed, that I had grown so much since beginning my OU studies, and that it wasn't fair to blame him for staying the same. And I had reminded myself of the damage that divorce does to children, and that even if I wasn't sure how much I still loved Daniel, his daughters did, and I had no right to deprive them of their father. What a supreme irony!

One thing I found very hard to cope with was the knowledge that Daniel was back in the UK, in the same town as us, but we had no communication. I didn't know where he was, what he was doing, what he was thinking. It was almost like losing a part of myself. Partly I was worried about whether he would stay away from the girls and me; but partly also I was worried about how he was coping. Even though I was angry with him, and horrified by his and his family's attitude, I still cared about him. Old habits die hard.

We had more evidence of the denial at work at the end

of April, on Tamsin's birthday. She received money from Daniel's parents and a small gift from his sister, Susan, as usual, and phoned them to say thank you. Her grandmother assured herself that Tamsin had spent all her money and then rang off. However, Susan asked to speak to me. We discussed what had happened in fairly friendly terms. I tried to describe how ill Tamsin had been, but Susan just said, 'Oh, well, she sounds all right now,' and ended the conversation. Of course she sounded all right; she could not have kept the abuse secret for five years if she wasn't good at pretending!

May 1997

2 May was a dreadful morning for me. No Conservative government meant no funding for assisted places at Tamsin's school and no place for Sam. Gloomily I read the paper as I ate breakfast. There was an article about the demise of assisted places. No more after the summer holidays – they intended to rush the legislation through.

Hang on! If they had to change the legislation, that meant there might still be some assisted places left now. I didn't say anything to Sam, but as soon as I returned from the school run, I began phoning all the local private schools. Most had no places left, but one or two did. I made appointments for Sam and I to visit two of them, both for girls only. One was very small, and the other larger. Each sent its prospectus and Sam and I pored over them.

The next week we visited both schools, the larger first. We had a long discussion with the headmistress, a wonderfully vibrant woman called Dr Perkins. She heard the whole story, and was very concerned that we should be quite sure that we made the right choice, and not at all concerned to push us into choosing her school. That impressed me. Sam and I then met the director of studies, Mrs Corcoran, who discussed how many Standard Grades Sam would want to do, and in what subjects. Sam had long ago decided she wanted to be a vet, and she wanted to take all three sciences, as well as a good range of other subjects. At St Andrew's School, she could take up to nine Standard Grades although, given the strife at home, Mrs Corcoran felt that eight would be more realistic.

Finally Sam was given a tour of the school by some of the girls who would be her classmates if she went to St Andrew's. She had been somewhat quiet and lethargic up until now, but she came back from her tour chatting to the girls nineteen to the dozen, full of animation and with shining eyes.

'I take it you like it here then,' I laughed.

'Oh, yes,' she gasped, 'it's brilliant! The biology department has its own small animal room!'

We arranged for Sam to return a couple of days later to do some tests, and to bring her school reports from the last few years. All the way home, and for the next few days, all she could talk about was St Andrew's.

We also visited the smaller school, but Sam said it felt too much like the one she already attended. I think she was determined to go to St Andrew's.

But first I had to visit the bursar, at a firm of chartered accountants, to see if we would qualify for an assisted place. Daniel had been earning so much that I knew that put us out of the wage bracket for any meaningful help. However, because we had separated in December the previous year (even though Daniel wasn't aware of it until March), they were allowed to use my income only, which qualified us for full remission of fees.

Now we just had to wait for the phone call, to see if St Andrew's would accept Sam. Every day Sam rushed out of school, demanding to know if it had come, and every day I had to disappoint her. Finally she persuaded me to call the school. I spoke to Mrs Corcoran.

'I'm so sorry,' she said, 'I didn't mean to keep you in suspense. I've just been waiting for the test results from the educational psychologist, but we'd be delighted to have Samantha as a pupil. Now we think she ought to start this term so as to be sure of her assisted place, because we don't know how quickly the legislation will change. She will be going into third year, and we would like her to start right after half-term, on the first Monday in June. Would that suit you?'

Well, of course it did! Mrs Lucas, at Sam's present school, had known since the beginning of the year that Sam would be leaving by the summer holidays at the latest, so that no notice period was required; and Sam just couldn't wait to start. St Andrew's had a uniform exchange, and the school secretary arranged for us to shop there. Just as well – we bought her winter coat and blazer there, and they cost £55 and £45 respectively. Fortunately I had asked my parents to lend me some money to outfit Sam for her new school, and we had just enough to buy the essentials.

Imagine Sam's disappointment when the school phoned to delay her start date by a week. She had been due to begin immediately after half-term, but the first week was to be occupied by term exams, and the teachers felt that wouldn't be the best start. So Sam had an extra week's holiday. She had already said her goodbyes at her old school, and felt it would be really embarrassing to have to return for another week, and I felt that a week off would do her no harm at all.

At the beginning of the month I had a consultation with the counsel who was to represent me in the divorce. One of the essentials for the assisted place was for me to get a temporary residence order for Sam, to show that I had care of her. Kim was also anxious to do everything in her power to safeguard my trust, as Daniel's solicitor had already tried to claim it as joint property. This was the first time that I realised what 'no fault' divorce means in real terms in cases like this.

In the vast majority of divorces there is fault on both sides, of course, and it is sensible to deal with the financial and legal aspects without apportioning blame. And I fully agree that no woman (or man) should think they have a meal ticket for life because they once married someone wealthier than they are. But there is no provision for exceptions; and when divorce is the result of intolerable behaviour such as Daniel's, no-fault divorce actually penalises the innocent parties.

Mr Donald, the counsel, assured us that since the trust monies had been left to me personally, Daniel had no claim on them. We were entitled to continue to refuse to supply any details, beyond a copy of the will. I had been shocked, and continued to be shocked, by Daniel's persistence in trying to get hold of half of my trust. After all, his father owned a half share in the farm in Switzerland which his family had owned for generations. Because of Swiss law, Daniel stood to inherit a substantial share, and the farm had been valued in 1984 at six million Swiss francs. In addition, Daniel's mother was wealthy in her own right, as she had inherited a whole terrace of houses in the north-east of England from her mother. In fact, Daniel and his solicitor continued to badger Kim and me until I suggested that if my future inheritance was to be regarded as joint property, then so should Daniel's. That shut them up for a couple of months.

Mr Donald agreed to press ahead with the residence order as a matter of urgency, but the remaining divorce proceedings had been suspended until Daniel was able to get Legal Aid. He had caused quite a lot of trouble by continually turning up at Kim's office and writing to her, despite being told repeatedly that she could not deal directly with him, only through a solicitor. But he had delayed retaining a solicitor until he had spent all his money and was therefore entitled to Legal Aid.

We briefly discussed dividing assets. I had already supplied an inventory of the household contents, indicating what I wanted to keep. Mr Donald was of the opinion that I should keep nearly everything. 'He's not going to need furniture in jail!' he joked. He advised Kim to write to Daniel's pension fund to get an updated statement of the assets it contained. We didn't have much else in the way of tangible assets, apart from the house, which was heavily mortgaged, and the endowment policies. I was very keen to have those, as I had already discovered that new life assurance was going to be very expensive, despite the fact that my condition is not life threatening. There was nothing much else we could do at present until Daniel's Legal Aid came through.

But again it was extremely difficult to be in the same

town and yet not talk to each other. Daniel had asked in his letter that, if we were to meet, we should at least be civil to each other. I have never in my life gone looking for a fight – I'm quite timid, really, and not very good at standing up for myself. I wasn't spoiling for a fight with Daniel, but I actually didn't – and don't – know how I would react if we did meet. I like to think I know myself well, and can predict how I will behave in most situations. So it's pretty frightening to feel that there's this one area that I can't predict.

I had an accident in the middle of May. I mostly use a wheelchair outside the house, but if I can park right outside a shop, I can walk in with the aid of a stick. That was what I usually did at the post office. One day, as I was waiting to cross the road to my car, a car which had been parked on the footpath began reversing, and backed right into me! I was desperately trying to get my feet out from under the wheels, and I sort of twisted out of the way and landed on the boot on my elbow. Fortunately, by this time, passers-by had alerted the driver, and he stopped. One of my sandals had flown into the air behind me, and the other was trapped under the back wheel of the car, which had just caught my big toe.

The driver got out and rushed round to see if I was all right. My toe and elbow were hurting, and I was pretty shaken, but mostly I was embarrassed and just wanted to get away. The driver retrieved my sandals and saw me across to my car, and then drove off.

'I should have got his name and address,' I thought vaguely, but all I really wanted to do was to leave the scene and collect Sam from school. But by that evening, my back was really sore. I saw the chiropractor the next day, but the pain just kept getting worse and worse. By the end of the week I could hardly move, and went back to the chiropractor. It seemed that my left sacroiliac joint had been quite badly damaged, probably from twisting out of the way. I didn't think the car had actually hit my body, and there was no bruising. But this was where the beauty of chiropractic lay. I had three treatments the following week, and two the week after that, and by then I was almost back to normal. Wonderful!

Tamsin sat all her exams, and seemed fairly relaxed about it. She was managing to stay at school without having freakies, and although she needed a lot of reassurance from me at the weekends, she seemed to be improving all the time.

Tamsin also had an accident that month. For the past year and a half, the girls had complained about getting electric shocks from the tumble drier in the garage. I had asked Daniel repeatedly to check the electricity supply, but he kept putting it off, until one day I lifted his tools out of the cupboard and insisted that he should do it. He went out to the garage and returned five minutes later saying everything was fine, and it was probably just static.

But one Saturday, while putting washing in the drier, Tamsin screamed and stumbled back into the house, clutching her arm and shaking violently. 'I got a really bad shock from the drier!' she wailed.

'Is your hand burnt?' I asked anxiously. 'Stick it under the cold tap.' I was concerned that there might be internal burns that were not visible, and so I phoned the local Minor Injuries Unit for advice.

'It's not burns we worry about,' said the nurse-practitioner, 'so much as the heart. Electric shock can cause arrhythmia – an unsteady rhythm – in the heart. We don't have the facilities to monitor her here, you'd better take her straight up to Accident and Emergency at the Royal.'

We were expecting an Australian friend of my parents' for a visit that day. Sam agreed to stay at home to meet her, as we could not contact her by phone. Tamsin and I piled into the car for the hot, slow journey through town. When we arrived, Tamsin was quite shaken and unsteady on her feet and so, getting my wheelchair out, I went in to ask for help for her. No one seemed very bothered. A porter strolled across and collected a chair to fetch her, and the receptionist turned to me in a bored fashion and asked what the problem was. I told her that Tamsin had had an electric shock, just as the porter was wheeling Tamsin in. Instantly her attitude changed.

'Straight through to Immediate Care!' she snapped to the porter, before turning back to me for Tamsin's details.

Tamsin was kept on a cardiac monitor for two hours, but her heart seemed unaffected, and by late afternoon we had returned home, with instructions for Tamsin to take things easy for the next day or two.

The following Monday I asked a local electrician to come and check the wiring. It took him all of two minutes to discover that when Daniel had replaced the fuse box, he had neglected to earth the power supply to the garage. It had been a time bomb waiting to go off.

I was so angry with Daniel! It just typified his lax attitude of the past few years. I sent the electrician's account to his solicitor with a demand for payment, since it was Daniel's fault, but he refused to pay.

Daniel's solicitor made me furious. His attitude appeared to be that Daniel was a poor, victimised soul at the mercy of a screaming, demanding harridan. He seemed to take no account of the fact that all this — the divorce, the court case, all the difficulties — were the result of Daniel's choices. Nobody made him abuse Tamsin. Nobody stood over him with a gun. He freely chose to do what he did, but now that it was payback time, suddenly he was the victim. To this day I don't know if that accurately reflected Daniel's solicitor's attitude, but to judge from his behaviour it certainly reflected Daniel's attitude.

Eventually I paid the electrician's bill myself, so that he wouldn't miss out, but I continued to demand that Daniel should pay. It wasn't a large bill, only £26, but it was the principle that mattered. Daniel had put all our lives at risk — he was lucky he wasn't being asked to pay funeral expenses instead of an electrician's bill.

I was still coping with grief, mostly for the girls — I think I used that as an excuse not to think about how I felt — and I was desperately worried about money and housing. But there was also a sneaking realisation of my new independence, which was really quite nice.

June 1997

Sam started her new school, and loved it from day one! It was so good to collect her in the afternoon and see her coming out of school wreathed in smiles. I think that really marked the beginning of her recovery. She had seen a child psychologist a couple of times; she was short-tempered with both Tamsin and me, most unusually for her; she was comfort-eating, and obviously finding life tough. But the psychologist, while sympathetic, felt that what Sam was experiencing was a normal grief reaction, which just needed time and support from me.

I received a kind letter from the reporter to the Children's Panel, sympathising with my awful situation. She felt that since I had reported the abuse promptly and co-operated with all the investigations, there was no need to have any formal protection structure in place for the girls, but she did suggest voluntary contact with the social worker for a few months. Great! More Tina asking how I feel about things! I felt quite angry that the one useful thing the social work department could have done — sending Sam to Tamsin's school — was the one thing they had refused to do. I had had no help with sorting out finances or housing, which were the two most urgent problems — just lots of manufactured sympathy which I didn't need, because I got the real thing from my small circle of friends.

Housing was really becoming urgent. I had discovered that if I sold the house, I could be regarded by the city council as having made myself voluntarily homeless. Not that I really wanted to live in a council house, but it beat living on the street.

One morning it all got too much. I laid my head in my hands on the table and, not for the first time, cried my eyes out. But it didn't change anything — I still had to find somewhere for us to live. I began idly flicking through the Yellow Pages. I stopped at Disabled Services and there it was: Disabled Persons Housing Service. I phoned them up and began to explain the situation; but then I broke down in tears! I managed to stammer that I would call them back, and hung up, crying bitterly and feeling disgusted with myself. Really I had to pull myself together! There were two kids relying on me to be strong, and all I could do was cry!

I made a cup of coffee, had a cigarette and tried again, this time with more success. I spoke to Olga, who offered to come to the house the next morning. When she arrived, she asked if I had registered with the council as potentially homeless.

'I don't know how to,' I replied helplessly. 'I don't know how to do any of this!'

'Well, let's go and see them now,' she suggested kindly; and so we did. We piled into the car and drove along to the local housing office. It was smack bang in the middle of an archetypal run-down housing estate, and my spirits sank. We sat in the foyer waiting to see a housing officer. The place was busy; there were groups of downtrodden-looking women sitting around, occasionally yelling at their recalcitrant children, who treated the place like a jungle gym. After a while we were called into a small glass-fronted cubicle to meet Mrs Williams.

Mrs Williams listened sympathetically as Olga and I, between us, explained my predicament. She agreed that we could register as potentially homeless, but everything depended on how many points we could amass. Points were awarded for factors such as length of time on the waiting list (none); children (yes); disability (yes); employment (not very likely). I had to fill in a medical form and take it away to be signed by my doctor, and then wait and see how many points we had.

Even though nothing much had changed, I felt so grateful to Olga. She had been an enabling force, making me feel that our situation was not hopeless. We went back to my lovely house for coffee, and she completed a long form for her own purposes. She mentioned a few housing associations which catered exclusively for disabled people; but at the moment I don't really need a wheelchair friendly house, and most of the houses were on the other side of town. I was prepared to move anywhere, but life would be much easier if we lived near Sam's school. By the end of the morning I had begun to feel more hopeful.

That month I received a letter from Uncle Bob's executor, telling me that Uncle Bob's wife had died a few weeks previously. It was not unexpected, and made no practical difference, as Uncle Bob's brother Joe was still alive, and the trust would not pay out until after Joe's death.

My parents came home for their annual visit in June. It was lovely to see them, and to have someone to talk everything over with. They had rented a garden flat ten minutes' drive from our house, and we spent a lot of time together. One of the first things they did was to book flights to Sydney for us for Christmas and New Year. We were to leave Heathrow on 7 December and stay for a month. It was indescribably wonderful to have that to look forward to. Whenever life became unbearable, I could look forward to December and our escape to the sun.

Tamsin became ill again towards the end of June. She had come home one Friday with a bad headache, which worsened as the weekend wore on. She was all set to go back for the last week of term, but I felt she should see the doctor, and so she stayed at home. The doctor felt it was a bad stress headache and that what Tamsin needed was some quiet time with her family; so that was what she got.

However, the following Thursday Tamsin, my parents and I travelled down to school for Open Day, a time for parents to meet teachers, and for the end of year concert and prize giving. It was the first time Sam had not been able to attend, but I had arranged for her to go home with a classmate until we returned, which made up for it. I didn't want her taking a day off school without a very good reason, but I also didn't want her travelling home and staying in the house alone. I was always very conscious that Daniel might be in Edinburgh, and was unpredictable.

He had moved out of the bail hostel and into a flat in the

east end of town; right next door to a primary school, it later turned out: in fact, the same primary school where a friend of mine taught. She was horrified to find he was so close to the school. I still wasn't used to thinking of Daniel as a threat to other children, and there was no evidence that he was, but every abuser has the potential to threaten any child who comes into contact with him.

In the last week in June, I received a letter from a firm of precognition agents. Never having been involved in criminal law before, I had no idea what they did; but it appeared that they wanted to interview me. There was a similar letter for Tamsin.

As gently as I could, I told her about the letters. Immediately she whirled around, ran upstairs and locked herself in the toilet.

'Tamsin, Tamsin, please come out and talk to me!' I begged.

'I don't want to talk to anybody!' she sobbed. 'The police said they didn't need to see me again. Why do I have to do this again?'

'Well, you don't,' I replied. 'You don't have to do anything you don't want to.'

'But if I don't, he'll get off! Why do I have to do this again?'

'I don't understand it either,' I admitted. 'Tell you what – I'll go and phone them and see if I can work out what's going on.'

I called the number at the top of the letter and spoke to the man who had signed it, a Mr O'Brien. Gradually it dawned on me that we were talking at cross purposes.

'Who do you work for?' I asked. 'The procurator's office?'

'No, no,' he replied somewhat testily, 'we work for the defence solicitors. We get a certain amount of information from the police, but we don't have access to witness statements.'

I explained about Tamsin's rocky state of health, and that I had been present every time she had spoken to the police. 'I'm quite happy to talk to you,' I said, 'and I can tell you everything Tamsin said as well.'

Mr O'Brien agreed to that and we set a date for the beginning of July. Immediately he rang off, I went up to Tamsin and explained.

'Is this going to help him or what?' she demanded from her refuge in the bathroom.

'I really don't know,' I admitted. 'I'll go and phone the procurator's office and see what they say.'

The Crown reference number was at the top of the letters, and I was able to speak to one of the lawyers handling the case. I explained that it was unlikely that Tamsin would be well enough to testify in court, and she advised me to co-operate fully with the precognition agents. 'That's the best way you can help to make sure he's convicted,' she said.

I reported back to Tamsin, who finally consented to come out of the bathroom. She didn't want any involvement at all in subsequent proceedings, and was quite happy for me to talk about her statement on her behalf. We arranged for my parents to take her out for the day when Mr O'Brien was to visit.

Somehow in the middle of all this chaos, I was continuing with my final year of study. It was cognitive psychology this year, very interesting. I had a summer school for a week in July at Stirling University. Because of my disability, I was expected to have a helper, a role which Daniel had previously filled.

As well as making friends with Jenny the previous year, I had also made friends with a fellow student, Rosie. She was a single mum with two daughters, older than mine, and worked in a centre for disabled people. She had lots of experience of pushing wheelchairs, and also lots of experience of summer schools, and so I had asked her to be my helper this year. She was delighted to be asked and I was delighted when she accepted.

I had some indication, when thinking about summer school, of the damage that Daniel had caused to me. It occurred to me that I was now effectively single again, and there would be lots of people at summer school, some of whom would be male, and single, and maybe even attractive. I dozed lightly while imagining the beginning of a new relationship – but when I imagined kissing a man, I woke up suddenly, feeling revolted and nauseous. This has not eased with the passage of time. I can't imagine anything worse than being tied to another man. I can't think of anything I could get from a man, including financial security, that would make up for having to have one in the house. And how on earth could I ever trust another man around the girls, if I couldn't trust their own father?

My parents had trouble booking a return flight and were to be in Edinburgh until the end of July. My sister Kate had already agreed to look after the girls, but was taking them to stay in her flat in Greenock; she didn't have room for the dogs too, so the plan had been that they would go into kennels. However, as my parents were still around, they agreed to stay in our house for the week before they left, and look after the dogs too.

Sam's residence order came through at the end of June. It had been unopposed – well, Daniel could hardly argue he was a fit person to look after her. Tamsin was now sixteen and no order was needed for her. Sam had repeatedly asked to see her dad, under supervision, of course. I was happy for this to happen, but when Kim wrote to Daniel's solicitor, he replied that Daniel had been advised not to see either girl before the court case. Poor Sam felt more abandoned than ever.

July 1997

Daniel paid money into my account on 3 July, and the bank duly transferred all the standing orders and direct debits on to my account. It was not until my bank statement arrived in the middle of the month that I realised that he had paid only £725. Kim wrote to his solicitor repeatedly, but Daniel just said it was a mistake and he would repay £50. But he didn't.

At the beginning of July Tamsin agreed to return to see Sheila, the counsellor at the Adolescent Unit. Her visits to the psychologist in Dumfries had not worked out well, what with exams and time off sick, and I felt it might be more helpful if Tamsin could see the same person every week for a couple of months. Her bad stress headaches led me to believe that she needed to talk, to get at least some of the anger out of the way, which would allow her to move on with her life.

Sheila suggested to Tamsin that it was now time to do some hard work, and Tamsin appeared to agree; she certainly didn't dissent when we made an appointment for the following week. But that night I was awakened by the sound of screaming. I rushed through to Tamsin's room and found her bolt upright in bed, screaming loudly but apparently still sound asleep. She was freezing cold and had obviously been like that for some time. When at last I managed to wake her, she became clingy and tearful and spent the rest of the night in my bed. That set a pattern for the following week. She was moody and difficult to deal with, flew off the handle at the slightest provocation, and slept with me, having frequent nightmares.

The following week she refused to go and see Sheila. I tried all the persuasion I could, but Tamsin was adamant. In the end I gave up and called Sheila.

'It sounds as though she's not ready to talk,' Sheila advised. 'You can't force someone to talk if they're not ready – I think we'll just have to leave it for now. But we're always here if you need us.'

I told Tamsin she didn't have to do anything she didn't want to.

'Can I go back to my own bed now?' she demanded aggressively, as though I had been forcing her to sleep with me.

'Whatever you like,' I replied helplessly. I was totally bewildered about the best way to help her, and decided to follow Sheila's advice and let her come to me. Tamsin seemed to have made up her mind that she wasn't going to be ill any more. She was fed up with it, and she was just going to get on with the rest of her life and forget the abuse, so there!

The house went on the market. We had lived there for only two years, during which time the market had been pretty static, and it looked as though we were going to lose money on the deal yet again. But the priority was to sell it quickly, so that I didn't have the responsibility of paying the mortgage any more.

I also had to give my home help, Chris, notice. I had discovered that when calculating our income support, the benefits agency did not take into account the £25 a week I paid for her; and much as I hated to let her go, I simply couldn't afford to pay her. I contacted social services and asked for a council home help; if Daniel was jailed, we would be back to living on income support, in which case my home help would be free. The co-ordinator visited us at home and agreed in principle that we were entitled to some help; but only for two hours a week, not six as I had been used to, and she wasn't sure when it would start.

Mr O'Brien came to see me, with Tamsin safely in her grandparents' care. Despite his testiness on the phone he actually turned out to be very nice, an ex-police sergeant with a world-weary air of having seen it all before. He apologised repeatedly for having to ask for all the gory details. I co-operated fully, telling him everything I knew and everything Tamsin had said.

Daniel had been charged with two offences: one relating to the specific assault which Tamsin had described from the previous autumn, and a more general charge of sexual abuse. Mr O'Brien didn't know what his intentions were as far as pleading, but he assured me that all the information I could give would help. Once again I had to go through the whole, sorry, disgusting tale. It didn't – doesn't – get any easier as time goes on.

The most exciting event at the beginning of July was

collecting my new car. It was bright red, and turned out to be a marvel to drive, full of oomph and with very positive steering. I walked around it in the drive, thrilled to bits, and polishing any dusty specks. It was much smaller than the Volvo, of course, and because it had only three doors, it was less convenient for the girls to get in and out of the back. But the five-door version had a much smaller driver's door, which would have made it difficult for me to get in and out, and that, I felt, was more important.

My sister Kate had arranged to collect the girls on Friday, the day before I went to summer school. Disaster! Tamsin had another dose of tonsillitis. She was not well on Thursday evening, and by Friday morning it was obvious what the problem was. We went to the GP for antibiotics; but then we had to decide if she should go with Kate or stay with Granny and Grandad. The girls had been so looking forward to going to Kate's; they didn't know her very well, but she had a horse, and they had planned to go to a major show on Saturday and Sunday, and Tamsin really didn't want to miss it. In the end she decided to go, and I was left alone for the evening.

Jenny and I had decided that as her son was on holiday and we were both child-free, we would go out for a meal that night. We went to a local restaurant overlooking the Forth. It was a beautiful summer evening, and we had a most enjoyable and relaxing time. In many ways Jenny has been my salvation through all of this. Her job takes her away from home a lot, but when she's around, she's always available, on the phone or in person. And of course, she can take a much more detached view of things than I can, and has the knowledge and experience to dispense good advice. But most of all, she's my friend, and that's priceless.

It was very exciting setting off for summer school the next day. The staff tutors who run the schools are usually top people in their field, and one or two have told me that OU students do in a week as much as their regular students do in a term. The pattern is the same for each week: we start with an icebreaker party and choose two out of four possible topics to investigate. I began this time with artificial intelligence and had a lot of fun writing programs in Prolog, a computer language specially designed for non-geek psychologists (and also used, incidentally, on Boeing 777s). The second half of the week was spent investigating eyewitness memory. In both cases we got some interesting results; indeed, our AI project was chosen to be presented at the final plenary session, thus fulfilling another ambition of mine.

I phoned the girls every night, of course. Tamsin's throat was much better by Monday, although she was disappointed that she had to stay in the flat and missed the horse show. Kate brought them home on Monday so that Tamsin could see her own GP if she needed to.

Towards the end of my week in Stirling I had occasion to speak to one of the tutors. She asked whether I had enjoyed the week, and if I was looking forward to going home.

'Not really,' I replied with a wry smile.

'Has it been as good as that?' she laughed.

'It's been wonderful, but it's not so much that Stirling is wonderful, more that home is so difficult,' I replied, and I told her what had happened. She was very sympathetic.

She confided that her father had abused her and her sisters for many years. 'My mother knew what was going on, but there was nothing she could do, really. There were no state benefits, and she had no way of making a living. We needed our father's money to survive. One of my sisters has never spoken about the abuse to anyone; I talked it all through with my mother after I had left home, but my sister has just cut herself off from the family so that she doesn't need to confront it. I know you're having a really hard time just now, but children are incredibly resilient, and with your support I'm sure Tamsin will get over it.' Our chat continued for some time, and was enormously comforting.

Rosie and I had enjoyed each other's company immensely during that week. It was a break that I really needed. I knew Tamsin and Sam were pining for me and wanted me at home, but I also knew they were being well cared for, and for one week I was selfish and put my own needs first.

On my return I found that the cheque for the Volvo had arrived. I took it out to the bank, but to my horror I found that Lisa had underestimated the amount to be repaid, and it was short by £300 − £300 that I didn't have. I couldn't partly repay the loan, and my new account manager − Lisa had moved on − advised me to use the money to keep up the repayments in the meantime.

The house was sold quite quickly. The buyers, a young couple, had already sold their previous home and were living with parents. I explained that I didn't yet have anywhere to go, and they were generous enough to be quite flexible about moving in. We agreed that if I found another house before the end of August, they would take possession immediately;

otherwise it would be left until the end of October. I had my final exam in October and wanted at least six weeks for final revision without having to move house in the middle of it.

August 1997

Tamsin's exam results arrived in early August. She had passed all six Standard Grades, with four at grade 2, one at grade 3 and one at grade 4 – brilliant results considering she had been absent for most of the spring term. I was so proud of her! It seemed to boost her confidence enormously, and she was determined to return to school and work really hard for her Highers.

Tamsin had come home one weekend the previous year and announced that she wanted to be a nursery nurse. She had an interview with the careers adviser, and this was what she had decided to do. It would have been my idea of purgatory, but it was her life and her decision. As preparation for this, she began to work for three days a week in a local nursery. She seemed to enjoy the work, although she was quite down to earth about the difficulties of spending all day with small children.

Tamsin had another accident in August: while carrying a basket of dirty washing for me, she fell down the stairs, right from top to bottom! She ended up in a heap at the foot of the stairs, with one leg doubled underneath her. I asked Sam to call an ambulance while I very carefully and gently moved Tamsin's leg, so that we could open the front door. She seemed to have hurt her ankle and her arm, which was already swelling and bruising – she had hit it against the stairlift rail.

The ambulance crew arrived quite quickly and fitted a neck collar. They thought Tamsin probably hadn't broken anything, but they lifted her carefully into the ambulance. Sam travelled with Tamsin while I followed in the car.

At the hospital Tamsin was X-rayed almost everywhere, but she had no fractures, just a sprained ankle and quite a few bruises. In a perverse way Sam enjoyed the day – it was the first time she had ever dialled 999 or travelled by ambulance! I was just thankful that no real harm had been done.

The council had agreed in principle to provide us with a ground floor tenement flat, without making a specific offer. I hadn't really wanted a tenement, but I wasn't given any choice. And at least most of the ground flats had their own gardens, an essential for the dogs. So we spent quite a few days that month driving around council estates, partly to see what they looked like, but partly also to look for unoccupied houses. Friends at church had obtained a council flat for their parents by finding an empty one near their home and asking the council if their parents could have it; and the sooner we got out of our home, the less money I would have to pay out on the mortgage. But we couldn't find any empty flats. I phoned Mrs Williams every week or two, but there was apparently nothing on offer. As August drew on, it became apparent that we were not going to be able to move until October.

Kim continued writing to Daniel's solicitor to try and agree a division of household goods. Despite what Mr Donald had said about Daniel's having no need of furniture in jail, I found that there had to be a division after all. I had drawn up an inventory in May, indicating what I would like to keep and what was available for Daniel, but he repeatedly said that it was far too early to think about things like that. It was very frustrating, all the more so because I felt that if we could communicate directly, we could have sorted it all out. But maybe that's wishful thinking. I'm not sure I could have borne to be in the same building as Daniel, much less in the same room; and his denial would have prevented him from being able to be honest – if he ever had been.

I worked off some of my frustration by taking a carload of bits and pieces to a car boot sale. Sam came with me, and we managed to sell almost everything, although for less than I had expected. We didn't end up making much money, partly because Sam saw a video game she had been looking for on another stall, which we bought. But at least it cleared out a load of junk. And if Daniel subsequently asked for any of the junk, I would simply tell him he ought to have decided what he wanted sooner.

Because the money Daniel paid us wasn't enough to live on and pay the bills, I began using the money from the sale of the Volvo. The girls needed shoes and trainers, and other items of clothing and stationery for school, and I just bought what they needed. I began to learn to live from day to day, not worrying about what might happen in six months' time. There was still an awful tearing anxiety about money and about where we would live, but I managed to suppress it most of the time. And when I couldn't suppress it, I escaped into my OU work – that never failed to take my mind off my worries.

Daniel had begun to convince himself and his solicitor that he would get off with a suspended sentence. He even began to convince my solicitor; she was now much less certain that he would be imprisoned. I had kept in close contact with the procurator's office, and the lawyers there spoke quite freely to me. I heard that there was to be an initial hearing on 22 September. At last some action was to take place.

September 1997

Tamsin and Sam returned to school. Tamsin was to study her remaining three Standard Grades in English, maths and computing; Highers in chemistry, biology and music; and National Certificates in psychology and philosophy. She was full of enthusiasm and determination. She was made a prefect, and that boosted her confidence.

Sam was just beginning her eight Standard Grades, and threw herself into school life with gusto. She joined a group working for the Duke of Edinburgh Bronze award, although she wouldn't be officially old enough until December. She began first aid classes, as all St Andrew's girls did for community service at Bronze level. She began judo as her sport, and loved it from the word go. Dog training was to be her hobby, and she also attended classes in map-reading and hill safety, in preparation for the expedition the following summer. She was soon asked to join the hockey team as goalkeeper, and went straight into the A team.

I had finally persuaded the girls that taking the rabbits

and guinea pigs to the council flat was not a sensible option. I had nightmares about finding their dead bodies on our doorstep one morning, although I didn't tell the girls that. Sam had talked about it at school and Mrs Corcoran, the director of studies, had offered them a new home. She already had some guinea pigs, and was delighted to add to her collection.

I was now allocated a council home help; but as a new client I had a succession of different helpers every week. All were pleasant and polite; but some were much more helpful than others. One evening we had baked potatoes for dinner, and one potato burst in the oven, making a dreadful mess. I find it virtually impossible to reach far enough into the oven to clean it, and asked that week's helper if she would clean it. She did – but only under protest.

I was very sad to lose Chris. She was an excellent worker – if she had finished the routine chores, she used to wash the paintwork, or tidy the garage – nothing was too much trouble. Sam, I think, missed her more than anyone, as she had always kept Sam's room tidy. But she was also a friend, always ready to listen sympathetically and very good with the girls.

I discovered from my bank statement that payment was not being made on one of the endowment policies. I immediately called my insurance agent, Jim Shepherd, whom I had met in June. There were two endowment policies in joint names, and payment of the premiums had been moved to my account in July. One company had sent a new standing order through the post, but the other preferred to have these matters dealt with by their agents. Jim had brought a mandate to the house for me to sign. I had seen no reason to hide from him the reason for the divorce, and he proved to be a good ally.

Jim said that the premiums on the policy were up to date. He investigated for me and discovered that Daniel had gone into the office and signed a new mandate to pay the premium himself. I couldn't understand what Daniel thought he could gain by such behaviour; the policy was in joint names and he couldn't cash it in or borrow against it without my consent. Kim wrote to Daniel's solicitor, but Daniel denied ever having signed the mandate. I still don't know what he was trying to do.

I phoned the procurator's office on 22 September to find out what had happened at the hearing. Daniel had not yet been allowed to plead, and we had no idea what would happen.

Daniel had failed to turn up. Apparently he was at sea and unable to attend, and so the hearing was adjourned until the end of the month. I began to wonder if I was going mad. How could he be allowed to get away with deciding for himself when it was convenient for him to attend?

I phoned Barbara at the Sexual Offences Unit, but she couldn't enlighten me, as once the police pass the papers over to the procurator's office, their involvement ends, apart from being witnesses in court.

In the meantime I had a 2,500 word essay to write before I began revising for the exam, which was to be on 24 October, the day before we had to get out of the house. But apart from phoning Mrs Williams every week, I couldn't do anything about that, either; the best thing to do was to get on with my academic work and ensure I got my first class honours.

Most of the time I managed it.

October 1997

The hearing finally took place on 6 October; but I could not find out what had happened. The procurator's office would tell me nothing directly and advised me to engage a solicitor but, as I was not the victim, it had to be done by Tamsin. She took Monday off school, and we visited a solicitor who specialised in representing children. Her name was Victoria, and she gained Tamsin's trust immediately, not an easy feat. She called the procurator's office while we waited and discovered that Daniel had pleaded guilty, but she wasn't sure to what.

That evening Victoria phoned again. Daniel had pleaded guilty to one charge of using lewd and libidinous practices, but she had been unable to find out what had happened to the other charge: it may have been left on file, or he may have been allowed to plead not guilty.

I'm still not sure what happened. Reading between the lines, my interpretation of events was that Daniel's solicitor had 'done a deal' whereby he would plead guilty to one charge if the other was not pursued; otherwise he would plead not guilty to both. With Tamsin unable to testify, the procurator's office had gone for the sure conviction. In some ways, Tamsin and I felt cheated that Daniel didn't have to answer for all of his crimes; but in other ways, it was a relief that he had pled guilty to one charge. He was now a convicted child abuser, and the girls were assured of being protected. But once more, I cried my eyes out, because it confirmed that this really was happening, it wasn't all just a bad dream that would go away.

The hearing had been adjourned for three weeks for background reports, which seems to be a sure sign that a jail term is being considered. Our contact with Tina had ended in June, but I managed to speak to the senior social worker who had attended the Child Protection Case Conference. She told me that it would be another branch of social services who would do the background checks. I waited in anticipation for someone to contact me. After all, I was Daniel's wife, I had lived with him for twenty years, no one knew him better than me. I could tell them about the effects of his crime on Tamsin, too.

I waited in vain. No one contacted me. No one enquired about the effects of the crime on Tamsin.

The hearing had a marked effect on Daniel. Before the hearing he was still refusing to agree a division of household contents; in addition, he wanted a letter from Uncle Bob's executor confirming that his brother was still alive. If I were to inherit in the near future, that would affect a division of matrimonial assets, as far as he was concerned. I was almost speechless with fury. I pointed out that Daniel could be receiving large sums of money from his parents; indeed, they could have died and Daniel could have inherited the farm in Switzerland, for all I knew.

In addition, he blamed me for his having paid the insurance premium for the last two months, and said that should be offset against the outstanding £50 aliment from July – this despite the fact that he had transferred payment of the premiums back to his own account.

But after the hearing, suddenly he repaid both the missing £50 from July and the £26 for the electrician's bill. And he finally agreed to say what he wanted in the way of furniture. We would have to buy a new suite, as he wanted ours – an Ercol suite – and we would also need to buy a washing machine and fridge-freezer, as ours were built-in. But at least I had a cooker – we had replaced the built-in electric oven and hob when we bought the house.

One Monday in early October I had a letter from the housing department, from a Mr Williams, telling me to go and view a house. I looked up the address on the map and my heart sank. It was one of the worst estates in north west Edinburgh. I drove to the address and as I turned in to the road, I began to cry. I drew up alongside the tenement and looked at it in despair. Then my despair left me, and I began to laugh through my tears. There were three steps into the tenement. The occupational therapist had insisted that there should be no more than two steps into the house – I could legitimately turn it down.

I rushed home and called Mr Williams, and shortly after that Mrs Williams called me. It had all been a mistake, she said. She was looking after us, she said, and she had a flat for us to see. We arranged to meet at the address, and for the occupational therapist to be there too. It was on what looked like a nicer estate. It was still a ground floor flat in a tenement, surrounded by other tenements. But it had its own front garden, and a shared back garden, and was neat and tidy inside. There were fitted wardrobes in the bedrooms – just as well, because we had fitted wardrobes in our present house, and so no free-standing wardrobes to move. The sitting room looked over the back garden, with the two bedrooms looking out to the front. The kitchen had plumbing for an automatic washing machine, and room for a fridge-freezer and tumble drier – just!

It was not suitable for indoor wheelchair use, and the occupational therapist was doubtful. But there were only two steps into the tenement, and it had a security door and entry-phone. We were desperate, and I managed to convince the occupational therapist that I really didn't need a wheelchair in the house. We took it.

That Friday evening I took Tamsin along to see the flat; Sam had already visited it and approved. Tamsin liked it too. There were only two bedrooms but I had already decided that it wasn't a good idea for the girls to share. They didn't get on very well together then, and I felt that Tamsin especially needed a private space. So I had decided to put a single bed for myself into the sitting room. I wouldn't be doing anything in it except sleeping.

We measured up all the rooms, and went home and measured all the furniture. We drew floor plans on squared paper, and drew and cut out scale models of the furniture, and juggled them around until they all fitted in.

That Saturday we went on a shopping spree. First we went to a discount carpet warehouse and chose new carpets, as the concrete floors in the flat were bare. Then we went to a discount furniture store. We found three sofas in the 'accidents' department. Two were pale blue and slightly soiled, and one was green and had a split in the fabric. The green one was £99 and the other two £109 each. Tamsin had been given a sofa bed for her room when we bought our present house, and Sam had been promised one when she turned fourteen, and so I bought the green one for her and the blue ones for the sitting room.

Next we visited the local DIY superstore, to buy tools and paint. Daniel had insisted on having all his tools returned, and anyway he had allowed them to rust quite badly. I bought myself a power drill and a set of bits. The flat was papered with woodchip and distempered cream all over, which we didn't really like, and so we bought paint for the whole place in colours which would complement the carpets. We also bought stencilling equipment, because the girls were to decorate their own rooms and wanted to try out different paint effects.

I arranged for a shower to be fitted in the bathroom, the week before we were to move in; I haven't been able to bathe for years, and that was a vital piece of equipment. We were taking over the tenancy from the 13th, so that we could decorate before we moved, and also because if we had delayed until the following week we might have lost the flat.

We went to a draper's and bought net curtains for all the windows. I had a sneaking feeling that privacy might be hard to come by, and anyway the metal shutters were to be removed on the 13th. If there were nets at the windows, no one could tell if the flat was occupied or not. I also managed to buy a reconditioned fridge-freezer and washing machine, which came with a year's guarantee.

It might seem that I was profligate in spending all the money that was meant to pay for the car loan. But I felt it was really important that the girls should see this move in a positive light, as making our own, new home without Daniel. The only real extravagance was the paint; we actually did need everything else, and I had no other source of funding.

Daniel had wanted to wait until after we moved out, and then go to the house to collect his belongings. But we were moving out on the day the buyers were taking possession; my exam was the day before, and I refused to move earlier, because I was to write my exam at home on the computer. I wasn't at all confident of being able to reconnect everything together and get it working again. So there was a frantic rush, the week before we moved, for Daniel to arrange for someone to collect his belongings and take them into storage. I insisted that he provided people to pack; he was taking our dinner service and some glasses, and I didn't see why I should have all the hard work of packing his belongings as well as my own. This was about the only opportunity I had to call the tune, and I made the most of it.

I was a bit naughty. The garage was full of odd bits of timber and assorted rubbish which Daniel had collected over the years; he got the lot!

I sold our double bed to friends and bought myself a single bed. I could see no circumstances in which I would need a double bed again, and anyway there wasn't room for it in the flat.

Tamsin had her half-term holiday the week before we moved, while Sam's was the week of the move. Tamsin began decorating that week, and Sam joined her in the evenings. I spent a couple of days painting the kitchen. I know, I'm not supposed to climb ladders; but it had to be done, and there was no one else to do it. I found I could reach the lower half of the walls and the skirting boards by sitting in a camping chair and tipping it forward: much easier than sitting on the floor.

I don't know if the paint fumes contributed, but Tamsin contracted another throat infection, and had to stay at home for the following week. As the time for Daniel's sentencing drew nearer, she was becoming less stable and more frightened. Even though she didn't need to testify herself, she seemed to be really upset by the court case. Her throat improved, but she stayed off school the whole week.

The day of my exam was also the day the carpets were being fitted in the new flat. Maisie, a friend from church, had agreed to come for the day and stay at the flat with the girls. She had spent a lot of time with me in the preceding couple of weeks, helping me to pack everything. By nine thirty that morning, girls and dogs were ensconced at the flat, and I was back at the house, nervously awaiting the arrival of the invigilator with my exam paper. The previous few weeks had not exactly been ideal preparation for an exam; all my revising had to be fitted around everything else, and I had not felt so badly prepared for an exam since I was at school. However, when it finally came, it seemed to go all right. I was able to quote from appropriate studies, although I couldn't remember dates and I knew I would be marked down for that. But, like so much else at that time, I could only do my best.

The exam finished at two o'clock and, as soon as the

invigilator left, I drove round to the flat, only five minutes away. The carpets had arrived and it was beginning to look like a real home. Sam had painted her room pale green and then sponged it with a darker jade green, and it looked wonderful! Tamsin's room was dark purple. She had intended to sponge it with pink, but didn't like the effect, and so purple it stayed. Sam had finished painting the sitting room pink just before the carpets arrived. I'll never know why I chose pink — I hated it all the time we were there. I suppose it was just the stress; I put an awful lot of things down to stress. We still had the bathroom and hall to do, but there was no rush for them.

Moving day went as smoothly as these things ever do. The only major problem was that we missed the telephone engineer and didn't have a phone; but fortunately I had my mobile, and we just had to make do with that for the weekend.

By the end of the day every room was piled high with boxes, with only narrow paths available to reach each bed. It took some weeks to sort things out.

On Sunday evening Tamsin insisted on returning to school. I really didn't feel she was well enough — she was strung up like her guitar strings — but she would not be persuaded to stay at home. Sam went off to school on Monday and I rang BT, only to find they were proposing to come again in two weeks.

'I can't wait that long!' I gasped in horror. 'My ex-husband is in court today for abusing his daughter — I need to be able to find out what happens!' Finally, after a lot of persuasion, they agreed to come the following day. I called Tamsin's solicitor and advised her that she should use the mobile number until further notice. Then I tried to occupy myself with unpacking as the day wore on.

At lunchtime Tamsin called. I wasn't really surprised when she told me she wasn't coping very well and asked if I could bring her home. The school was two hours' drive away, which meant that I didn't have time to fetch Tamsin before I collected Sam from school at five o'clock, after judo, but I assured Tamsin we would arrive as soon as possible. Still there was no word from Tamsin's solicitor.

At five o'clock I collected Sam from school and we set off, fortified by sandwiches and soft drinks. It was dark when we left, and it seemed like a long journey. We found Tamsin in the main building, and she made me a large mug of strong coffee before we returned. She fell asleep shortly after we left school, and it was Sam who kept me awake most of the way, before she too fell asleep half an hour before we arrived home.

It wasn't too bad then, at the flat. The flat above us and the one opposite were both empty, and we had met the other occupants of the tenement, who seemed friendly. We were glad to get home and into bed.

It was the following day before I heard from Tamsin's solicitor. Daniel had been sentenced to twelve months' imprisonment and five years on the Sex Offenders Register. I didn't know how to feel. I was glad he had been jailed – maybe now he would realise the seriousness of what he had done – but twelve months! And he would probably be out in six. Even taking into account that he denied it had been going on for five years, his sentence for what was paternal child abuse seemed lenient.

Tamsin slept most of the day. I woke her in the early

afternoon before we went to collect Sam, and told her about Daniel's sentence. She was pretty subdued, although glad he had been jailed. When we told Sam, she insisted that we had to go out and celebrate; so we went to our local restaurant for a meal. Just before we left the flat, Maisie called. There was a small report of the court case in the evening paper; just a filler at the bottom of a column. But with a name like Schenker, it would be obvious to everyone who he was. At least Tamsin wasn't named. All we could do was hope that none of Sam's classmates would read it.

We had our meal, and chatted brightly. But when we got home, Tamsin collapsed in tears. We had talked about what might happen to Daniel in jail; how the other prisoners would probably beat him up, because 'honest' criminals like robbers don't like child molesters. Maisie's daughter worked in the prison service and she had told us some examples of what had occurred in the past.

Sam's attitude to her father had completed reversed. Last Christmas she had begged Tamsin and me not to bad-mouth Daniel in front of her. But now she bad-mouthed Daniel, and men in general, probably more than either Tamsin or me. Sam recounted Maisie's stories with glee before going off to her room. But Tamsin was heartbroken.

'He's still my dad!' she sobbed. 'All I ever wanted was a nice dad, who would spend time with me. Not too much to expect, was it?'

All I could do was hug her. I was crying too, because I had wanted her to have a nice dad, but all my attempts to give her one had failed miserably.

November 1997

Tamsin went downhill quickly. She insisted that she didn't need any help; she just needed to be left alone to 'get her head together'. She didn't sleep at night, but slept most of the day.

Sam and I gradually got used to our new life. The flat was closer to school than our previous house, so that we could leave for school a bit later in the morning. Sam now had to walk the dogs alone. I used to accompany her on my electric buggy, but that was now in a friend's garage, as there was nowhere to store it at the flat. I had bought a metal shed, and had permission to erect it in the garden; but I needed a gate put in the metal fence, and I was running out of money fast. The proceeds of the house sale had been divided equally, but by the time the mortgage, estate agent and solicitor had been paid, I received just over £2,000. And of course aliment had ceased. We had received a terse letter from Daniel's solicitor, saying that since Daniel was now in jail, he could no longer pay aliment. My fault again.

As we had changed addresses, we also changed home helps, although as I had never had a regular helper, it wasn't much different. But we now had a regular home help, called Anne. I found it difficult working with her, as she was in her sixties. She was quite fit, of course, much fitter than me, but it still felt quite awkward telling an older woman to clean my home.

Kim phoned one day in a bit of a panic. Daniel had been asking what had happened to the money from the car sale. The car loan was in joint names, and he was concerned that he might be chased for payment if I couldn't keep up the repayments. Now he was threatening to send in the bailiffs.

'There's not much here that they can take,' I said, trying to sound unconcerned. 'The TV and video are both still on hire purchase, and there's no furniture worth anything.'

'But what about your new car?' asked Kim anxiously.

'It's not mine,' I reassured her, 'it's on contract hire from Motability. He can't touch it.'

I heard no more about the bailiffs. But I couldn't believe Daniel could be so mean! He knew I would be literally stuck in the house without a car. He had never been mean when I knew him; if anything, quite the opposite. He was liable to spend money we didn't have, buying presents for me. But since his return in March, I had gradually come to see that the Daniel I knew was only a part of the whole person. There were depths to him that I had never suspected existed. I know now that I was incredibly naive, but I had expected Daniel to react in the way I would have reacted myself. If I had abused my child and been jailed, I don't think I could have borne the shame. I don't see how I could have lived with myself; but then, I would never have abused my child in the first place.

When people asked me how I was coping that year, I used to tell them I had pencilled in a nervous breakdown for November, because that was the only time I had free. In the event, it didn't happen. I didn't have the time, because Tamsin and Sam needed all my time and energy. I spent my days unpacking and trying to find places for all our belongings. It's very hard moving from a semi-detached house with two reception and three bedrooms, to a flat with one reception and two bedrooms.

I began to try out my new tools, putting up shelves and a rail for the shower curtain. The shelves were quite successful, but the shower rail was a disaster. The walls, I soon discovered, were plasterboard, with cinder brick behind; but in most places the cinder brick was about two inches behind. This meant I had to use plasterboard plugs, which I hadn't used before. One of the men from the choir came to put up my book-shelving system, and showed me how to use the plasterboard plugs, and I tried them myself with the shower curtain rail. The first time I attached the sockets to the wall, the rail sagged alarmingly, and I decided I would have to start again. But it was very hard to pull the rail back out of the socket. Eventually it came out suddenly, and I catapulted backwards out of the bath. Well, that did my back the world of good. Thank heavens for chiropractors!

Shortly after the 'bailiff' scare, Kim and I received an offer of settlement from Daniel and his solicitor. The only asset of any note was Daniel's pension fund, of which £60,000 was to be treated as jointly owned; if equally split, I would be entitled to £30,000. Against that was to be set my half of the car loan, the overdraft on the joint account and the credit card bill; so they estimated that I was owed about £21,000. As poor Daniel was in jail, he had no means of paying me; so they proposed that Daniel should pay the premiums of one of the endowment policies for the next fifteen years. When it matured it would pay out £19,000 plus terminal bonuses. If I agreed to that, Daniel would take over payment of the car loan from 1 January.

This was just a nonsense. Apart from the difficulty of ensuring that Daniel paid the premiums, £21,000 invested for fifteen years would more than double. And we needed money now; I had two teenagers to support.

We had another consultation with Mr Donald. He was of the opinion that, given that Daniel's behaviour was the sole cause of the divorce, and given that I would be unable to work, both because of my physical condition and because Tamsin was likely to need a lot of nursing, that the assets should be split 60:40 in my favour. We agreed that Kim should write in such terms to Daniel's solicitor, and I put all thought of the divorce settlement out of my head.

Less than a week after we moved in, there was an incident in the tenement. The soundproofing was non-existent, and in mid-afternoon, I heard what at first sounded like a child and its father, the child trying to defend itself. The child's voice began to cry, and eventually I realised it was the young girl who lived in the top flat with her boyfriend and their baby son. There were sounds of crying and arguing, and screaming, and I stood irresolute in the hall of the flat. I didn't know what the 'form' was in places like this; should I call the police? The noises continued; there was crashing and banging accompanied by screams, and then someone ran down the stairs and out of the building. Shortly afterwards there was a knock at the door. Someone had called the police and a constable stood there; had I seen anything? Would I make a statement?

I described what I had heard, and despised myself for not having had the courage to call the police. The constable left, and half an hour later came another knock at the door. It was Mikki, the young girl who had been so distressed, coming to thank me – she, too, thought it was I who had called the police. We chatted for a few moments, she saying that it was 'just an argument that had got out of hand'. Then, to my astonishment, her partner Dave joined her and they went off together quite happily.

One day I got a call from my insurance agent, Jim Shepherd, to warn me that Daniel's mother was trying to find us. She had spent the past two days on the phone to Jim, trying to persuade him to divulge our new address. Daniel's solicitor had been told that mail would be redirected from the old house for at least a year, and anything from Daniel or his family should be sent there; but that wasn't good enough for Mrs Schenker.

I thanked Jim for the warning, and spent the next couple of days phoning everyone who knew our address, to warn them to keep it private. I felt it was important for Tamsin's security that Daniel and his family should remain ignorant of our whereabouts. I was still prepared to be on friendly terms with his family; Sam especially was very fond of her grandpa. George, the minister, had asked if the grandparents could see the girls.

'Of course they can,' I had replied. 'But they'd have to see me, too; I'm not prepared just to put them on a train to Glasgow.' I heard no more about visiting the grandparents.

One Saturday morning I was waiting for the girls to dress before going shopping when there was a knock at the door. It was the woman from the top flat, opposite Mikki's, and she told me that my car had a flat tyre. I went outside with her and, sure enough, the front nearside tyre was as flat as a pancake – and slashed. I thanked her for telling me and went indoors to call the AA to change the wheel; I have changed many wheels in the past, but now they are too heavy for me to handle. The AA promised to be as quick as possible.

Just after I put the phone down, there was another knock at the door. When I opened it, there stood Mikki's partner, Dave, looking very ashamed of himself. He confessed that it was he who had slashed the tyre. He had been drunk the previous evening and thought he was in a different part of the street, slashing the tyre on someone else's car. He was full of apologies and offered to change the wheel, and to pay for a new tyre. Bearing in mind that I was going to have to live in the same building, I accepted his apologies and told him not to worry. I was fairly sure that I would not have to pay for a new tyre, and after his fight with Mikki, I was not at all anxious to fall out with Dave.

The tyre was replaced without charge, and Dave promised it would never happen again. He would watch over the flat while we were away and he would help us to decorate when we returned. I accepted his offers and tried very hard to be friendly.

Sam attended a school disco that Saturday evening. Because her school was for girls only, they often arranged social events in conjunction with one or two boys' schools. This disco was to be at a very posh school on the other side of Edinburgh.

Tamsin had great fun helping Sam with her make-up and hair, and they had spent hours in the preceding week deciding on suitable clothes. When the evening came, Sam looked lovely! We arrived at the school and discovered that all the boys were wearing their 'dress' uniform of kilts.

Sam seemed to have a very enjoyable evening – when we collected her, she confessed that she had a boyfriend. Her first ever! Because we were due to leave for Australia the following week, they had exchanged phone numbers, and David had promised to phone Sam in January.

As the weeks drew on, it became obvious that Tamsin wasn't getting any better; in fact, she was getting worse. She was having nightmares, and waking up screaming and in a freakie. The only saving grace about freakies was that she didn't appear to remember anything about them afterwards; so although it was extremely distressing for Sam and me to witness, at least Tamsin was unaware of her behaviour.

I gave her three weeks and then I insisted that she should get some help. She was very reluctant; but I talked it over with Sheila, the counsellor at the Adolescent Unit. She promised to talk about nothing that Tamsin didn't want to talk about, and finally Tamsin agreed to see her. Our GP continued to supply diazepam to be used as sparingly as possible, and gradually with Sheila's support and the prospect of going to Australia, Tamsin began to improve.

December 1997

It was nearly time to leave – we were so excited! The choir carol concert, in which I was taking part, was on Friday 5 December, the day after Sam's birthday; on Saturday we took the train down to London, and stayed overnight at a motel near Heathrow; and on Sunday morning at nine thirty we boarded the flight to Vienna, and on to Sydney. It's a very long way and we were profoundly grateful to arrive, with a missing suitcase the only trauma.

We had a wonderful time in Australia. As well as a holiday from home, in many ways it was a holiday from our situation as well, something we all desperately needed. We went on trips around the area with friends, but quite often Dad would drive the three of us down to the beach for the day, and we would lounge around the swimming pool. Other days we just stayed at home and read books, and sewed, and chatted, and generally relaxed.

Maisie had keys to the flat and had agreed to go in just before Christmas to see if my exam results had arrived. She phoned early on the morning, Sydney time, of Christmas Eve — Continuous Assessment Score 91, Exam Score 90. I had my first! Now we really had something to celebrate.

My sister Kate was in Australia at the time, on a long holiday. She was staying at a friend's house nearby, and joined us every day. She took the girls out without me some days, to give me a complete break. Some days Mum and Dad took them out while I sat in the sun and relaxed. Perfect.

January 1998

The New Year began with a bang – literally! Dad drove us up to Bayview on the Pittwater to see the fireworks, and we ended up sitting about fifty feet away from where they were being released.

On New Year's Day, we all went down to Manly Harbour, and found a grassy bank to sit on, with a good view of the start of the Sydney to Hobart sailing race. We were quite near a swimming pool, and the girls were able to cool off there. I swear Sam was a dolphin in a previous life.

Kate had borrowed a friend's car for a couple of weeks, and the four of us had a few trips. We spent one glorious day at Palm Beach, where 'Home and Away' is filmed. Palm Beach is situated at the tip of a long peninsula, with the ocean on one side and the huge inlet which is The Pittwater on the other.

Our last week in Australia sped by all too quickly, and soon it was time to return to our real lives. We were looking forward to seeing the dogs; Tamsin seemed much better and was determined to go back to school and work hard; and Sam was looking forward to her return to school, with her beautiful tan.

The flight home seemed much longer than the flight out. The first part of the journey was from Sydney to Melbourne, and on to Kuala Lumpur. Imagine our astonishment when we learnt that our captain was none other than Nikki Lauda, the owner of the airline. We had a four-hour wait in Vienna, and were exhausted when we arrived in Manchester. While in Sydney we had booked and paid for a night at the airport hotel, but when we arrived it became clear that the booking had not been passed to the hotel. However, they had plenty of room, and we were able to stay the night.

We had train tickets home for the next day but, because of a power failure, we had one delay after another, and didn't reach Edinburgh until five o'clock. Jenny was there to meet us. We dropped the luggage off at the flat, and had a cup of tea with Jenny before going out to the kennels to bring the dogs home.

We found that both the empty flats had been let while we were away. I soon had to fix a 'Disabled Driver' sign outside the flat, because the new tenants had no scruples about filling up the parking spaces. The people in the ground floor flat were nice enough, but the ones upstairs – oh, dear. They all seemed to wear size twelve lead-lined boots. It was hard to work out who actually lived there; there was one man who was always there, and who had his bed directly above mine. He got up for work at five o'clock every morning, and there seemed to be another man there, who I later discovered was his son. They were quite unabashed about shouting to each other, watching TV, running up and down, all at five in the morning.

Even with my sleeping pills, I was being woken every morning. It was difficult to sleep during the day, because of noise, and we couldn't even have early nights; we could hear the TV from upstairs until late in the evening. I don't cope very well with sleep deprivation.

The big news in the tenement was that Mikki's boyfriend, Dave, was in jail. She had kicked him out after yet another beating. He had begged to be allowed to return and, when she refused, he threatened to 'get himself jailed'. Mikki had remained adamant, and so he had carried out his threat. I never discovered exactly what he had done.

Shortly after we returned home, I arranged to see the director of postgraduate studies at the philosophy department at Edinburgh University. We discussed the one-year taught MSc they offered, and I decided to apply. I was hopeful of obtaining a grant, as a disabled single parent. After all, our new government was all for getting disabled people and single mothers into work. My only realistic option for work was tutoring and/or research, and this was a way forward.

I was very disappointed when we arrived home to find not so much as a Christmas card for the girls from anyone in Daniel's family. I had sent cards and gifts to his parents and sister and her children, and told them they could write to us at our previous address, as I had arranged for mail forwarding; but nothing came back. What we did find was a letter for each of us, from Daniel. Normal letters as though he were away on a ship, instead of sitting in jail because of what he had done to Tamsin. He was fine; he had a nice little job in the woodwork shop, and he was doing a course in business studies in the evening. He warned me darkly to 'let the girls make up their own minds'. If only he knew! I didn't need to say anything to either of them. Tamsin knew from personal experience what a creep he was, and Sam had learnt from watching Tamsin just how much damage her dad had done.

Tamsin didn't even want to read hers, and I felt soiled by touching paper he had touched. Only Sam was glad to hear from him. I asked my solicitor to pass on a request for Daniel not to write to any of us except Sam.

In view of our abandonment by the Schenkers, I could see no good reason for keeping their name. Tamsin had wanted to start using my maiden name of Charles the previous summer; but I was still hopeful then that, once Daniel's family had recovered from the shock, they would realise that we were innocents worthy of help and support. But if they couldn't even be bothered to send a Christmas card! In spite of all my resolutions, I couldn't help feeling deeply hurt by the way Daniel and his family had abandoned us.

I talked it over with the girls. We had to decide now, because if I was reverting to my maiden name, I needed to let the Open University know immediately for graduation. Tamsin was desperate to shed her father's name; even Sam was disappointed at the lack of support, and so it was agreed. Sam wrote to her father and told him, and I waited for an explosion. I had had it impressed on me from the time we met, what a privilege it was to carry the name of Schenker; when Tamsin was born, Mrs Schenker had told me what a very special baby she was, because she was the first of the next generation of Schenkers to carry the name. I was beginning to feel soiled by the name; also it was about the only way I had of striking back and hurting his family; so my motives were not very honourable, but understandable.

Daniel wrote back to Sam quite soon. He said he had always thought I would revert to my maiden name, but one day Sam would be able to make up her own mind. I suppose all his mail was being censored, and his letters had to be pleasant. But I don't think he had the courage to tell his mother: she still addressed mail to the girls by his name.

So we changed our surnames to Charles. I wrote and told everyone. There is no need in Scotland for any formal procedure; you can call yourself by any name you wish, as long as it is not for fraudulent purposes.

Because we had been away for a few weeks, our home help had been allocated a new client, which meant we were back to a different person every week. But after a few weeks, we were allocated a permanent helper, a friendly woman who was most obliging, but again much older than me.

Sam's holiday seemed to have done her the world of good: she had only one chest infection that month. True to his word, her new boyfriend David called soon after our return, and they went on a date, a visit to the cinema. But Sam made it quite clear that she was not at all prepared to do any of the 'kissing stuff', to use her expression. So David gave up; he called her one night and broke off the relationship. But Sam was not in the least upset: if anything, she was relieved. She is still quite adamant that she doesn't want anything to do with boyfriends — one sign of the damage which Daniel has caused her.

Tamsin's new resolve, brought back from Australia, didn't last long. She had been back at school for only a couple of weeks before she came down with flu, and then she started having nightmares and freakies again. Soon she was back to hiding in her room all the time, refusing to go to school. We couldn't go on like this indefinitely.

February 1998

By the beginning of February, Tamsin was becoming really ill, and even she could see that she needed help. Finally, fifteen months after she disclosed the abuse, she agreed to talk about it. We discussed it with the Adolescent Unit and with her school, and decided the best option was for Tamsin to have counselling on Monday afternoons, and for me to drive her to school on Tuesday mornings. Her school timetable had undergone a radical revision; she had dropped Standard Grade computing and Higher music (too much maths) the previous term; the National Certificates had perforce been dropped because she had missed the second half of the autumn term; now it was decided that she should also drop the remaining Highers, chemistry and biology, and concentrate on Standard Grade English and maths. Dropping the Highers would have no effect on her plans for a nursery nursing college course.

The new arrangement began the following week; and for the rest of that term and the whole of the summer term, that was our routine. We would set off about ten o'clock in the morning, buying sandwiches and drinks at the garage, and then stop for an early lunch just after we had completed the twisting section of road through the Dalveen Pass. We arrived at school during the lunch break, and I was back home in good time to collect Sam. I loved driving my little car along the winding roads. It has tremendous acceleration which makes overtaking easy and safe, and the front-wheel drive makes it a joy on twisty roads.

The counselling seemed to make a huge difference to Tamsin. She became more like her old self, full of fun and laughter, teasing Sam, generally being more like a normal teenager. She wanted driving lessons for her seventeenth birthday; I couldn't see at the moment how I could afford it, but she was understanding about the money situation.

Sam was Sam: helpful, reliable, cheeky, full of nonsense. She had made friends with Josie, a thirteen-year-old girl from the first floor opposite. Her mother had three other children, and Josie was expected to spend most of her time looking after them. Her mother's partner was a heroin addict who was quite free with his fists. I felt very sorry for Josie, and she spent quite a lot of time in our flat.

Sam was continuing with her Duke of Edinburgh work. She had completed her first aid certificate the previous term, and it had just been returned to have the surname changed. She had a judo grading just before we went to Australia, and had risen by a whole belt, three mons, which apparently is quite something to achieve in such a short time. I know nothing about judo, but I was very proud of her. She had obtained a grant from an educational charity for music lessons, and she spent a lot of her spare time playing her flute, except when she was having yet another chest infection. She seemed happy and settled, and to have recovered from the worst effects of her father's betrayal.

The noise from our upstairs neighbours continued unabated. One Friday night they had a party, and the whole building shook. At eleven o'clock Tamsin announced she was going upstairs to ask them to turn the sound down – I thought she was very brave, and maybe foolhardy, but she would not be dissuaded. It was quite amusing in a perverted sort of way. In our sitting room, Sam and I could hear when she arrived at the front door; we could hear them turn down the music so that they could talk; we heard her request, and a girl's voice assented. Then as Tamsin came back down the stairs, we could hear an argument upstairs, before the music was turned up even louder.

At eleven thirty I called the police; I was exhausted, I wanted to go to bed, I couldn't stand the noise any more.

At midnight the music stopped, and they started vacuuming! Then they went out and silence descended. I called the police back and told them not to bother. The desk sergeant was apologetic; they had had lots of calls to answer. Were these people causing trouble regularly? I explained some of our problems, and she offered to send the community policeman round the next day. I agreed to that and then we all went thankfully to bed.

The community policeman came the next morning. There was a neighbourhood reconciliation service available; it was much less threatening than a visit from the police or a complaint to the council. It sounded like a good idea to me; after all, I could call the police any time, but after they went away, we would still be here, and so would the man upstairs. I was very conscious of how vulnerable we were, both physically and emotionally. I didn't want to cause any trouble, but I need my sleep, and we were all becoming exhausted.

Kim and I had finally had a reply from Daniel's solicitor. Far from me being entitled to more than Daniel, he argued that because Daniel had been imprisoned, his employment opportunities would be limited, and so he should get the bigger share. I was utterly disgusted. Once again we were being made to feel like we were the bad guys for putting Daniel in jail. Neither he nor his solicitor showed any appreciation of the fact that the only person who put Daniel in jail was Daniel.

Daniel was now prepared to offer a cash payment of £7,500 in full and final settlement – I have never felt so insulted in all my life. £7,500 – was that all that I deserved for twenty years of looking after Daniel, making a home for him and his children, putting up with his bad temper? I was so hurt, and angry, and bitter.

Kim suggested I might want to think about accepting a smaller capital payment, say £15,000. But I felt Daniel should pay what he owed regardless; so I said unless they were prepared to offer the full amount, with no strings, I wasn't interested. And there it was left.

March 1998

I heard from the Open University that my graduation would be in Edinburgh on 9 May. I was getting quite excited about it now. I also received a letter from Edinburgh University with an offer of a place on the MSc course in philosophy. It began to look as though my life was getting back into some sort of shape. I had obtained the application forms for a grant from the Student Awards Agency for Scotland – SAAS – and filled them in after much consultation with Jenny. Jenny provided a stunning reference for me, as did my tutor from the previous year, Adrienne, and I sent them off full of hope. Adrienne was a senior lecturer in the faculty of education in Glasgow. She had been told that priorities for funding were single parents, disabled students, mature students and good firsts, and I fit all four categories.

I also wrote an article about the effects of child abuse on the child, and the way abusers are protected. Daniel had never been made to face up to the damage he had caused to Tamsin. No one stood up in court and said how ill she had been. And now I heard from George that Daniel was being protected in jail too, by being housed in a separate wing for sexual offenders. It just felt like every effort was being made to help the abuser, but the victims – oops, sorry, not allowed (by Tamsin!) to use that word – the survivors were given no help once the case was over. It felt like we had been used to secure a prosecution and then discarded as being of no further importance.

I sat down and wrote the piece in a couple of hours. Then I began phoning newspapers. I was concerned that our confidentiality might not be respected, but this was a groundless fear. Eventually the article was published in the *Guardian*, and I was paid £250.

I was absolutely delighted. Now I could buy some material and make posh clothes for us for my graduation! We had been living on income support since Daniel was jailed, and money was desperately tight. Mum and Dad helped out when they could, but they were not rich themselves. And the car loan was bleeding me dry. I couldn't find nearly £200 a month out of £143 a week, and so the bank was increasing my overdraft by £200 a month to pay it.

One thing gave me pause for thought. While speaking to the features editor at the *Guardian*, he had mused, 'It's very well written. The bitterness comes across quite clearly.' Bitterness? I didn't want to be bitter. I didn't want to be angry. I thought it over for a long time, and finally concluded that the prolonged wrangling over money was doing me no good at all. I didn't like myself very much then, because I was bitter and angry; justifiably, without doubt, but I have to live with myself.

I called Kim and instructed her to offer to settle for

£15,000, plus the car loan, plus the endowment policies. She felt that was a sensible offer — I felt it was bloody generous of me in the circumstances, but it was worth it to me just to get the whole divorce business out of my life. I also mentioned to Kim that we should investigate getting a new interdict to keep Daniel away from Tamsin after his release; but to my horror she told me that we could only do that after Daniel had tried to contact her. I was almost speechless; if Daniel did approach Tamsin, I thought it was most likely that she would immediately retreat into a freakie, which could put her life at risk, depending on where she was. It would also do her enormous damage, just when she was beginning to recover; but that's the law, believe it or not.

We had more trouble with the neighbours that month. One night there was a terrific argument upstairs. That wasn't unusual in itself: sometimes if there was nothing worth watching on TV, we would switch it off and listen to the live 'soap' going on upstairs. But this argument went on for several hours. The girls went off to bed, and I settled down and tried to sleep. At about one o'clock in the morning, I heard loud footsteps going along the hall upstairs, out of the door, down the tenement stairs — and then there was a terrific crash at the front door! I heard the tenement door bang a moment later.

The next morning I took the dogs out to the garden as usual. It wasn't until we were coming back into the flat that I noticed broken glass all over the floor. Then as I pushed the front door open, I discovered shards of glass sticking out of the wood of the door, by cutting my hand. Someone had crashed something made of glass into the door.

That same night the front windows of the other ground floor flat had been broken. After that, when there were arguments upstairs, the girls would bring their bedding into the sitting room and sleep there with me; their bedrooms looked out over the front of the tenement, and they were afraid that the windows might be broken while they were in bed.

A few days later when I opened the front door in the morning, it was covered in spittle. Charming people we lived with.

April 1998

Just to make life in the flat more interesting, we had an infestation of ants. We tried the stuff which the pest control officer left, but it made absolutely no difference. Then I heard that the ants were in every flat in the block. We bought some stuff which my parents used in Australia to keep the cockroaches out, and that worked – we had no more ants.

I had given a lot of thought to my graduation party. I couldn't afford to hire a hall and a band; and after all, if the flat was good enough for us to live in, it was good enough for us to have a party in. If people wouldn't come because of the address, it would sort out real friends from those who were just friendly.

I had an illustration of that very point that month. I discovered that people whom I had thought were my friends, whom I have know for many years, had been writing to Daniel in jail. They didn't tell me; I found out by accident. I talked it over with Jenny and Rosie, who were both horrified.

'He's just using them to get at you,' advised Jenny. 'It's a way of showing that he can reach you even when he's in jail. It's just another power game.'

I could see the sense of that. I knew these people were trying to behave in a Christian way; but what they didn't or couldn't understand was that by treating him as a normal person, they were reinforcing what seemed to me to be his belief that he had done nothing very wrong, and was being unjustly punished because of his vindictive ex-wife. Certainly that was the way he made me feel, because he never once tried to explain why he abused our daughter, and almost seemed to play down the whole child abuse aspect of his crime. Of course, maybe our friends weren't aware of how much damage had been done to Tamsin, and to Sam and me, but they only had to ask to find out.

I had a major argument with George about this. I was hurt and angry that people who were supposed to be my friends were supporting the person who had torn apart our lives. But George didn't seem able to appreciate how much damage Daniel had done, and he insisted that I had no right to tell other people what they could do. He was also quite adamant that he had no right to tell Daniel to stay away from the church on his release.

I was bitterly upset by all this, and decided that I couldn't go to church for a bit. I was hurt and angry about the letters, and also by George's attitude. I thought it all through for a couple of weeks, and eventually decided that the reason I went to church was not to meet friends, but to worship God. Then I decided that I didn't want to go to a different church because I enjoyed being part of the choir, and felt I made a valuable contribution. So I returned to church, but for me, not for anyone else.

I have found that very few people are prepared to talk about child abuse. Maybe they don't want me to think they are prying. But this conspiracy of silence protects only abusers, while the innocents who have been hurt are left to struggle on unsupported. We have done nothing wrong; we have committed no crime; on the contrary, we are survivors of a crime. But the institutions of this country don't want to know.

I feel enormously let down by the church. Maybe I have been unlucky; maybe we would have had more support from a different congregation. Or maybe the church simply doesn't know what to do with victims/survivors.

As Christians we know how to treat criminals. We must forgive them, sustain them, help them to see the error of their ways. We visit them in prison, we write letters to them, we assure them of a welcome if they would like to return. Daniel has had more support than we have. He was visited in prison; people wrote letters to him. They were quite prepared to welcome him back into the congregation, even if that meant that I left.

But we really don't know what to do with those who have suffered from a crime. Our minister was most reluctant for anyone to know why my marriage broke up. Most people in the congregation do know, because my parents told them – they saw no reason to protect an abuser, which is all that secrecy does.

I think it is time the church took a long, hard look at its attitude to those who have suffered through crime, especially where the criminal is also a member. At the moment it seems it's much easier just to ignore the innocents and try to rehabilitate the offender.

Fair enough, if rehabilitation was being carried out. But to my knowledge, Daniel was offered no 'treatment' in prison, and in my opinion he would not have accepted any without coercion, because as far as he is concerned, there is nothing wrong with him. If that is the case, then Daniel has been protected from having to face up to the consequences of his behaviour, and that is wrong. Lack of rehabilitation in prison suggests that if the opportunity arose again, the sex offender would be likely to think nothing of taking it. As a result there seems very little point in jailing that offender in the first place. And from Daniel's point of view, I couldn't see any evidence that he was being educated to acknowledge the seriousness of his crime. Indeed there was more evidence to suggest that he was being protected from having to appreciate the consequences of his behaviour.

Before his arrest, I wrote a letter to him, begging him to be honest to prevent Tamsin's having to testify against him, and outlining some of the difficulties she was facing; but the police refused to give him the letter, because they had a duty of care towards him, and felt that he might not be able to cope with such an emotive letter. The first hearing was adjourned for background reports, but nobody bothered to find out the consequences of his behaviour on any of the three of us, so he didn't find out. While in prison, he was kept away from non-sexual offenders for his own safety. And from my point of view, prison life didn't seem to be much of a punishment. By all account he was quite comfortable, thank you.

I had a feeling that Daniel would be released at the end of April, but again I had inordinate difficulty in finding out. I did have a genuine need to know; if I couldn't protect

Tamsin and Sam with an interdict, at least I could try and find out where Daniel was likely to be. In the end it was SACRO, an organisation set up to help ex-offenders, who were the most helpful. They discovered that Daniel was to be released on 27 April – six months to the day since he had been jailed. I had a long chat with one of their officers about Daniel's crime and his attitude; I was advised that Daniel would continue to pose a threat to the girls and me as long as he persisted in his denial, and nobody was doing anything to try and confront that denial.

Although Daniel had to sign the new Sex Offenders Register, the police were not allowed to tell me anything about his whereabouts. He could be given a council flat in the next street and I wouldn't know anything about it. A lot depended on how easily he found work; I knew that being unemployed would destroy Daniel faster than anything else. I was afraid that if he was unemployed for any length of time, I would get the blame, and he would come looking for me. And I can't run away. But we couldn't get any legal protection until after he caused trouble.

All we could do was to be less predictable about where we went and when. I was determined not to be prevented from going to church and choir practice, and I arranged to give a friend a lift to and from choir practice, so that I would not be alone on Thursday evenings. There were always lots of people around on Sunday mornings, and Maisie promised to let me know if he had turned up, before the choir entered the church.

Daniel didn't know which school Sam attended, and the office staff at St Andrew's knew not to give out any information about her.

The only thing Daniel could predict with any certainty was that Tamsin would be meeting or leaving the school bus at Waverley station on Fridays and Sundays. I talked it over with the school staff, and we arranged for Tamsin to be collected and deposited on the outskirts of Edinburgh instead.

Tamsin continued to see Sheila, and to do well. She also got a holiday job. I came home one morning to find that she had lined herself up a job as a chambermaid at a large hotel. It didn't last long, though; she had to get up at some unearthly hour to catch the bus in the morning, and she was too slow to get through all her work in the allocated time. A couple of weeks was long enough, then she gave in her notice and went to work at the local McDonald's restaurant. She seemed happier working there, although as a new starter she nearly always got the early shift and had to start at 7 a.m.

Kim sent me an offer of compensation from the Criminal Injuries Board. It was for repeated abuse, but included nothing for mental distress. I felt that Tamsin had been quite distressed enough to qualify for compensation, and so returned the offer with an explanation, and a list of people who could confirm what I said about Tamsin.

One day we had an unexpected visitor. There was a knock at the door. Sam went to answer it, and there was a sudden flurry before the front door was slammed, locked and bolted. I got up quickly to see what was happening and found Josie's mother standing in the hall, shouting abuse through the door to her partner. She laughed rather shakily as she came into the sitting room.

'I got off lightly there — he put me in hospital the last time!' Suddenly her druggie partner appeared at the window.

He couldn't see in because of the nets, but he jumped up and down, screaming abuse as he banged the window. The dogs went berserk, barking and snarling furiously as I stood frozen with terror, and I think it was the dogs that persuaded him to leave. He ran off across the garden and over the fence. Tamsin checked that it was safe and then went upstairs to fetch their baby while I made a cup of tea. I tried to persuade Josie's mum to call the police but she was having none of it.

'He's not usually like this,' she said. 'He must have got some extra-strength stuff. He'll be okay when it wears off. I'll just go to my sister's for the night.'

She phoned her sister and collected her children and left. I honestly don't know how or why women put up with such behaviour, except that maybe they've never known anything else. Or maybe there is still such a stigma against single women in that sink estate culture that any man is better than none. But the result for us was that we felt even more frightened and vulnerable in the flat.

The neighbourhood reconciliation people came to see us: a middle-aged American woman and a younger Scotsman. I wasn't really sure how much of what was happening was a real problem and how much was due to our inexperience of living in a flat. However, they seemed to think that the noise levels were a bit excessive, and promised to go and see the man upstairs.

In the meantime I was putting the finishing touches to our graduation outfits. I had made myself a trouser suit in a charcoal pinstripe. I never wear skirts because if I can't see my feet, I don't know where they are and then I trip or fall. For Sam I had made a trouser suit in a lovely hyacinth blue, which suited her really well. By now she was taller than Tamsin, about five feet nine inches, and was developing a more adult figure. I also made blouses for both of us. Tamsin had a peach-coloured silk jacket she had bought in Australia, and to go with it I made a sleeveless dress in a cream patterned cotton. Mum had bought me a beautiful blouse in Sydney: cream-coloured with lots of green embroidery. I was planning to wear that for the evening, and so I made a pair of green trousers to go with it. We were all looking forward to the great day.

Towards the end of the month Kim called. Daniel had made a counter-offer of £12,500 in cash, plus the endowment policies, and he would pay off the car loan. I told her to accept; I was just grateful that we had reached a deal. She sent me a copy of the offer which I forwarded to the bank, and after that they were much more relaxed about my ever-increasing overdraft.

Tamsin turned seventeen at the end of the month, and I scraped together the money to give her five driving lessons. She was thrilled to bits! By the time she had used up the gift token I gave her, she would be earning enough to continue paying for driving lessons herself.

May 1998

My parents arrived from Australia for their annual visit at the beginning of the month. I had booked a bed and breakfast for them for the first couple of weeks; when we arrived there, it turned out that Mum and Dad already knew the owners. They had previously run a local market garden and flower business, and they had provided the flowers for many family occasions.

It seemed no time at all until graduation day arrived. The ceremony was at three o'clock, but we had to be in the hall by two o'clock. As well as the girls and me, and my parents, my sister Kate came, and so did Rosie and Maria, Sam's godmother, and Jenny.

The McEwan Hall is a wonderful place. The walls and ceiling are covered in beautiful classical paintings, and I gazed around in wonder as I waited for the ceremony to begin. I don't remember much about the actual ceremony, except concentrating fiercely on not falling as I walked across the stage. But I do remember feeling quite proud of myself!

Afterwards we all crowded around outside, taking photographs and having them taken.

We had arranged to go to our local restaurant for a meal; my parents drove down with Kate in her car, while Jenny and Maria squashed themselves into my car with the girls and me. We were in high spirits as we drove through the late afternoon sunshine, through the city and down to the riverside. We had a wonderful meal, with lots of fun and laughter.

More guests had been invited from eight o'clock onwards, and the evening passed in a blur of talk and laughter. Jenny made a most embarrassing speech about my academic prowess before proposing a toast. Most of the guests left by half past ten, leaving Jenny, Maria and the girls and me to loll around, drinking wine and talking. Maria was staying the night, but Jenny eventually left by taxi at about midnight.

Jenny and I had spent a lot of time together since the beginning of the year. I used to go along to her flat for the day about once a week. I loved her flat; it was in a quiet, broad street, and when you walked in the door, it sort of welcomed you. You felt that happy people had lived there. It was an oasis of peace amid the chaos of my life.

Then Jenny dropped a bombshell. She was leaving Edinburgh. Her contract with the Open University would expire in a year, with no guarantee of renewal; there was a vacancy in Belfast for a staff tutor, and she had applied for that with mixed feelings. She originally came from Northern Ireland, but had lived in Scotland for twenty years. But she had a son to support through university, and couldn't afford to take a drop in salary until he was safely on his way. She had been offered the Belfast post, and decided to accept it.

I would miss her so much! But, we rationalised, Belfast isn't so very far away, and no doubt Jenny would be in Scotland on business from time to time, and there was always the phone.

An idea began to form in my mind. Jenny had two cats, and her flat was privately rented. Would the owner agree to having dogs? I was very concerned that Jenny shouldn't feel I was jumping into her life, but I sounded her out about it. She was actually relieved. She had been dreading telling the owner of the flat that she was leaving; but if she could suggest a new tenant, she would feel much better about it.

Jenny wouldn't be leaving until the end of the summer, but she agreed to ask the owner if she would think about letting the flat to us. At last! There was hope on the horizon.

Calling in the neighbourhood reconciliation people had been a mistake. The man upstairs – Fairy Feet as we called him – now thought we were trying to have him evicted. His manner towards us, always difficult, was now downright truculent. I just had no idea of how to handle the situation, and decided to ignore it as much as possible; we wouldn't be there for much longer, God willing! We didn't talk about it much, the three of us. I didn't want the girls to know how frightened I was, because I felt that would make them even more frightened. And I couldn't admit to myself how bad it was, because I had to go on living there. But looking back, it was truly dreadful.

I had a consultation with Kim and Mr Donald, to discuss

Daniel's offer. Mr Donald was most reluctant to accept it. He felt I was being seriously cheated. But as he himself pointed out, if we went to court, it would be the following year before a hearing could be held. And Daniel's fiftieth birthday was in March 1999, after which he could empty his pension fund. I might get a judgement for forty thousand pounds but no way of collecting it, and we needed money now.

I had to sign a statement acknowledging that I was acting against legal advice in accepting Daniel's offer, so that if I later regretted it, I would have no comeback on the lawyers. I signed it without hesitation; I needed money now, and I just wanted to be shot of the whole affair.

We had heard and seen nothing of Daniel since his release from prison. But now he was suddenly and mysteriously unavailable to sign the papers. His mother said he was 'travelling around', and I became suspicious that he was working. I spoke to the Child Support Agency and reported my suspicions in writing, but nothing happened.

We heard of a happy event: my brother and his wife had twin boys. They were a little premature and had to stay in hospital for a few weeks, but soon began to catch up. We were all delighted, although our delight was tinged with sadness. They lived in Australia, and were moving to California in the autumn – we didn't know when we might be able to see them.

One morning Mrs Jameson phoned from school, to tell me of the events of the previous night. Tamsin had gone missing. She had had an argument with her friend, Jane, and had gone for a walk in the grounds to cool off. She told me later that she sat down under a tree and had a good cry – and then she fell asleep. She was wearing only a sweatshirt and jeans and, by the time she woke up at midnight, she was too cold to move.

In the meantime her absence was discovered at ten o'clock, bedtime, and the staff had spent a frantic two hours searching for Tamsin before they called the police. Tamsin was found just after that, and had to be taken indoors and put in a hot bath before bed. She was none the worse for her adventure, but everyone had had a real fright. Months later she told me that in fact she had had a freakie, and had no recollection of how she came to be lost in the grounds.

Apart from that escapade, though, Tamsin was generally much better. She had had an interview at the college and had an unconditional offer of a place on the nursery nursing course. Having finished her exams, and having no more school work to do, she was spending most of her days in the nursery section of the school, helping with the little ones. That included going swimming with them twice a week, which she loved. At the weekends, she was almost back to normal, helping with household chores and teasing Sam in a good-natured way. It seemed that for Tamsin, the worst was over.

June 1998

At the beginning of the month I finally collected the cheque from Kim's office. £12,500 — I had never seen such a big cheque! I took it out to the bank, and came home to find a frantic message from Kim on the answering machine, to give her a call asap.

It turned out that she should not have given me the cheque at all. I was only entitled to the first £2,500 — the rest was supposed to go to the Legal Aid Board, to be held to pay my legal fees. I had immediately to write a cheque for £10,000 and hand it over. Kim thought she could ask for another £4,000 to be released, but the rest had to stay with the Legal Aid Board.

This was the first indication I had of what the likely bill would be. I had asked Kim, and she had said it would be 'into four figures', which to me meant a couple of thousand — maybe £3,000 at most. Now it seemed that it would be well over £5,000. I was bitterly disappointed. We had been busy planning a fabulous holiday in Kenya; if I kept all the money I would lose my income support and have to spend the money on everyday expenses, and I had been advised that after all we had been through, it was justifiable to spend a lot of money on a holiday. I had a £2,500 overdraft to pay off as well. Kenya was now out of the question; we settled for two weeks in Dumfriesshire.

Later in the month I visited Kim's office to swear an affidavit. This was a statement to the court explaining the circumstances of the divorce and the settlement agreement. If I provided an affidavit, and someone else could provide one confirming what I said, there would be no need for me to go to court. Jenny provided the second affidavit; but mine had to be revised, as it included our council flat address. Normally a copy of the affidavit would have been sent to Daniel's solicitor, but in this case I refused to allow this, and Daniel's solicitor accepted my position. The only copies would be mine, those in Kim's files and those in court; and I was assured that Daniel and his family would not have access to the court documents. I felt I had done all I could to safeguard our whereabouts.

There was still no word of whether Daniel was working; nothing at all from the Child Support Agency. But also no sign of Daniel hanging around, which was good. His mother was making a great fuss about having an address so that she could contact the girls, as she wasn't convinced that I would continue to redirect the mail. After a lot of consideration, I thought the best option was for her to send mail to the church. They would always know where we were, and would pass on mail promptly. Kim wrote to Daniel's solicitor asking him to pass on the message.

I kept myself busy making summer clothes for all of us.

With both girls at school, I was alone most of the day, and it was generally too noisy to read; so I sat at my sewing machine and listened to the radio. I had bought a tape of Verdi's Requiem, and when the noise from upstairs became unbearable, I could blast that out. Very satisfying!

Mum and Dad returned to Australia in the middle of the month. They had enjoyed their Scottish break, but were glad to be going back to their lives in Sydney.

Tamsin left school at the end of the month. She was still working at McDonald's at the weekends, and was using the money to pay for driving lessons. One of the choir members was a driving instructor, and he charged a reduced rate for friends; Tamsin was able to have two hours' instruction a week, and seemed to be making good progress.

Sam completed her expeditions for her Duke of Edinburgh Bronze. One fine weekend they had a practice expedition in Perthshire, which seemed to go well. They camped overnight beside a loch, and Sam came home sunburnt and covered in midge bites. The following weekend was the test expedition; and it rained! Somehow they managed to dry out some of their clothes overnight, and it wasn't too cold, but they were all thankful when it was over.

I think Sam took quite a lot of stick from the other girls for being a slow walker. The difference in length between her legs was by now twenty three millimetres, and to avoid ruining the Vibram sole of her walking boot, the orthotics technician had designed an insole to raise her heel by twenty three millimetres. Unfortunately, that meant that her foot was only just inside the boot. That, combined with her asthma, made it very heavy going for Sam, and for her Silver award, she was hoping to do an exploration, which is less strenuous.

Sam had another judo grading at the end of term, and once again raised her standard by a full three mons. She seemed to love judo: she is tall and strongly built, and it's a good way of getting rid of stresses. She also won a share of a prize at school – a new trophy had been presented for the best performance of a school team over the year, and the third year hockey team won it. They worked out that they should each hold it for about ten days.

From being freezing cold in the winter, the flat now became stuffy and airless. And, of course, eternally noisy.

July 1998

At the beginning of July I received a copy of the Minute of Agreement regarding financial affairs in the divorce, which had now been registered with the courts. I had signed it before Daniel, and this was the first chance I had to see his signature. He had signed it in Aberdeen and had it witnessed by someone from Hull. To me that meant only one thing – he was definitely working. That explained his sudden co-operativeness to get the divorce settled. If we had gone to court when he was working, he could have been ordered to make payments to me from his salary.

I wondered out loud how we could find out which company had been foolish enough to employ him. Then Tamsin piped up.

'I'll do it!' she said. 'I'll phone them up and say I'm trying to find my dad, 'cos my mum won't let me see him or talk to him!'

And she did – she was brilliant! I still had copies on the hard drive of the computer of all the letters he had sent in

September 1996, when he was looking for another job, and we tried all of those — no joy. One personnel manager suggested trying the union and, as I was looking through the address book to get Daniel's union number, I came across the number for Jim Morris at Jepson's, who had been so keen to employ him before his arrest. Tamsin tried that number — bingo! He was working for them, and was presently in Hong Kong.

I couldn't quite work out how he could be allowed to work in the Far East when he was supposed to be on the Sex Offenders Register and on parole, but never mind. I immediately faxed the Child Support Agency with the name and address of the company — the rest was up to them.

We were busy preparing for our holiday. Jenny was going to join us for the middle weekend, and we were really looking forward to it. I was still waiting to hear whether my grant application had been successful. I phoned SAAS, but they wouldn't give details over the phone. Jenny agreed to drop in and collect mail on her way down for the weekend.

And so we set off. I had found a garage to rent, quite close to Jenny's house, and had reclaimed my electric buggy and trailer from the various friends' houses where they had spent the winter. We loaded the buggy, Sam's bicycle and most of the luggage on to the trailer, but there still wasn't much room in the car, what with three of us and three dogs. We ended up letting Sally, the smallest and oldest, sit in the front, because she was bossing the other two around and they wouldn't settle. We stopped at Abington for a break and arrived at our chalet in late afternoon.

The chalets were beautifully situated in the grounds of a

derelict manor house. Some of the outbuildings had been converted to holiday cottages, and six wooden chalets had been built on a flat, grassy site. They were about a mile and a half from the road, down a twisting, rutted track which made the buggy bounce wildly in the trailer. Fly couldn't believe her eyes: there were rabbits everywhere. She peered out of the windows intently. There were also sheep in the nearby fields, which she eyed with interest; we would have to watch her. Lucy thought it was all quite interesting, and Sally just barked her head off as usual.

The chalet was lovely: beautifully furnished, and very comfortable. There was a double bedroom which I bagged, and a room with bunks which reminded Tamsin of school. We unhitched the trailer and Sam and I went back to Castle Douglas, the nearest town, for some shopping, while Tamsin took the dogs for a walk.

We had a lovely relaxing week. We went for lots of forest walks, nearly always getting bogged down with the buggy at some point; but the girls managed to extricate us, and did it with giggles and fun, not bad-temperedly as Daniel would have done. The weather wasn't brilliant, but we were out most days.

The girls went riding at Sandyhills, about half an hour's drive away. I didn't watch them to begin with. It still hurt that I could no longer ride, as horses had been a very import-ant part of my life when I was younger. But one day I returned while they were still in the outdoor school, and discovered that I could now watch without feeling torn apart.

I was really impressed with Tamsin. Although she hadn't ridden regularly since she was twelve, she sat in the saddle as if she had grown up there, and was fearless about jumping. We were discussing it on the way home one day, and somehow she decided that she should abandon nursery nursing and look for a career with horses. It turned out that the careers adviser at school had offered her veterinary science (too many exams for Tamsin's depleted confidence) or nursery nursing – nothing else.

There were horses in a field near the chalet, which we discovered belonged to a teacher from Tamsin's school. She gave Tamsin some names and addresses to contact after we went home, and that produced yet another improvement in Tamsin's general mood.

On Friday morning we went into Castle Douglas to meet Jenny. She arrived in an enormous hired car, and we set off back to the chalet. As soon as we arrived, she dug out the mail. As I was reading the letter from SAAS, Tamsin announced with great glee that she had passed her written driving test. My news was not so good.

'I didn't get a grant,' I said, trying not to sound too dismayed.

'Oh, no!' said Jenny. 'I'm so sorry.'

'Oh, well,' I said with forced cheerfulness, 'I always have to fight for everything.'

'But it would have been nice, just this once,' said Jenny, and it was hard not to agree.

I managed to put my disappointment to one side for the rest of the holiday. That afternoon was hot and sunny and we spent it on the beach, going for fish and chips for tea. The following day we drove right across Galloway to Portpatrick. Jenny had often visited it as a child, coming over from Northern Ireland by fishing boat, and she was very pleased to return. On the way home we drove from Newton Stewart up towards New Galloway, and then through the Raider's Road, a Forestry Commission drive which meanders through some lovely countryside.

On Sunday it rained all day. We played Monopoly: individually to begin with, but then Jenny teamed up with the girls; but it still took them three hours to beat me. Jenny left that afternoon, but we continued our holiday happily. We toured around the local countryside: it was an area I knew well, as my parents had once owned the village shop in the area, and I enjoyed showing it off to the girls.

Jenny had brought us some good news: her landlady had been pleased to hear of a new tenant, and would contact us on our return. So we had that to look forward to. It was about the only thing that made returning to the flat bearable.

We returned on Saturday afternoon, and unpacked and washed clothes to the accompaniment of noise from upstairs. Fairy Feet's son had moved out and his teenage daughter had moved in, and it was no improvement. She didn't work or go to school or college. She sat in the flat all day, playing loud pop music and entertaining friends. That Saturday evening she seemed to be having a party with her friends, and the noise was incredible.

The following morning I noticed a pile of empty alcopop bottles on the ground outside our kitchen window. 'I bet that's from her upstairs,' I mentioned to Sam. Unfortunately Sam told Josie, and soon the word was all over the tenement. In the middle of the afternoon we had a visit from Fairy Feet. He stood on my doorstep and yelled and swore at me. He was going to get me evicted; he was going to make the council get rid of the dogs (who I'm sure protected us from much worse); he went on and on, and I couldn't get a word in edgeways.

I was so pleased that I'd had a call from Jenny's landlady, Pat Owens, that morning. She was quite happy to have dogs in the flat: she had five herself, and understood what an important part of the family they are. She had no objections to the rent being paid by housing benefit, and she had invited us to go and meet her at her home that evening. We were glad to get out.

Pat turned out to be a lovely woman. As well as dogs, she had ponies, too, and the house was full of tack, which made it feel very homely to us. We told her something of our experiences, and she felt only too pleased to offer us a home. We wanted somewhere to stay for the foreseeable future, and she wanted a long-term tenant, and so it was agreed. We drove home feeling happier than for a long time. At last we were to have a comfortable – and safe – home.

August 1998

Tamsin lost no time in buying a copy of *Horse and Hound* and applying for positions. I discovered that she wanted to go into racing. I spent a fortune buying equipment and paying for train fares. She tried out at a few stables, but didn't really have the experience needed. She rode well enough, but her stable management was not up to professional standards. After three false starts I contacted the local agricultural college and discovered they were still interviewing for the course for a National Certificate in horse management. Tamsin's interview was set for the beginning of September. She had finished her counselling and stopped taking her betablockers, and although I thought it was a very short time to recover from abuse, both Tamsin and Sheila seemed to feel they had covered everything.

Tamsin asked me to cut her hair – we couldn't afford a hairdresser, and I can do basic styles. When I worked with horses, I learnt how to take the hair off a horse's heels without leaving any scissor marks; horses look much better bred if they don't have hairy heels. At this time, Tamsin's hair was shoulder length, but she wanted it really short, so that it would be quicker and easier to wash every morning. I cut it to a couple of inches long. Tamsin lived with it for a day or two, then demanded it should be shorter. She wasn't satisfied until it was about half an inch all over. But she has a well-shaped head, and although it was extreme, it suited her.

Sam was spending a lot of time with a friend from the year below her at school, called Nicola. Sam was firmly resolved to go to vet school, and to gain admittance she needed agricultural experience, as well as lots of Highers at grade A in one sitting. She and Nicola had volunteered as helpers at Gorgie City Farm, and they spent a lot of time there. Sam also spent a lot of time at Nicola's house. Nicola had visited us once, and been scared to death. I didn't mind at all when Nicola's mum asked if Sam could visit there; I could understand Nicola's feelings only too well.

We received another offer of compensation from the Criminal Injuries Board; however, it was for the same amount. The only person they had contacted was the psychologist in Dumfries, whom Tamsin had seen only a few times. I sat down and wrote a description of Tamsin's ordeal of the last year and a half, and again gave them a list of people to contact, such as Sheila, the counsellor, our GP, and teachers at Tamsin's school. I was notified shortly afterwards that my request for an independent assessment had been granted, and they expected a hearing would take place the following March.

I also heard from the Child Support Agency. According to them, Daniel was earning around £18,000 a year, and had been ordered to pay £73 a week for the girls. That wasn't right — I had done a lot of the negotiation with the new company on Daniel's behalf, and the company had been offering over £30,000 a year. I wrote and asked for a second tier review, telling them I knew from personal experience that he should be earning more and was suspicious that the details he had given were incorrect, but it was turned down. Daniel had provided payslips for May and June of that year.

I couldn't understand it. There were only two explanations I could think of: either he had been on UK rates for those two months — why else confirm he had been working in May? — or else the rest of the money was going into his pension fund. I wrote and asked for an appeal, which was granted, and would be heard probably at the beginning of the following year. In the meantime we would continue to receive income support.

I kind of fell apart a bit in August. I had just had too much to cope with in too short a time. I found myself bursting into tears for no reason, and if the girls said anything wrong, I buried my head under my duvet and howled! I went to see my GP, who referred me to the Community Psychiatric Nurse, and also suggested a counselling service.

I suppose it was to be expected. The girls now seemed well — it was almost as if I had been waiting to give myself permission to feel again, and suddenly all the feelings were there at once. And I had so much to do! I had another house move to organise, and I was still trying to find a way to go to university.

I contacted my local MP, to see if he could persuade the Scottish Office to pay my fees, if nothing else. I also worked out that as a last resort I could borrow enough from the endowment policies to pay my fees, and we would just have to go on living on Income Support until the Child Support Agency caught up with Daniel. I was determined to go to university – I couldn't bear the thought of another year of doing nothing.

At the end of August Sam and Lucy competed in the final of the Scottish Beginner of the Year in obedience training, having won the first show they entered. I didn't see them compete; I had worked Penny, my first collie, in obedience, and she never did well when the family accompanied us. Lucy seemed to do everything right, but Sam felt she had made a few mistakes. But they ended up sixth overall, which was pretty good. I was certainly very proud of them!

I had an indication that month that Tamsin was not as stable as she appeared. She had been continuing to work at McDonald's at weekends, but I discovered that the manager had been harassing her. She had difficulty in operating the tills because of her specific learning difficulties; she had been quite open about it at the interview, and had been assured that there were plenty of other jobs she could do. But Alan, the manager, continually shouted at her when her till didn't balance.

One Friday night, when she was due to begin work the next morning at seven o'clock, Tamsin asked if I would phone and say she was ill. That was when I found out about the harassment. From her point of view, it was too close to the abuse for comfort: another man in a position of power, giving her grief. I thought for a while: it was after ten o'clock at night – would there be anyone in authority available? I decided to phone the largest branch, and was pleased to find that I could speak to a senior manager. She advised me to contact the branch manager, but when I explained that he was the culprit, she understood the difficulty. She suggested that Tamsin should change to a different branch, and mentioned a new branch opening in the town centre. We agreed that Tamsin would report there at eight o'clock the next morning.

I went through to Tamsin's room to tell her the good news, and found her sitting on her bed, staring vacantly into space, and scratching furiously at her arm.

'Don't you dare have a freakie!' I exclaimed in alarm, and she 'came to' quite quickly. I explained what was to happen, which pleased her greatly. She worked happily at the new branch for a couple of weeks until it was time for her college interview; but it was a warning that she was still pretty fragile.

September 1998

I began counselling at a local charity organisation. They
charged only what people could afford, and I paid only £1
per session. I quickly grew to like and respect my counsellor, Hilda. She was older than me, and quite motherly,
and she helped me to see that I hadn't really thought about
what Daniel had done to me. I had understandably been
caught up in helping the girls, especially Tamsin, and I had
been vaguely aware that I was avoiding facing the issue
squarely. One night I cried myself dry, thinking of how we
had started out together with such hope, only to end in
such tragedy. That was a turning point for me. Until then
I had trouble in saying Daniel's name – it was always 'him'
or 'his nibs' or 'Mr Schenker'. Now I could say 'Daniel' much
more easily.

That is not to say that I suddenly recovered – Daniel has
damaged me permanently. I watch pictures on TV of fathers
and their newborn babies, and I think, 'How can all that
tenderness turn to predation in a few short years?', and it

brings tears to my eyes. I see fathers with their children at the supermarket, and want to rush up and tell their mums to watch out for their children.

Counselling allowed me to begin the long task of unravelling my confused feelings. One of the difficulties when a relationship ends like this is that there is no proper ending, no closure. I never got the chance to say goodbye to Daniel. People didn't expect me to grieve for Daniel because of what he had done; but this was the man I had spent half my life with, the father of my children (ouch!), the man I expected to spend the rest of my life with. We had supported each other through good times and bad, and faced the world as a team, whatever our private disagreements. Grief was, and still is, allowed; more than that, it is necessary − without grief there can be no final acceptance, and without that acceptance we are doomed to live in the past.

Another insight was the realisation that the pain of Daniel's betrayal − and it was a betrayal, of all of us − will never go away. Nothing can cure it. Again the answer is acceptance, because without acceptance nothing changes. I have friends who are men, but at the moment I can't see that I would ever want another relationship. I accept that my views are abnormal, but that's how I am, and how I feel comfortable. And feeling comfortable with myself is the first step to recovery.

Tamsin dressed in her best breeches and coat for her interview at the agricultural college, which went very well. She was offered a place on the course which began in two weeks. Fortunately I had borrowed some money against the smaller of the endowment policies to pay for the removal, and I used some of that to pay Tamsin's room deposit and to buy the rest of the equipment that she needed. It is a residential college, and she would come home for two weekends out of three: the students took it in turn to stay for the weekend and look after the horses.

Sam had returned to school for the second year of her Standard Grades. Having completed all the sections for the Duke of Edinburgh Bronze, she now had to get her logbook signed by the dog trainer and judo trainer, and she was all set to receive her award in October.

I was busy packing for our move. I had sorted out our housing benefit, although not until after our local councillor had stepped in, and the community psychiatric nurse helped to arrange a team from the community service people to do the actual move. I had organised a plumber to move the shower and fit a gas supply in the kitchen for the cooker. There was still noise and harassment from our neighbours but with the help of my counsellor, the community psychiatric nurse and the knowledge that we would be leaving soon, I got by, and gradually began to feel better.

Details of my course came through; we were moving on 5 October, and my course began on the 6th. Wonderful timing yet again!

We were all sorry to see Jenny leave at the end of the month, but we promised to keep in touch – and we have.

INTERLUDE

When I began writing this in August 1998, I believed that we were coming to the end of our difficulties. Tamsin seemed happy at college, and although she didn't receive much learning support, she seemed to be coping, if only by spending all weekend catching up on her notes. Mentally she seemed to be back to normal. She was her usual noisy, disruptive self, but also very helpful in the house, being quite happy to cook evening meals. She began going to Scotland rugby matches – she could buy cheap tickets at college – and became a huge fan of the Scotland team. She had one boyfriend after another at college, but mostly she seemed happy. I was so glad; after all she had been through, it was fitting that she should now enjoy life.

Sam was settled at school: back into the routine of hockey matches, judo and study. During the summer Lucy had become increasingly lame and we discovered that she had hip dysplasia, which had caused quite bad arthritis even at her young age. But a course of anti-inflammatories had settled it down. She was not allowed to work in obedience any more, though, and Sam started training Fly, my collie. Fly had about a year's training as a puppy, before my back became too bad, and it seemed to come back to her quite easily. The school nurse spent a lot of time trying to find an alternative expedition for Sam for the Duke of Edinburgh Silver award, and it was she who discovered the exploration option and found a group Sam could join.

I began my course at the university, and loved every minute of it! There were seven of us on the taught MSc, ranging in age from new graduates in their twenties to older people like me; and we were two Americans, a German and four Brits. The first term was quite pressurised, as we had three courses: one in history of philosophy, for which I chose ancient, one in current issues, and one special subject, which for me was philosophy of mind. We were plunged straight in at the deep end, and lots and lots went flying straight over my head; but I was more sure with every day that this was the right thing for me to do.

We still had money problems, of course, but I was less freaked out by them, and learning to take things a day at a time. Our new home helped enormously; it was wonderful to be in a quiet environment.

My divorce arrived at the beginning of October – at last!

So our lives seemed to be settling down. Every so often, I felt this strange feeling coming over me. It was pleasant but unfamiliar, and it took me quite a while to work out what it was – happiness! We had survived! We had come through together!

Never relax when life is going well. You have no idea what is just around the corner.

December 1998

The first sign of trouble came at the beginning of December. Daniel's mother sent Sam a birthday card with a cheque as usual; but rather than sending it to the church, she had sent it to our council flat, with the words 'Please Forward' on the envelope. She had addressed it to Claire Schenker, not Claire Charles, and so the mail redirection did not operate; someone had written our new address on it in ink. I had been very careful not to leave word of where we were going with anyone, and extremely careful not to let Daniel or his family have our council flat address: what was going on here?

I always knew that if the Schenkers were prepared to pay a tracing agent, they could find out where we were. It's not that hard; in fact, it's really quite difficult to hide. You are not allowed to remove your name from the electoral register, for instance. The Schenkers had been told repeatedly that they could write to our original address in Edinburgh and that mail would also be forwarded to us through the church. I wasn't trying to deny them any knowledge of how their grandchildren were, but I knew that Tamsin must never have contact with Daniel; the potential consequences for her would be horrific.

Fortunately, Sam's birthday was on a Thursday, and Tamsin was safely out of the way at college. We burnt the envelope, and with reluctance I wrote to Daniel's mother. I told her exactly how ill Tamsin had been, and that she was just beginning to see a future for herself. I told her that the only reason we had kept our address secret was for Tamsin's sake; I had done nothing wrong and had nothing to be ashamed or afraid of. I pointed out that it had not been my choice to cut her off from her grandchildren; Daniel had made all these choices for us when he began sticking bits of his body into his daughter. I begged her, for Tamsin's sake, to write via the church, even if she had our present address.

I contacted Kim, my solicitor, and asked if she would write to Daniel via his solicitor.

Then I began writing to everyone who had our address. I wrote to the new tenant of our council flat, told her of our circumstances and begged her to destroy any trace of our new address. I wrote to gas, electricity and phone companies, insurance companies, everyone. As part of this exercise, I also called the agricultural college where Tamsin was studying and spoke to the registrar, Lesley. She listened in silence, thought for a moment, and then asked, 'What's his name?'

'Daniel Schenker,' I replied.

'That's who it was!' she exclaimed, and described how they had received a series of phone calls, three in one day, from a Mr Schenker, looking for his daughter. He was persistent and abusive; he had been told his daughter was definitely a student there, and he wanted to be put in touch with her.

This was awful! It sent shivers down my spine to think how close he had come. Lesley hadn't recognised the name because Tamsin had always been Tamsin Charles to them, and of course Lesley wouldn't have released information anyway. But she promised to let the wardens know quietly, so that if anything happened, they would be aware of the situation.

I could not for the life of me understand how Daniel had come so close; but he had, and I had no choice now but to write to him. I tried to impress on him the harm that he had already caused, and the harm he would cause if he did manage to find Tamsin. I begged him to leave her alone. He had signally failed to protect her in the past, but now he had another chance. Maybe, I wrote, if he left us alone for a year or two, Sam would forgive him, and maybe even Tamsin would come round. That was probably holding out false hope, but I had to use every lever I could to make him see that he must leave Tamsin alone.

I also called the police and spoke to an officer at the Sex Offences Unit. She suggested contacting police headquarters and speaking to the person in charge of the Sex Offenders Register, which I did immediately. He was very helpful. Daniel had signed the register and was complying with the conditions, but he was due for a visit soon. The sergeant said he would contact the local police force and ask them to warn him about his behaviour; but that was the most they could do. He asked if I knew where Daniel was living.

'I have no idea,' I replied.

'Well, I can tell you that he's down south,' the sergeant said. 'I'm not supposed to tell you even that much, but at least he's not living in Edinburgh.' And with that I had to be content.

That was a really difficult weekend for me. Tamsin came home on Friday evening for the annual carol concert. It was a belter that year! We had a huge audience, more than 700 people, and it went really well. I was so proud of my girls when I saw them selling programmes. They both had new outfits. Tamsin had allowed her hair to grow out, so that although still very short, it looked fluffy and appealing. She was very slim and fit after her exertions in the stable yard, and she wore light grey pinstriped trousers and a fluffy grey sweater. She looked so poised and assured – many of my friends did not recognise her at first.

Sam, too, looked lovely. She was by now five feet ten inches tall, and wore high-heeled mules, which made her look even taller. She wore a claret-coloured velour top and black moleskin trousers. She had been growing her hair from the chin-length bob she had had for the last few years, and it was just long enough to tie up.

We spent Saturday and Sunday relaxing, but this was the first time in Tamsin's life that I had not been a hundred per cent honest with her. The problem with Daniel and his family was at the front of my mind, but I was determined not to let Tamsin know, as I was quite sure it would be very harmful to her. She returned to college on Sunday evening none the wiser, and I breathed a sigh of relief.

That week I received the final payment from my divorce settlement. My divorce had cost me £6,100 in legal fees. Here was another injustice based on no-fault divorce. This divorce was undoubtedly Daniel's fault; but I had to lose almost half my settlement to pay for it.

I had to get some work done the next week. We were supposed to have three 3-hour exams at the end of term, but we had discussed it with our director of studies. We students felt that memorising facts for an exam was a poor use of our time; we all had firsts or upper seconds and had proved our ability to memorise facts. He agreed; he had been considering a 'take-home' exam, and so it was decided. At noon on the following Friday we would pick up our exam papers; by noon on the Friday after that, we had to complete nine essays of 1500 words each. It was going to be a hellish week; we were all tired, but once it was done, we had four weeks off over Christmas.

At the beginning of the week I saw my director of studies and the head of department, and explained the circumstances of my marriage break-up, and that I had reason to believe that Daniel might come looking for me. I also told my fellow postgrads, the PhD students as well as the MSc students. We are a small but generally happy bunch; we get on well together, and everyone helps everyone else.

I did a lot of reading that week, and felt fairly well prepared. I had written a lot of essays for my degree, and with all my notes and books to hand, I was confident of at least passing, if not passing well.

The real trouble began two years to the day after Tamsin disclosed the abuse. On Friday morning I was sorting out my work space at home, ready to begin writing, when the phone rang.

'This is Ronnie, the warden at the college,' a male voice said. 'We're a bit concerned about Tamsin. She's shaking violently and lashing out at people, and doesn't seem to be able to hear us.'

Omigod, I thought, she's having a freakie!

'We've called the GP and we're waiting for her to come out, but we thought we should let you know,' Ronnie continued.

'Yes, of course, thank you,' I said, my head whirling. Had Daniel turned up at college? Had his mother written to Tamsin at college? 'I need to make a couple of phone calls and I'll be straight out,' I told Ronnie.

Never mind the reason for now, I thought, she's obviously having a freakie and I'm the best − probably the only − person who can get her out of it. I called my director of studies, Graham, and explained. 'I'm probably going to have to do a bit of nursing this week,' I told him.

'Well, just forget about the time limit for the exam,' said Graham immediately. 'No one's going to mark the papers before the start of next term anyway. Good luck!'

I drove out to the college as fast as traffic permitted, and met Ronnie and the principal in Ronnie's office. The principal was very disapproving, and gave me a lecture on how dangerous it would have been if this had happened while Tamsin was on a horse. I was to take Tamsin home until the beginning of next term, and she would need a doctor's certificate before she would be allowed to return.

I still didn't know myself exactly what had happened, or was happening. I tried to explain what I believed was happening, but it made no difference to the principal's attitude. And I could see his point; he wasn't to know that freakies needed a trigger, and he had the safety of all the students to consider.

Ronnie told me that Tamsin was in her boyfriend's room,

and we made our way up to the flats. The doctor still hadn't come, but I knew what to do.

'I've brought some diazepam with me,' I told Ronnie, and he laughed ruefully.

'Well, I hope you have better luck than we did last night,' he said. 'We couldn't get her to take anything!'

We went into the building and were met by Andrew, Tamsin's boyfriend, who took us to his room. Tamsin was asleep in his bed. I sat down beside her and tried to rouse her. She began moaning and shrugging me off.

'Will we just leave you to it?' asked Ronnie, and I nodded.

'Wake up, Tamsin,' I said gently, over and over. 'It's Mummy, you're safe, it's all right, sweetheart.'

After a few minutes she came to and lifted her head sleepily.

'Hello, sweetheart.' I smiled at her. 'How are you feeling? What's been happening?'

Tamsin seemed confused and sleepy, and not at all surprised to find me in Andrew's bedroom. I gave her some diazepam, and sat with her for another ten minutes or so, until I was sure she was awake and not about to lapse back into the freakie. Then I went along to the kitchen where Ronnie and Andrew were waiting.

'She's okay,' I said. 'She's awake and all right. Does she have any clothes here?' I asked, for she was wearing only a slip.

'No,' replied Andrew.

'I'll go down to her room and fetch some,' I said. 'Could you make her a cup of tea? She's very thirsty.'

Andrew put the kettle on and I collected Tamsin's keys and fetched her some clothes. While she dressed, I spoke privately to Andrew.

'I'm not going to play the heavy parent,' I reassured him; he looked worried and tired, and quite apprehensive. 'What happened last night? Has her father phoned or written to her?'

'Not that I know of,' replied Andrew. 'She just seemed to collapse in the bar. She hadn't drunk all that much, but she couldn't walk or talk. She never said anything about her father.'

'Do you know about her father?' I asked him.

'I just know she's really frightened of him.'

'She's got very good reason to be frightened of him!' I said grimly, and he nodded as though he understood. I didn't know what Tamsin had told him and I didn't feel I had the right to tell him exactly what Daniel had done, so I didn't say any more.

By now Tamsin was dressed and ready to leave, and we started the drive home. She told me in the car what had frightened her. At the beginning of the term she had gone out for a couple of weeks with a boy called Duncan, and then dropped him because he could be as nice as ninepence one minute and really horrible the next. When she ended the relationship, he had thrust his face into hers and said, 'I'll kill you!' quite seriously.

A week or two later, Duncan had been seen walking around the campus with a sack of ammonium nitrate, looking for some diesel so that he could make a bomb and blow up a car. Tamsin and a couple of friends had told Ronnie, and as far as they knew, Duncan had been expelled. Then suddenly he had reappeared the previous Sunday, and had been hanging around Tamsin all week.

It took me a few weeks to piece together what actually happened that night. Tamsin had collapsed in the bar; she could hear and see and was aware of her surroundings, but she couldn't move or talk. Andrew had carried her up to his room, and the paramedics had been called. They thought it was either a bad trip or an acute psychotic episode, but Andrew would not let them take her away. He had stayed with her all night and made sure she came to no harm.

I had a lot of respect and liking for Andrew. He had been going out with Tamsin for only two weeks before this, but he obviously cared deeply about her. He was older than Tamsin, twenty-eight, which is probably why he coped so well.

I was very glad that Tamsin's freakie had not been caused by her father or his family; hopefully I could keep their attempts to find us secret. Tamsin had another sleep that afternoon and woke looking refreshed and well. But later that evening, she began to act strangely. She was lying on the settee watching TV when she began to murmur to herself. She moved her arms as though she was doing something, but there was nothing there. After a few minutes I became convinced that she was hallucinating. I tried to talk to her but she ignored me. Suddenly she got up and walked out of the room, and locked herself in the bathroom.

Sam and I looked helplessly at each other. Tamsin came back in and lay down on the settee with her back towards me.

'Are you coming to bed now?' I asked her.

'No!' she replied in a childish voice.

'Why not?'

'Because I don't like you! You made me drop the purple daisy, and the inside people won't give me any more.'

This was too much for me to deal with alone. I called the emergency doctors and asked to speak to the duty GP. By the time he called me back, Tamsin had gone from peaceful contemplation, through heavy over-breathing, to screaming loudly and slapping at herself, and I was really worried. I held the phone out so that the doctor could hear her screaming. He was very sympathetic.

'She certainly needs to be seen,' he said, 'but we're just about to change shifts. I'll pass this on as an urgent call, and someone will be with you as soon as possible.'

Tamsin continued to alternate between peaceful murmuring, over-breathing and screaming. Finally the doctor arrived at half past midnight, just as Tamsin again locked herself in the bathroom. It was a female doctor, and she was obviously not sympathetic to psychiatric problems.

'I haven't got time to wait until she comes out of the bathroom,' she snapped, just as Tamsin unlocked the door and returned to the settee. 'Tamsin! Tamsin! What's the matter?' she snapped again. But Tamsin ignored her.

'You could take her up to the psychiatric hospital yourself,' she suggested. 'The only other option is to call an ambulance and have her sectioned, and I haven't got time for that.'

I felt so helpless. Tamsin obviously needed professional help, but she wouldn't listen to me or talk to me, and the doctor was worse than useless. Then Sam stepped in. She began talking soothingly to Tamsin.

'Come on,' she said, 'we'll go and see the head of the inside people and he'll give you another purple daisy.'

Tamsin seemed to listen to Sam, although she was violently opposed to having anything to do with me. Sam talked to her soothingly and managed to get her into the car, although without a seat belt. I climbed into the driver's seat as quietly as I could, and began a nightmare drive. The hospital is at the other end of town, and I was very conscious of the lack of a seat belt. Sam sat in the back and kept talking soothingly to Tamsin, who continued her cycle of behaviour.

When we arrived at the hospital, Sam tried to take Tamsin in; but there is an automatic door at the entrance, which is quite noisy when it opens and closes, and Tamsin wouldn't go anywhere near it. Sam tried to keep Tamsin at least near the door while I got the wheelchair out of the car and went in.

The GP had phoned ahead, but the duty registrar was not there yet. I sat in the entrance hall, crying quietly, while watching Sam's attempts to stop Tamsin taking off. After a bit, a couple of police officers came into the hall from the hospital, and I begged them to help. One of them was a woman, and she went outside and gently talked Tamsin into the hall. Tamsin sat on a chair at the opposite end of the hall from me, and I tried to sit silently and not look at her.

At last the duty registrar arrived, a Dr Bowie; a tall, thin New Zealander with a shock of curly hair. He squatted down and looked into Tamsin's face.

'What's happening, Tamsin?' he asked gently, and she burst into tears.

'I don't know!' she sobbed in her normal voice. Dr Bowie and the duty staff nurse took Tamsin away to talk to her, and then I really did cry. Sam sat holding me. 'It's all right, Mum, she'll be all right,' she soothed. What a kid!

Eventually Dr Bowie came back and asked us to join him. I explained Tamsin's background as he took copious notes. Tamsin was asleep in a chair, her arm shaking violently, murmuring under her breath.

'We think she may have delirium tremens,' said Dr Bowie, and I was shocked. But Dr Bowie pointed out the violent tremor and the undoubted hallucinations, and I had to bow to his knowledge.

'We've got a bed for her in Ward One,' he continued, 'so we'll take her up there. Tamsin! Wake up!' Immediately Tamsin woke up obediently, stood up and followed Dr Bowie.

'Wow! Can I have a tape recording of your voice?' I asked him, amazed. 'She never gets up like that at home!'

We followed Tamsin and Dr Bowie through the sleeping hospital to the ward, where we were taken to a pleasant sitting room. Tamsin had 'come back' now; she knew who I was and wasn't angry with me any more. While the admission procedures went on, she drank copious amounts of squash; she seemed to be very thirsty. The night nurses were friendly and reassuring. They apologised that there were no single rooms available, so that Tamsin would have to sleep in a dormitory; but she was quite happy with that, and I explained that she had been at boarding school.

Sam and I said goodnight to Tamsin in the corridor, as the wheelchair was much too noisy to go into the dormitory, and we drove home, exhausted. My mind was in turmoil. DTs! Surely Tamsin hadn't had access to alcohol in large enough quantities for long enough to have a physiological dependency. At home I looked it up in my Family Medical Book, and sure enough the symptoms fitted. I went to bed feeling confused and uncertain, and desperately worried.

The next day we returned to the hospital in the late morning. Tamsin was up and dressed, and sitting in the 'smoking' day room. She began smoking at school when she was about fourteen, I think, although I didn't know about it then. She had managed to stop, but had started again when Daniel was released from prison, and had begun smoking openly last summer. I wasn't pleased; but with a habit like mine, I wasn't really in a position to lecture her either. At least it wasn't drugs.

Tamsin seemed subdued and tired, and still had a violent tremor in her leg. Soon after we arrived, the duty doctor saw her and discharged her. We brought her home again. Waiting at the traffic lights, the car began to shake, and I wondered what was wrong with it, before realising that it was Tamsin who was shaking, not the car.

At home I gave her the medical book to read, and tried to talk gently to her about drinking and the dangers of alcohol. She continued to protest that she hadn't had much to drink that week, and I left it for the moment.

We spent a happy afternoon together, making mince pies for Christmas, and then Tamsin helped me to cook dinner. She didn't remember much about the previous night, and was as close and affectionate as ever. After dinner, we were about to wash up together, when she walked out of the kitchen. I found her on her bed.

'The inside people have come back, and they won't go away!' she cried. I wasn't sure how much diazepam I should give her, and I knew I had to phone the emergency doctor; but before I left her, I gave her my teddy, Buddy, to hold on to. 'Just keep tight hold of Buddy, and he'll keep you safe,' I said, and ran for the phone.

By the time I had spoken to the doctor, it was too late. I couldn't get Tamsin to take any medication, although she was still clinging tightly to Buddy. This time it was Sam who was the 'bad guy', and as long as I phrased my requests through Buddy, Tamsin obeyed. We managed to get her into the car again, and although she started in terror when I fastened her seat belt, I reassured her through Buddy.

When we arrived at the Emergency Doctors Unit, I sent Sam inside to ask the doctor to come out. Tamsin was slipping further and further away from me, and I wasn't sure how long I could control her. After a few moments the doctor came out, tried to speak to her and shook his head. 'You'll have to go back to the hospital,' he said. 'I'll call and let them know you're coming.'

While we were waiting to see the duty GP, and during the subsequent drive to the psychiatric hospital, Tamsin kept up a one-sided conversation in quite a normal voice. She tipped her head to one side to listen, and then answered. At one point she said, 'But I haven't got much fingernails.' She listened again, shrugged her shoulders and then said, 'All right, I'll try.' And she began to scratch her arms fiercely. I couldn't stop her and drive the car at the same time, and so I just kept driving.

I wasn't sure where to take Tamsin: we parked outside the ward and Sam went inside to enquire. I let her out of the car and got back in, locking the doors. Tamsin had now gone completely, and the usual insensate stranger was sitting beside me. Sam came out and I opened the window.

'We have to go back to where we were last night,' Sam said, and I unlocked the door to let her back in. Quick as a flash, Tamsin opened her door, twisted out of her seat belt and ran off into the night.

'Go after her!' I yelled to Sam. 'I'll go inside and get help!'

With my stick I staggered in through the door of the ward and called, 'Can somebody help, please? She's run away!'

One of the male nurses came up. 'We can't actually stop her,' he explained, 'it would be assault.'

'She's got no idea of where she is or what she's doing,' I cried frantically; I was very aware that there was a busy main road near the hospital – why didn't they understand? 'My other daughter's gone after her, but she's only a kid!'

The nurse said he would call the emergency team, and I went back outside. I was terrified. I stood by the car, smoking and sobbing and shaking and looking into the darkness. After a few minutes the nurse came out.

'There's no sign of them!' I said. 'You have to do something!'

'Why don't you come into the ward and wait?' he suggested. 'The emergency team are looking for them and there's nothing you can do here.'

I got the wheelchair out, locked the car and wheeled inside. The nurses tried to reassure me and brought me a mug of tea; but I just sat, shaking and terrified. Then a nurse came round from the office.

'They've got her,' he said. 'They're coming up to the ward now.'

What a relief! At least both girls were safe now.

Soon the ward door swung open and Tamsin marched

in, still clutching Buddy and closely followed by Dr Bowie and Sam. Sam peeled off to join me as Tamsin and Dr Bowie went through to the office. The nurses spoke reassuringly while we waited; but Tamsin began to scream again. I asked if I could wait in the smoking room: if ever I needed a cigarette, it was now.

'Of course you can,' the nurse replied, and so Sam and I waited there.

After a while Dr Bowie came to see us. 'Phew!' he said as he sat down. 'It's hard to say what's going on here. She's quiet now. We've given her some medication and that's settled her down. I don't think it's psychotic, because she comes out of it too quickly. I don't think any more it's DTs, either.' He questioned me about her drinking habits, and I explained that she had had access to alcohol only since September, and as her bursary was just £14 a week, she didn't have enough money to buy much alcohol. He also asked about drugs, but Sam told him that Tamsin was violently opposed to drug use.

'I think it's more likely to be a hysterical dissociation,' he said at last. 'She's being admitted, of course, and we'll see what happens. She seems to be hallucinating about spiders, which is what causes the screaming fits.'

I was so glad to hear that it wasn't psychotic, as that was what I had feared — it must just be a recurrence of her freakies, if a bit more extreme.

Tamsin joined us shortly after that. She had 'come back' again, and once again was drinking jugfuls of squash. This time she was given a single room, and we saw her comfortably settled before leaving her for the night.

While we drove home Sam told me a bit about what

had happened. She had run after Tamsin, who legged it through the hospital grounds. Gradually Sam had managed to get in front of Tamsin and had then shepherded her back towards the entrance hall. Tamsin kept running until she came to the building, and then crouched down in a dark corner. She wouldn't let Sam anywhere near her, and so Sam had just kept Tamsin safely corralled until Dr Bowie with his magic voice arrived. He spoke to her for a few moments and then managed to coax her through the noisy automatic door, which still terrified her. Sam had followed them into the building, staying well out of reach.

Sam began to have really severe headaches, which were obviously stress-based. She had had responsibility for getting Tamsin into the hospital both times we had taken her there, and she had seen her sister in enormous distress. No one of fifteen should have to see anyone like that; but to see your sister, and to be responsible for her – no wonder she had headaches. She stayed off school for three days the following week, and returned on Thursday.

Tamsin stayed in the hospital for a week. She was in an adult ward, as there were no adolescent beds at that time, and she was on 'shared care', which meant that the adult consultant would have responsibility for her jointly with the consultant from the Adolescent Unit. She was confused for much of the time. Sometimes she had freakies, sometimes she hallucinated. It turned out that she had had two permanent 'voices' since last September. Peter was a mate, they talked things over and had a laugh. Paul, she told me, 'is a bit like you: he disapproves of everything I do but he keeps me safe.'

'I don't disapprove of everything you do!' I protested.

'You disapprove of me smoking, you disapprove of me drinking, you don't like my boyfriends,' she pointed out.

'I don't disapprove of Andrew,' I told her, 'he's good for you. I'm not really in a position to disapprove of your smoking, I just don't like to see you doing things that hurt you.'

I spent most of my time with Tamsin at the hospital. I knew I had to write my essays, but I had until early January to do them, and Tamsin was more important. On Tuesday of that week, I spent all day with her, and then went home at teatime. 'Will you be all right if I don't come this evening?' I asked her. 'I'm really tired.'

Tamsin agreed quite happily. I called her on the ward pay-phone that evening and she sounded quite relaxed. But when I arrived the next day, she had a large bandage around her left wrist.

'What happened here?' I asked her.

'Oh, I just scratched it a bit,' she replied unconcernedly. Then, fiercely, she said, 'It wasn't my fault!'

'No, of course not,' I agreed, and she relaxed again.

'It's really deep,' she said, quite proudly, 'it's right down to the bone!' And then, again with that air of unconcern, she began talking about something else.

I had a word with the nurse when Tamsin was watching TV. They had found her the previous evening scraping away at the skin of her wrist with a knife. They took the knife away and explained to her that they were quite happy to spend time with her and talk to her, and she didn't need to hurt herself to get attention.

A short time later, they had found her with a deep wound

in her wrist; apparently she had continued to scratch with her fingernails. But it was important for Tamsin's sake to focus on her mental health, rather than on any injury she had, and so I followed the nurses' lead and ignored the wrist.

That night, while Tamsin was in the toilet, I was tucking her sheet in when I found a pair of sharp scissors secreted under the mattress. I pocketed them quickly before she returned, and after that always checked while tidying her bed.

A couple of days later I was in the ward when Tamsin's wrist was dressed, and she asked me to come and watch. There was a deep hole, about an inch across, and although the nurse denied that it was 'right down to the bone', she did admit it had reached the joint capsule.

Tamsin explained that the bad voices, The Doctors as she calls them, had told her that she was being poisoned by the hospital food, and had to let the poison out of her bones, so that was why she had done it. Some months later she told me she had actually used the scissors I found under the mattress. The Doctors had told her to say she used her fingernails, so that the staff wouldn't find the scissors.

On Friday I had a chat with the adult consultant, Dr Brown. He said they weren't sure what was going on. He questioned me about the abuse: was it real?

'It was real, all right,' I replied grimly. 'Her father got twelve months for it.'

'But still, this might have nothing to do with that,' he said. 'We're fairly sure now that it's not alcohol withdrawal. I'm going to start her on some tranquillisers, and she can come home on pass for the weekend.'

I discovered that 'on pass' meant that Tamsin could come home with us, but she was still technically an inpatient and could return directly to the ward at any time, if she needed to. Sam was going to judo camp that weekend – she had just had another grading and gone up another three mons! – and so it would be just Tamsin and me. She had seemed a little better in the last couple of days and I was confident of coping.

I took Sam to her judo camp that afternoon, at a leisure centre in one of Edinburgh's satellite towns. She went off quite happily, and I picked up a McDonald's to take into the ward for Tamsin's tea. We spent a happy evening, chatting together. Her mind was much clearer and she was able to explain what she had been seeing and hearing.

'I have to do what The Doctors tell me,' she said, 'otherwise they punish me by covering me with spiders.' Tamsin has been phobic about spiders for years, and this was about the worst thing they could do to her; so they had a lot of power once they were in control.

It was very difficult not to talk about The Doctors as if they were real people. To Tamsin they were very real, and she was very frightened of them. She had and has no desire to hurt herself, but if The Doctors told her to do it, she had no choice. You can understand where the belief in demonic possession comes from when you see Tamsin under the control of The Doctors.

The following day I arrived to collect Tamsin from the ward at lunchtime. Her medication had not arrived from the pharmacy; in fact, it had not been ordered until that morning and, because the hospital pharmacy was closed on Saturdays, we had to wait for it to be brought from another hospital. We didn't get away until after four o'clock.

We had a lovely, quiet time together. Tamsin and I shared a bedroom; because she was at college when we moved, we thought she would be home only for weekends and holidays, and Sam needed her own space to work for her exams. I was sick of sleeping in the sitting room, and wanted a bedroom, and so we had agreed that Tamsin and I would share.

We didn't do much; Tamsin slept a lot, and we watched TV and videos. On Sunday afternoon we went to collect Sam. She had had a marvellous time, letting off steam mostly, but learning as well. She had also become close friends with a girl from another school, and they saw each other quite often.

On the way home, we bought our Christmas tree. We had wanted a container-grown tree, so that we could plant it in the garden; but there were none left, and we had to make do with a cut tree. Sam and I installed it in the bay window of the sitting room and Sam and Tamsin decorated it.

The next day Tamsin returned to the ward. We were able to report that she had had no problems, and it was anticipated that she would come home on pass on Wednesday, in good time for Christmas Day on Friday.

Relating all these events, it might seem that I was cool, calm and collected. I wasn't! I was calm with Tamsin, but I cried every night on the way home from the hospital, and I kept bursting into tears at other times, especially if I had to deal with any sort of business. I couldn't bear to think of not having Tamsin home for Christmas, and I refused to buy any extra food until I knew she was coming home.

Mrs Schenker replied to my letter the week before Christmas. First of all she took me to task for 'taking that tone with her'; then she said that she had sent the card, not Daniel; that she hadn't been told to write via the church; that she'd got our address from the divorce papers; and that Daniel had left Christmas presents with her for the girls, but if that was the way I felt, she wouldn't bother passing them on.

Well, I thought, I'll take any tone I like, so long as you get the message to leave us alone! If she wasn't told about writing via the church, she should take it up with her son. I checked with my solicitor, and it is just not possible for her to have obtained our address from the divorce papers; and in any case, the only way she could know that we had left that address was by making enquiries. I felt profoundly grateful that she was not going to pass on gifts from Daniel; that really would have freaked Tamsin out!

In part, I feel very, very sorry for Daniel's parents. They are elderly and not in good health: his mother has diabetes, and his father is crippled from a stroke in 1990. It must have been horrible to have to deal with a son who turned out to be a child molester.

But in part, I feel very, very angry with Daniel's parents. They have shown precious little compassion for their grand-children. It has been very difficult to live in poverty, knowing that it could all have been very different if Daniel and his family had taken responsibility for his actions.

Christmas passed peacefully enough. It wasn't really like Christmas for me, because we didn't go to church at all. Tamsin was fearful of being with a lot of people, and I was not prepared to go out without her for more than a very short time. But I enjoyed just being at home with my girls, in safety and security. We watched lots of TV and videos, and I spent some time working on a cross-stitch sampler for the birth of my twin nephews. I also began working on my essays, just for an hour or two each day.

Tamsin returned to the hospital the Monday after Christmas. We discussed her education with the consultant. Dr Brown saw no reason why she should not continue with her course; but I had been in touch with the college. The principal was insisting that if she was going to withdraw, it had to be by 4 January. If she did that, she could recommence the following January with no loss of bursary; otherwise she would not get another bursary. Tamsin and I had talked it over. She was behind with her practical assessments, because she had torn her shoulder ligaments and missed four weeks of practical work; and she was getting no help with her learning difficulties. She was not keen to return to the college, and I felt that, because she had appeared to collapse from nervous stress, the last thing she needed was a return to a pressurised environment. The only part of college Tamsin missed was contact with Andrew; but he had kept in close touch, phoned almost every day and had visited her in hospital.

January 1999

Tamsin was released on pass on Wednesday before New Year, and we passed another peaceful long weekend. We returned to the ward the following Monday. Dr Calder, the consultant from the Adolescent Unit, was absent because of flu, otherwise Tamsin might have been discharged then; but they wanted to be sure that follow-up arrangements were in place. A brain scan had been booked for the following Tuesday morning at nine o'clock at another hospital, and Tamsin was asked to go back into the ward on Monday night, to ensure she arrived for the scan on time.

Tamsin was reluctant to return to the ward the following week. She had been quite content there to begin with; I think she was vaguely aware of how ill she was, although she doesn't remember much about those weeks. But now that she was feeling better, she really didn't want to be there. However, it was only for one night.

She phoned me from the ward at eleven o'clock the next morning. She had had her scan, and was all set to come home. I went up to collect her, and we made arrangements to return the following day to see Dr Brown, as Dr Calder was still absent. She was discharged the next day, and her medication reduced, as she had had no recurrence of the problems. We were told that the Adolescent Unit would contact us about follow-up, and went cheerfully home.

Daniel began paying child support in January. He had been assessed on his (bogus?) salary of £18,000 to pay £73 per week, which worked out at just over £300 per month. However, he was to begin at £250, gradually increasing to £317 by July. £250 a month – that was only about £59 per week. I phoned the Child Support Agency for an explanation. Apparently, according to their records, Daniel had 'overpaid the Secretary of State' at some point in the past, and so he was to begin with a reduced payment. Regardless of how much I pointed out that we had received no benefit from his overpayment, they were adamant. Yet again, Daniel was being given the benefit of the doubt at our expense. Not only was he being assessed on what I felt were false income figures, he was being allowed to pay a tiny amount.

A tiny amount – but added to my disability benefits, it took us over the limit for income support by a couple of pounds a week. Now I had to pay prescription charges, and more rent – overall we were considerably worse off.

Sam returned to school, to two weeks of exams. She was still having headaches, and by the end of the first week, she also had a chest infection. Somehow she managed to struggle through the exams, and came out with some remarkably good results, given the circumstances. But once the exams were over, she had yet another chest infection, and needed two weeks off school and two courses of antibiotics.

Tamsin soon got fed up sitting around at home. She contacted the local riding school and volunteered her services, which were cheerfully accepted; and so I began to drop Tamsin on the way to school with Sam, before going on to university myself. I had no lectures this term. I had a current issues tutorial once a fortnight, and a tutorial on Aristotle once a fortnight, for which I was given two presentations to write – gulp! In addition I was expected to attend three seminars a week. Most of the work I could do at home, so that I could be on hand if Tamsin needed me; but she seemed to be doing fine.

However, it didn't last long: within a couple of weeks she was beginning to hear voices again. I spoke to Dr Calder, who had not known that Tamsin's medication had been reduced. She authorised an immediate rise in the levels, and said Tamsin might need to go back into the ward for a few days. The following day, Tamsin herself said that she wanted to return to the ward; and so we did. She was becoming increasingly confused and having freakies again, and we both felt she would be safer in the ward for a few days. She was admitted on a Friday late in January. That night she cut the back of her hand with a table knife.

There was a very ill male patient in the ward, called Malcolm. He was a classic paranoid schizophrenic: he believed that devils were trying to steal his soul, and he spent much of his time in the smoking room, building shrines out of books, ashtrays, anything that came to hand. He would kneel in front of them, arms extended, totally unmoving, for long periods of time. At other times, he would pace around, muttering to himself and tossing lighted cigarettes around. Sometimes he spoke to other people, and he showed classic signs, like disordered and repetitive speech. From the point of view of a psychologist, it was fascinating to see; but even I found him creepy and frightening, and Tamsin was very scared of him.

On Sunday morning, I took Sam to get her sight tested, as she was still being bothered by headaches. She did need new glasses, and we waited for them before going to the hospital. We were met at the door of the ward by a nurse, who asked us to go the office with him. Omigod, I thought, omigod, what's happened? Please let Tamsin be all right.

'Tamsin's not here right now,' the nurse began. Frantic thoughts dashed through my head: she's hurt herself and been taken to the general hospital! 'She was a bit agitated this morning, so the recreation nurse took her for a walk. But as soon as they left the hospital grounds, she legged it, and the nurse couldn't keep up with her.'

'What's happening? Who's looking for her? Have you called the police?' I asked, trying to stay in one piece.

'We can't call the police. She's a voluntary patient, so they won't do anything. We're just waiting to see if she comes back. I think you should go home and wait, maybe she'll turn up there.'

I couldn't believe it! Tamsin was out there, on the streets of Edinburgh, maybe in a freakie and unaware – it was my worst nightmare come true! I didn't have the mobile phone with me, the battery needed charging, and so we agreed that I would go home. If there was no sign of Tamsin, I would charge the phone and then go and look for her myself. I would call the ward as soon as I got home.

Sam was just incredible – so calm. I was falling apart inside, shaking, trying to drive, trying to think: Tamsin doesn't know Edinburgh well, she doesn't have any friends here that she might visit.

'Let's go round by the church,' Sam suggested, 'that's where she was going when she ran away two years ago.' So we drove round, but the building was closed up. Then I remembered: it wasn't being opened that day because there was a joint service at another church. We drove past St Andrew's School on the way home, as that was about the only other place Tamsin knew well, but there was no sign of her. We drove home: no Tamsin.

'You have to eat, Mum,' said Sam, and so I forced a sandwich and some tea down my throat, followed by my usual painkillers; they were essential if I was to keep going. I began phoning people I knew who lived near the hospital, asking them to watch out for Tamsin. I kept myself together that afternoon only because of Sam; she was so calm and practical, and every time the situation threatened to overwhelm me, she talked to me and hugged me and kept me going.

I phoned the ward every half-hour, but there was still no news. After we had been home for an hour, with no sign of Tamsin anywhere, I told the nurse I was going to report Tamsin missing to the police. 'I know they won't look for her actively yet, but at least if someone sees her acting strangely and reports it, they will know what the situation is,' I explained as calmly as I could.

'All right,' said the nurse, 'I'll call them and let them know. It's better if it comes from the hospital.' I was so glad that at last someone was doing something that I didn't argue.

We sat on, Sam and I, waiting for the mobile to charge. It takes only two hours, but the minutes crawled so slowly.

Finally the charging light went off. I stretched out my hand to call the ward, to let them know to call the mobile, but before I could touch it, it rang. I snatched it up. It was one of the nurses – Tamsin had been picked up by the police in the city centre and was on her way back to the hospital. Oh, thank you, God!

We set off for the hospital straight away, arriving just a few minutes after Tamsin. She was in the kitchen, making a cup of tea, which she took through to her bed. She wouldn't look at me, she wouldn't talk to me, she certainly wouldn't hug me. We followed her through to her bed, and she climbed in fully clothed and pulled the quilt over her. She was very cold, having been on the wintry streets for three hours. I kept talking to her and gradually realised that she thought she was going to get into trouble for running away. I tried to reassure her.

'It wasn't my fault!' she cried. 'I don't know what happened. One minute I was in the ward, trying to tell the nurses that The Doctors were back, and the next minute I was at The Mound!'

Gradually I pieced together what had happened. The nurses thought that Tamsin was agitated and were trying to teach her distraction techniques, so that she wouldn't have to rely on drugs all the time. But Tamsin had 'gone' before she left the ward, and had suddenly 'come back' to find herself in the city centre, with no idea of how she'd got there. She couldn't remember our phone number, and she was frantically searching through her purse to see if she could find it, when a group of homeless lads approached her. She must have been in obvious distress; they asked her what was wrong.

'I'm not supposed to be here,' she cried. 'I'm supposed to be in the hospital, and I don't know how I got here or how to get back!'

One of the gang had called the police on his mobile (!) and they had immediately collected her. I was so grateful to that gang, although there was no way of showing it. The whole thing could have had a much worse ending.

Tamsin was obviously still very distressed, and eventually the nurses consulted the duty doctor and gave her something to calm her. Gradually she drifted off to sleep. I took Sam home because she was exhausted, and returned a couple of hours later.

Tamsin was very difficult to deal with that evening. She didn't want to be in hospital; she was bored; there was nothing to do. She was hostile towards me; maybe she felt I was chaining her to the hospital bed. I tried to calm her all evening. At bedtime, I tucked her in and held her as she cried.

'Please, please let me come home!' she begged over and over.

'Maybe tomorrow,' I said. 'Let's wait and see what Dr Calder says.'

'You don't want me! That's it!' she cried at last. 'You just want to have Sam at home, you don't really want me, I'm just trouble! Well, you just go! Go and stay with Sam and leave me here!'

I couldn't help myself, I began to cry as well as I tried over and over to reassure her. 'Of course I want you at home! But you have to get well, and it won't happen overnight. What if you ran away at home? I can't run after you, and it's not fair to expect Sam to.'

'But I won't!' she sobbed. 'I only ever hurt myself in the hospital and I only run away from here! I never do these things at home! It's this place!'

What could I say? I felt so helpless. All I could do was hug her and rock her and hope that she would soon fall asleep. That night I howled all the way home in the car. I was so angry with God.

'How can you call yourself a God of Love and let a child suffer like that?' I raged. It just felt so unfair. Daniel was out of prison, back to his old life at sea, earning pots of money and handing over peanuts to keep his children. As far as he was concerned, it was all over. But poor Tamsin just went on suffering, with no end in sight.

The following morning we saw Dr Calder. She wanted to triple Tamsin's medication, and she explained to Tamsin that she had to stay in hospital while that was done. I saw the look on Tamsin's face.

'It's just for your safety,' I explained. 'It's not a punishment!'

'Am I missing something here? Is that what you think?' enquired Dr Calder, startled, and Tamsin nodded miserably.

'Really, sweetheart, it's not that at all!' exclaimed Dr Calder. 'We know now to be careful about when we take you out, and we also want you to meet the staff at the Day Unit, so that when you come as an outpatient, you'll feel comfortable there.'

Tamsin had to be content with that.

February 1999

As the week wore on, Tamsin gradually improved, but her opposition to being in hospital remained implacable. It didn't help that the night staff suddenly began to ask me to leave at 9.45 p.m. Tamsin's last medication was at ten o'clock, and usually I stayed until she'd had that and was settled in bed.

However, there was another teenager in the ward, who had a 'professional hospital mother'. Her children had all been in and out of hospital, and she knew everything about everything. She ordered the nurses around like private servants; she regaled us all with tales of how she had held parties in the smoking room until midnight or later. No wonder the staff wanted all visitors out by 9.45 p.m.

On Friday morning I had a phone call from Kim, my solicitor. She had finally received a reply to her letter. Daniel categorically denied having made the phone calls to the agricultural college, and was visiting his solicitor in a couple of weeks. Could I get a letter from the college? I certainly could! I had it within a couple of days.

I managed to see Dr Calder alone that day, and explained what Daniel had been doing. I was trying to collect enough evidence to get an interdict, to keep Daniel away from Tamsin but, because Tamsin was over sixteen, she might have to do it herself. I was fearful of the consequences of Tamsin knowing that her father was looking for her.

Dr Calder agreed that just knowing would be very bad for Tamsin; but it might be unavoidable. We agreed to keep in touch without saying anything to Tamsin for the moment.

I also had a chat with Tamsin's nurse that day, who told me that Tamsin was taking antipsychotic drugs. I didn't say anything to her, but I was deeply disturbed. Dr Brown had said the drugs were tranquillisers, and Dr Bowie had seemed quite certain that Tamsin was not psychotic. So why was she on antipsychotics? I resolved to talk to Dr Calder the following Monday.

I looked up psychotic illness in one of my textbooks. As I had thought, there are two types of psychotic illness: mood disorders, such as manic depression and psychotic depression; and thought disorders, the schizophrenias. Schizophrenia is not a single illness, rather a group of illnesses, caused by a chemical imbalance in the brain. Mood disorders are treated with lithium, and thought disorders with antipsychotics. As I looked down the long list of signs and symptoms which might indicate a schizophrenia, I had to admit that Tamsin showed a lot of them.

I brought Tamsin home and we had a peaceful weekend. The drugs made Tamsin very drowsy and she slept a good deal. She was reluctant to return to the hospital on Monday, but I was fairly sure she would be allowed out on pass again soon.

Early that week I received the letter from the college, confirming that a Mr Schenker had phoned in late September/early October, looking for his daughter Tamsin. He had been persistent and rude; he had called three times in one day, and on at least one other occasion. I took the letter to Kim.

'I can't get you an interdict with this,' she explained sadly. 'It's a horrible situation to be in, and all the sympathies are with you, but because Tamsin is over sixteen, any interdict would have to be applied for by her.' She looked thoughtfully at the letter for a few moments and tapped her teeth with it. 'Just stay here for a minute and I'll show this to one of my colleagues who does criminal work.'

She returned a few moments later. 'He says you should take this to the police,' she told me.

I went home, called the police and explained what was happening. But they were adamant. They could do nothing without an interdict.

'I do not understand why these men are released from prison without some sort of restriction on contacting their victims!' I raged.

To my utter astonishment, she replied, 'They are. He was the subject of a restraining order while he was on parole. But all his restrictions have ended now, and there's nothing we can do until your daughter has an interdict.'

'Well, if that's the case,' I said, 'he made the phone calls while he was under the restraining order.'

'It doesn't matter,' she replied, 'it's too long ago. If it had been reported at the time, we could have done something, but it's too late now.'

I put the phone down, enraged and bitter. Once again

Daniel had broken the law and been allowed to get away with it! And even though his first contact with Tamsin would certainly cause a lot of damage, and might result in her taking her own life, still he was allowed yet another 'first bite'! Was there no end to his protection? No beginning to Tamsin's protection? Why weren't we told that he was the subject of a restraining order while on parole? It would have meant a lot less worry for us. And now, when we did have evidence of an attempt to contact, Kim had discovered that it had happened too long ago for an injunction to be granted; we would need concrete evidence of an attempt to contact that had occurred within the preceding two to three weeks.

I saw Dr Calder at the end of the week and explained that there was nothing I could do personally to obtain legal protection for Tamsin, because of her age. We looked at each other.

'We're going to have to tell her,' said Dr Calder, and I nodded.

'Well, let's leave it until Monday, and we'll do it together,' she suggested, and I agreed. Then I asked her about Tamsin's medication.

'Dr Brown seemed quite certain that she does have a psychotic illness,' she told me. 'People hear voices for all sorts of reasons, but Tamsin has repeatedly given us clear descriptions of hers, and that's usually a good sign that they are psychotic.'

'Well, if she is schizophrenic, she's been schizophrenic for the past two years!' I exclaimed. 'She's been having freakies since December 1996 – the only difference now is that she's got the voices added, and she's hurt herself more seriously.'

'We think she's been developing it for some time,' Dr

Calder agreed. 'You have to be born with a tendency to psychotic illness, but it also needs a trigger, and it seems certain that for Tamsin, the abuse was the trigger.'

'I'm aware that I have a bias towards psychotherapy,' I began carefully, 'but I do think Tamsin needs to talk more about the abuse.'

'Sheila seems to think she's covered just about everything,' Dr Calder replied. 'But in any case, psychotherapy is contraindicated because of the psychotic illness – it would make it much worse. It's too intense.'

We chatted for a few minutes more, and then Dr Calder brought Tamsin into the consulting room, and we discussed her psychotic illness with her. This was the first time either of us had really been told what was going on.

In the car going home, Tamsin turned to me and demanded, 'What exactly is wrong with me, then?'

I explained what I knew. 'It doesn't mean you will always be ill; lots of kids have a psychotic episode in their teens or twenties, and then recover and lead completely normal lives. We just have to get your medication right.'

'So I've got schizophrenia,' Tamsin announced.

'It's a form of schizophrenia,' I temporised, 'but it's too early to say whether it's temporary or permanent.'

Tamsin laughed. 'It was so funny this morning, watching you and Dr Calder tiptoeing around it and talking about psychotic illness! Why not just come right out and say it? Everybody knows what hearing voices means!'

We discussed it over and over, until Tamsin was satisfied that she knew everything that I did. And I had had a reminder of just how bright she is, and a warning not to underestimate her.

The following Monday, Dr Calder and I explained as gently as we could what Daniel had been up to. Tamsin heard us out in silence, looking serious.

'Are you all right?' I asked her.

'Yes,' she said. 'It's just a bit of a shock! It would have been nice if people told me what was going on.'

'It's the first and only time I have not been a hundred per cent truthful with you,' I said. 'I have never lied to you. I just didn't see any point in saying anything unless it was essential.'

'It's okay, Mum,' she replied with an impish gleam in her eye, 'I've used that distinction myself!'

We agreed to increase Tamsin's medication again, and Tamsin was formally discharged, to continue attending the day unit four days a week. But from that moment, she began to go downhill sharply.

We made an appointment to see a solicitor specialising in child law in two days' time. Her name was Elizabeth King, and she had guided Sam through the residence order proceedings.

Sam had recently decided that she wanted to sue Daniel. After all, Tamsin was in line for several thousand pounds in compensation. Sam had certainly not suffered as much as Tamsin, but she had suffered nevertheless, and would continue to suffer financial disadvantage in the future, compared to what her circumstances would have been if Daniel had been a decent man. Elizabeth had explained that she could take only a preliminary statement from Sam, before applying to the Legal Aid Board for funding to take statements from me and other witnesses.

Tamsin had decided to apply for income support, and to

sue her father for maintenance. I introduced Tamsin to Elizabeth and showed her the letter from the college. 'This is too old,' she told me sadly. 'We would need much more recent evidence that he has been looking for you. Have you got any?'

'No,' I explained, 'but we only found out about this by accident,' and I explained about Daniel's mother and Sam's birthday card. 'It's very hard to find out what's going on behind your back.'

'Well, it's a horrible situation to be in, but we really can't do anything without more recent evidence. If you find out anything more, get in touch immediately and we'll go straight to court. In the meantime, I'd like to see a copy of the Minute of Agreement from the divorce, to check if there is any age limit on child support. You certainly have an excellent case for damages against your father, Tamsin, but I think you have to be in education for him to maintain you.'

Although I was careful not to let Tamsin see, I was incandescent with rage! Once again Daniel had escaped. All Elizabeth could do was to write to Daniel via his solicitor. Kim had written again, confirming that we had documentary evidence of the phone calls, and telling Daniel that his daughter had schizophrenia, and if he cared at all for her, he should make sure he kept well away.

At home I looked out the Minute of Agreement and read it idly, then suddenly with more interest. I had forgotten! Daniel had agreed in the Minute not to contact either of his children. I called Tamsin's solicitor but she couldn't discuss it with me, only with Tamsin, and so we saw her again. But still there was nothing she could do until we had more recent evidence. Another round to Daniel! And what had been the point of registering the Minute of Agreement with the court if we could not enforce it?

Since Christmas we had got into the habit of keeping all the knives in the house in a locking cupboard; Tamsin had asked for this, and we were happy to comply. A couple of nights later, Tamsin was really unwell. She had voices in her head, although not The Doctors, and she complained about her skin feeling crawly and itchy. I gave her some diazepam, and then suggested she should go and have a shower. I cleared the bathroom of razors and laid out towels for her, and she went in.

A couple of minutes later, I knocked on the door, to see if I could use the toilet before she went into the shower. There was no answer. I couldn't hear anything, and so I knocked again. Still no answer. I opened the door and went in, to find Tamsin sitting on the toilet lid, shaving the skin off the back of her hand with a razor which I must have missed. She was completely silent, concentrating intently on her task and unaware of my entrance.

'Oh, Tamsin, don't do that!' I cried and snatched the razor away. She seemed to 'come to' and began to cry as I pressed toilet paper over the raw patch on her hand.

'Don't be angry with me,' she begged. 'I didn't want to do it. It was The Doctors; they made me!'

'I'm not angry with you,' I reassured her.

'You sounded angry!'

'I'm just angry with myself for not being more careful,' I said gently as I looked at the damage. Fortunately I had reached her quickly, and there were just a couple of scrapes. I took her through to the sitting room, hugging her and talking gently, while Sam went through the whole house, removing anything with which Tamsin could conceivably hurt herself. I called the duty doctor at the hospital and was advised to increase her medication again. She was now on the maximum dose.

Tamsin was also having a lot of nightmares at this time, and was prescribed sleeping pills to help her over the next week or so. And she had lots of diazepam. But she just got worse and worse. She would not go to the Day Unit. She would not go out with me unless I insisted, and she certainly would not go out alone. She would not even go into the garden, in case her father saw her.

I tried to reassure her. 'He won't come anywhere near you while you're with me,' I said. 'He's far too much of a coward!' But she sank further and further into her own world.

That Thursday morning I had a tutorial which I had to attend, as I was giving a paper. It was also the day that Daniel was to see his solicitor in Edinburgh, and I really wasn't prepared to leave Tamsin at home alone. It was just possible that Daniel and his mother had our new address and would be unable to resist at least driving past. And if Tamsin saw them . . .

I tried everyone I could think of who might be able to look after Tamsin. There was nowhere at the hospital where she could go. Most of my friends would be working. I tried social services, but because Tamsin had not been formally assessed for community care, they were unable to help.

The only solution was for her to come with me. There is a tiny postgrad common room, which we share with the photocopier, and there are tea- and coffee-making facilities there. It is right next door to the office. I cleared it with the secretaries, and introduced Tamsin to a PhD student before leaving for my tutorial. He and Tamsin apparently spent most of the morning together, and it reinforced Tamsin's desire to go to university.

I had another tutorial the next day, but Tamsin was exhausted from having risen so early the previous day. She insisted she would be fine sleeping at home; and she was.

But the following week just got worse. On Monday night she had a visit from The Doctors. On Tuesday night she was as low as I've ever seen her.

'I can't see any point in going on,' she cried to me. 'I keep wanting to hurt myself! It's the only thing that helps the pain in my head. I've got so much pain in my head, and I just can't bear it!'

I just didn't know what to say to her. She was in such agony! I couldn't help crying myself, and she apologised for making me cry. What a kid! In the depths of her own misery, she could feel sorry and guilty for making me sad.

Eventually I suggested that we should call the Samaritans. 'You won't get through,' Tamsin said hopelessly. 'I've phoned ChildLine so often, and it's always engaged.' And it was engaged. But I kept trying, holding Tamsin and talking to her all the time, and at last we got through. I explained the circumstances and then handed the phone over.

Tamsin began by crying, but gradually the counsellor engaged her in conversation, and she calmed down. She talked about Sam and me, and about Andrew, who was still as attentive as ever. After about half an hour, Tamsin said she'd better get off the phone, so that other people could get through.

After that, she settled down for the night. I called the

hospital the next day. Dr Calder couldn't see her that day, but she was given an appointment for Thursday morning. That night The Doctors returned. Sam and I were used to it by now; we would put Tamsin's favourite Dr Hook CD on to play, and hold Tamsin and rock her and encourage her to sing along while the diazepam took effect. Eventually she settled down and fell asleep.

The next day I explained to Dr Calder what had been happening. She questioned Tamsin gently. It turned out that, as the drugs cleared her mind, she had begun to recover a lot of bad memories. There was now only one incident of abuse where she had a blank spot. Memories of the abuse made Tamsin want to hurt herself, although the rational part of her didn't want that at all. Dr Calder sat back.

'There are two illnesses going on here which are interacting with each other,' she said. 'But we can't do much about the memories of abuse until the psychotic illness is more stable. I think we need to change your drugs, and you need to come into the ward for that. Is that all right with you?'

Tamsin agreed. She seemed relieved that someone else was going to take control for a while. The only reservations I had were about Tamsin's safety. She was always much worse at night, but the night staff wanted me to leave before she was asleep. 'There are only three nurses,' I explained, 'and with the best will in the world, they can't watch everyone all the time.'

Dr Calder said that was no problem – they would arrange for Tamsin to be constantly watched. We set off down to the ward. Tamsin was given a single room, and seemed quite content. I spoke to one of the nurses before I left.

'Dr Calder didn't have a chance to tell you this herself,' she explained, 'but we would like you to stay away during the day. Tamsin doesn't talk to us while you're around, and we can't do a proper assessment if we can't talk to her.'

I thought it was highly unlikely that Tamsin would suddenly start chatting to the nurses just because I wasn't there. It had taken me nearly eighteen years to teach her to talk to me, and I didn't think she would suddenly start talking to the nurses. But I agreed; I could see their point, and who knows, maybe she would talk if I wasn't there.

Sam stayed at home that evening; she had a lot of home-work, and didn't want to visit the ward. When I arrived, Tamsin was obviously very angry with me.

'I don't want to be here!' she cried. 'I want to come home tonight! Why did you make me come here again?'

'But you agreed,' I stammered, astonished.

'No, I didn't!' she snapped. 'I don't want to be here!'

'Did they tell you I'm not allowed to visit during the day?' I asked.

'Yes!' she cried, bursting into tears. She allowed me to hug her as I tried to explain the thinking behind the visiting ban, but she would not be consoled. She was still quite angry with me as I helped her into bed and tried to settle her.

After twenty-four hours, Tamsin was taken off constant observation and put on fifteen-minute observations. She had made no attempt to harm herself and, apart from still being angry with me, she seemed to have resigned herself to some time in the ward. The weekend went very slowly; it was hard being at home all day while Tamsin was in hospital. But I had work to do, a presentation to write and lots of reading. Somehow I was keeping up, although I read up on only one current issue, the one on which I intended to write an essay at the end of term.

Tamsin improved rapidly on the new medication. She phoned on Monday and said she had an overnight pass. I collected her in the late afternoon, and was almost as glad to have her at home as she was to be there. We snuggled up together on the settee all night, and she slept until lunchtime the next day. She returned to the ward in time for tea.

She stayed in until Friday, going to the Day Unit from the ward, and then came home for the weekend. She was so much better! No voices, no fears. We had taken all the knives out of the cupboard. The nurses had explained that Tamsin had to be allowed access; she had to learn not to hurt herself, because she could not stay in a protected environment for ever.

On Monday we returned to the hospital, but Tamsin insisted on going to Outpatients rather than the ward. Dr Calder saw us sitting there.

'Are you waiting to see me?' she asked. 'I've only got a couple of minutes.'

'It'll only take a couple of minutes,' Tamsin assured her, and she laughed. We told her that everything had been fine, and she agreed to discharge Tamsin. She still attended the Day Unit four days a week, and she began to see a clinical psychologist for neuropsychological testing. 'We think that her illness may have affected her academic performance,' Dr Calder explained, 'and now that she's getting treatment, it should improve.'

At the end of the month I had a letter from Kim, passing

on a letter from Daniel's solicitor. (It all gets very compli-
cated when everyone has a separate solicitor!) Daniel still
categorically denied having made phone calls to the college.
He had been in South East Asia for the whole of that period
of time, and could produce ship's records to show that he
had not called. He said he was concerned for Tamsin's
welfare and would not attempt to contact her.

Then there was a large paragraph about how upset Mrs
Schenker had been by my letter, and by letters which my
mother had written to Daniel and his mother. They had
already asked us not to write again – setting up the conditions so that they could get a non-harassment order
against me! Surreal! Bizarre! Obviously Daniel's solicitor
had read the letters and told them they had no grounds
for a non-harassment order; but there was a request that
any future correspondence should go through Daniel's
solicitor.

I thought about it for a while. When Daniel and I were
in South East Asia in 1980, we had been able to go into any
hotel and call the UK; and telecommunications had
improved a bit since then. Showing that he had been in
South East Asia and producing ship's records proved
nothing. As for his daughters' welfare, I thought bitterly,
if Daniel was so concerned for it, why didn't he tell the
Child Support Agency the truth and start supporting them
properly?

I was sorry Mrs Schenker had been upset; but she had no
one to blame but herself and her son. She had begun all
this by writing to our council flat address, and her son had
begun all the trouble in the first place. I didn't want any
contact with any of them, for the rest of my life. But I am

not prepared to stand by while Daniel hurts Tamsin yet again. I think they understand that, now.

Sam received some bad news. When she had visited the solicitor, Elizabeth, she had described only the difficulties which she had experienced since Tamsin had become ill the previous December. The Legal Aid Board had refused any further funding, as they did not believe that a case could be made against Daniel. I asked Sam how much she had told Elizabeth, but she couldn't remember. I wrote to Elizabeth myself, explaining the return of Sam's asthma, her schooling difficulties, the loss of her home, our poverty – all that Sam had suffered since December 1996, and would continue to suffer for the foreseeable future.

At the end of the month, we had a silent phone call. I dialled 1471 but it was not a number I recognised. I wrote it down – I don't know why.

March 1999

In the first week of March we had another two silent phone calls. One was 'Number Withheld', and the other was an English area code which I didn't recognise. I wrote these down, too. After thinking about it for a while, I called the Nuisance Calls Bureau and explained what had been happening. The investigator put a trace on the line, and we waited to see what, if anything, would happen.

Because Tamsin was now receiving income support, I no longer received child benefit for her, and Daniel no longer had to pay child support for her. The CSA recalculated his payments and sent me a new schedule – still with an alleged income of £286 per week. I called them.

'You know these earnings figures are completely bogus, don't you?' I suggested.

'No,' came the reply.

I explained again that I had negotiated the job for Daniel, that Jepson's had been offering £30,000 a year, that he had been earning £29,000 a year before he was arrested. I also explained about Daniel's attempts to find Tamsin and the silent phone calls.

'Do you have any evidence?' I was asked. I didn't, of course, have anything on paper from Jepson's, but I did have a fax Daniel had sent in January 1997 with the new pay rates. I also had the letter from the college, and the correspondence between our solicitors, and the fact that Daniel had underpaid child support in February and March. I bundled it all up and sent it off. Eventually I learnt that Daniel had been asked for a more recent pay slip, and was in fact earning £420 a week. The final assessment gave us slightly more for Sam alone than we had been receiving for both girls.

The independent review was finally held, at which I was told I should have asked for a 'change of circumstances' review; but because I had not supplied all the information I had until March, the increased payments could not be back-dated to the previous July. Another round to Daniel! I reckon he cheated us out of around £1,500.

The next three weeks were the best of the year so far. Tamsin attended the Day Unit happily, and even began to come home by bus. This was a major step for her. She has always got lost easily because she has so little spatial awareness, and finds it hard to make maps in her head, unlike most people.

I threw myself into my work. I had two 3,000-word essays to write by the end of term, and I was also beginning to put together a PhD proposal. The deadline for grant applications was the end of April.

I had talked over the possibility of staying to do a PhD with Graham, my director of studies, and he was very encouraging. I went to see the head of department, Spiros

– everyone is on first-name terms at postgrad level. He had been tutoring us in Aristotle's philosophy, and had seemed impressed by the two presentations I did for him. He, too, was encouraging about my aspirations, which was very good for my self-esteem.

I wrote Spiros' essay and handed it in on time. The other essay was for Graham who is a little less scary, and he had given me an extra week.

The following Friday, Tamsin came to me as we were settling down for the night. 'I need to talk about it,' she said, and I knew she meant the abuse.

'I'm quite happy to talk about anything with you,' I explained carefully, 'but I don't want to hear details about what Daniel did. It puts pictures in my head that I can't get rid of.'

Unfortunately that was exactly what Tamsin did want to talk about. I was desperate to ensure that she didn't feel I was pushing her away; but at the same time, I was aware that if I had to listen to the details of Daniel's behaviour, I wasn't sure how I would cope with that. And I needed to stay in one piece, for the girls' sakes.

So we called the Samaritans again. I left Tamsin in the sitting room to talk, and I left the sitting room and bedroom doors open so that I could hear if she called me, but I couldn't hear what she was saying. She talked for about half an hour, and seemed much more cheerful when she came through to bed.

The next day found me hard at work on my second essay. It was on a subject which I didn't wholly understand, and I was striving for understanding and trying to write at the same time. Tamsin was supposed to be cleaning the dog droppings off the grass in the garden before Sam cut it. Tamsin came in, satisfied that she had completed the job; but Sam complained bitterly that she was having to redo it because Tamsin had missed parts. Tamsin refused to go back out and also refused to tidy her part of our bedroom. In other words, it was a normal family situation, and Tamsin had been so well for the past three weeks that I forgot how ill she still was. I remonstrated with her and so did Sam.

The afternoon wore on. Tamsin stormed through to our bedroom after another complaint from Sam. After ten minutes or so I went through to see her.

'Look, what's the matter?' I began, as she stared stonily at the wall. 'Why are you being so difficult? It's not unreasonable to ask you to help.'

There was no reply.

'Are you feeling all right?' I continued. 'Are you just being a normal teenager or is there something wrong?'

Still no reply.

'Oh, well, I tried.' I shrugged, and went back to my essay. A couple of minutes later I heard Tamsin's voice, softly at first and then rising to a scream: 'No, no, no . . .' I rushed through and found her slapping at herself: the spiders were back!

I hugged her tightly and crooned to her. 'There are no spiders, it's all right, I'm sorry I was cross, honestly there are no spiders,' and gradually she came round. Sam rushed to get the diazepam and a drink, and we held Tamsin until she was calm. Then she explained that The Doctors had been around for the past hour or so. They had told her that I was evil and bad, and that she had to kill me; but she wouldn't do anything to hurt me, and so they sent the spiders.

I immediately increased Tamsin's regular medication, and made a mental note that in future, if she needed to talk, she also needed her medication increased for a few days. She settled down over the next couple of days, although she had a few bad nightmares. But she had planned a visit to stay with Andrew and his parents for two days the next week, and she was determined not to miss that.

We discussed the events of the weekend with Dr Calder on Monday, and she agreed that we would need to address the abuse as a matter of some urgency. Tamsin admitted that she hadn't really talked about anything important to Sheila. She was extremely reluctant to talk to anyone at the hospital; she felt it would be too embarrassing for them to know everything that had happened to her, if she had to see them every day. Dr Calder agreed to try and find an outside agency which could provide counselling while liaising closely with the hospital staff.

On Tuesday morning, we met Andrew at the station, and he took Tamsin home to his family in the west of Scotland. I had finished my essay and, with help from Spiros (who turned out not to be so frightening after all) I began writing a PhD proposal for funding applications. Sam was still at school, but term ended on Wednesday at lunchtime. I met Tamsin at the station on Thursday, and took her straight up to the hospital, to meet the psychologist for testing. Tamsin said she had been fine while she was away – no voices and no nightmares; and she agreed to come home by bus.

She was perfectly all right that evening, quite her usual self – until she got a phone call from a friend from school. Although Karen is a couple of years younger than Tamsin,

April 1999

Tamsin had another nightmare that night. She was rather subdued the following day. She went off to get ready for bed quite early, but came running through, screaming, 'The Doctors are back!'

We had worked out a routine by now, Sam and I. I held Tamsin tightly while getting out the diazepam, and Sam fetched her a drink. We put the music on, and sang, and did all the usual things, and eventually The Doctors went. But it took twenty milligrams of diazepam to chase them off.

Tamsin slept most of the next day. It was Easter Saturday, and we enjoyed a rugby match on TV in the afternoon. We were watching TV in the evening when Tamsin got up and left the room. I hardly noticed, or if I did I assumed she had gone to the toilet. But she didn't return, and suddenly my 'antennae' began to prickle. I went to find her, and discovered her sitting on the bedroom floor, cutting the back of her hand with a pair of scissors.

I took them gently from her, and she began to cry. 'I didn't mean to hurt myself! I didn't want to do it. It was The Doctors – they made me!' She hadn't had enough time to do any real damage, and Sam and I swung into the diazepam-and-drink routine. I sat on the settee and hugged Tamsin, as she told me that The Doctors had appeared and told her not to tell me they were there. She was to go through to the kitchen and cut her hand. She had gone into the kitchen and picked up the first knife she came across.

I had cooked a turkey that afternoon for the following day. We didn't have room in the fridge to store it whole, and so I had carved it at teatime. The first knife I used was blunt but, rather than wash it, sharpen it and reuse it, I had just taken another knife.

Tamsin had picked up the blunt knife and drawn it across the back of her hand, but it had hurt a lot because of its bluntness. That was why she had decided to use scissors instead.

'You've got a guardian angel somewhere!' I told her. 'If you'd picked up the sharp knife, you probably would have cut the tendons.'

'I hope I don't have to go into hospital!' she said. 'I don't want to go into the ward.'

'Well, you probably won't,' I reassured her.

'But maybe it's the best place for me just now,' she suggested. Given her dislike of being in hospital, I had to take that seriously. We discussed it for a few minutes, and then I rang the duty doctor, who agreed that she certainly should be seen that evening.

We drove up to the hospital. Tamsin was floating in and out of hallucinations, and she had a couple of attacks of 'the spiders' before we arrived. It seemed to take ages for the doctor to see her — he was trying to find her notes — and all the time Sam and I sat holding her hands to try and keep her with us.

We told the duty doctor what had happened; he left the final choice to us of whether Tamsin should be admitted, and Tamsin decided she would feel safer in the ward. It was one o'clock in the morning before all the admission procedures were complete, and Sam and I could come home.

The following evening I was sitting in the smoking room with Tamsin. We had discussed what she could do to let me know if The Doctors came, without speaking, and we had agreed that she would flick her lighter without lighting a cigarette. At eight o'clock the signal came — The Doctors were back!

I went to get a nurse and returned to Tamsin. When no one came within a couple of minutes, we decided to go and find someone together. But as we went along the corridor, Tamsin began to talk to The Doctors.

'No, don't do that! I'm sorry I told! No!' and she began to scream and hit her legs.

I held her hand tightly and told her over and over that there were no spiders, as a nurse came running with medication.

'Are you sure?' Tamsin demanded desperately. 'I can see them!' and she began hitting herself again.

'Do you honestly think I would be sitting right here beside you if you were covered in spiders?' I laughed; for I don't like spiders any more than Tamsin does.

Soon she calmed down, and the rest of the evening passed without incident.

Tamsin stayed in the ward until the following Wednesday.

There were no restrictions on visiting, and her treatment was not altered at all. She steadily improved; it seemed she just needed a safe place to be, to recover from the events of the weekend. Dr Calder was absent that week, but Tamsin was given a two-day pass on Wednesday. She returned to the Day Unit on Thursday and Friday, and was given a weekend pass.

We saw Dr Calder in the ward the following Monday.

'There's a pattern beginning to emerge here,' she said, and I agreed. What seemed to happen was that the anti-psychotic drugs cleared Tamsin's mind, which enabled her to recover a lot of bad memories. She then needed to talk about those memories, which stirred up the psychotic illness. It was a bit like walking a tightrope: every so often we fell off one side or another, but we learnt to cope.

Tamsin had another admission at the end of April, this time because of the excitement of her birthday. She had visits from The Doctors and the spiders every night for a week before her eighteenth birthday, but we coped at home. Tamsin was determined not to go into hospital for her birthday.

On the big day she managed to hold everything together really well. When we were on holiday in Spain in 1989, she and Sam were given a benjamin of champagne each, which I said they could drink on their eighteenth birthdays – and we still had them. Tamsin managed to get through the whole day without diazepam, so that she could drink at night. We had discussed this with her consultant, who had authorised a small amount of fizz just for one day – but only if Tamsin had not taken diazepam!

Sam and I began her birthday by collecting croissants for

breakfast. I also bought her a bouquet of roses, while Sam bought her a 'Taz' helium balloon. Once the coffee had brewed, we woke Tamsin and gave her her presents. I had bought gold earrings for her, and Sam had bought her a cigarette case and lighter, which Tamsin thinks is the height of sophistication. My parents sent her a gold cross, something for which she had asked, and she was thrilled with it.

By the time Tamsin had opened her presents and eaten breakfast, it was time to leave for the Day Unit. Sam was on exam leave for her Standard Grades, and stayed at home to do some work. I dropped in at the university for a while before collecting Tamsin and bringing her home.

Andrew arrived at five o'clock, while we were in the throes of dressing and make-up. We were going to our local restaurant for a meal. Andrew had brought Tamsin a beautiful necklace, and also a lovely brooch from his parents.

We enjoyed our meal, and came home to crack open the champagne. I had a bottle of Martini Brut for Andrew, Sam and me, and Tamsin had a glass of that, too. But that wasn't a good idea – it wasn't long before she was feeling sick and dizzy.

Andrew stayed the night in Sam's bedroom, while Sam slept on the sitting-room floor. Not the best preparation for her English exam, but she didn't seem to mind. Tamsin was fine all the next day, but became really ill at night. Suddenly the spiders had begun to appear without any warning from The Doctors. It really freaked Tamsin out; she could under-stand – just – that these were hallucinations, but she does hate spiders, and it must be really hard to see them and feel them, and yet convince yourself that they are not real.

On Saturday morning Tamsin woke up hallucinating

spiders; they were all over her, me, her bed, her clothes — everywhere. And now The Doctors were threatening to hurt me if Tamsin didn't take an overdose. So it was back to the ward for a few days.

Part of the problem was because of another memory which had surfaced, which shocked all of us. Tamsin suddenly remembered that when she was about eleven, a friend called Grace complained that Daniel had made improper remarks about her figure.

Although the remarks made both Tamsin and Grace feel very uncomfortable, they didn't really understand then that there was anything sinister about his behaviour. Children believe that adults have their best interests at heart, even if what they do doesn't feel right. I was horrified to hear about these remarks. It was totally inappropriate behaviour towards an eleven-year-old and it made me extremely concerned about Daniel's motivations.

May 1999

I felt that this was something I had to report to social services, because Daniel seemed to have been assessed as 'low risk'; but his remarks to Grace seemed to suggest he might be a potential danger to other children. Once again, the police were called by social services; they wanted to interview Tamsin again, but obviously it had to be handled very carefully. Eventually it was decided that the interview should take place at the hospital with Dr Calder in attendance. I did not sit in on this interview – I do not want to know any more details of what Daniel did to Tamsin. Maybe this sounds selfish, but I needed to stay in one piece for the sake of both girls. Tamsin apparently coped really well with the interview. By this time she had remembered nearly everything that Daniel did, and gave a very full statement.

Once she was finished with Tamsin, the policewoman asked to see me. She said that they would want to interview Grace before talking again to Daniel; but, if Daniel admitted the truth of any of it, he would be charged again.

(Grace confirmed that Daniel had made suggestive remarks to her.) Whether accidentally, or 'accidentally-on-purpose', she had left Daniel's file on the table, and I had read most of the address almost before I realised what it was. I now knew which town he lived in; and I also knew that this was the town from which one of the 'silent' phone calls had been made.

In the meantime, Tamsin was once again admitted to hospital within days of giving her statement. Her medication was changed again, but she had to stay in the ward for almost two weeks without even an overnight pass before she was well enough to come home.

Sam sat all her exams. She sat her maths exam with a chest infection, and was robbed of revision time by being ill. But she was very laid-back about the whole thing. We would just have to wait until August to see how well she had done.

In the meantime I was working as best I could on my Master's dissertation. I was now working exclusively with my supervisor, Thomas, who (I later discovered) has two PhDs – one in biology and one in philosophy. As we got to know each other better, I often wondered if he could be dyslexic – he displayed a lot of the problems that Tamsin had shown. One day he asked me outright, and I agreed that I thought he probably did have dyslexia. He was astonished: 'All those exams I sat, and I never got extra time for one of them!' he exclaimed, laughing.

My work was, as always, an escape for me from the fraught tensions of everyday life: the constant underlying terror that something would happen to Tamsin, the more normal levels of anxiety about Sam, and the continuing struggle to put together enough money to live on. Our situation had recently become much worse: my housing and council tax benefit were cut by £120 per month, simply because Tamsin was now 18 and I no longer received a dependant's allowance for her. I got some help with that, though – I applied to the university's Hardship Fund. Normally, if one does a one-year course, one is expected to have enough funds for the year. But because of the extraordinary circumstances, they awarded me a grant of £400. Shortly after, I heard that I had won an academic prize of £500. As well as boosting my self-esteem, this gave us enough to live on for a few more months.

Then we heard that Tamsin had been awarded Disability Living Allowance at the highest care rate and the lower mobility rate, as well as Severe Disablement Allowance. The DLA was backdated to 1 February, and Tamsin received a cheque for around £1,300. We agreed that she would keep her SDA and give me the whole of her DLA, £68 per week, to cover her living expenses. For the first time in this whole sorry business, we now had just enough coming in each month to live on. What a relief that was! Tamsin also gave me £400 from her lump sum, and gave Sam £150, and we had a couple of wonderful 'shopping days'.

My parents came back to live in Scotland permanently at the beginning of June. They were truly shocked to see the sorry state Tamsin was in, and determined to do all they could to help. It was very reassuring having them close by, if only to have someone to talk to.

At last it seemed that life was getting back on an even keel. There was only one blot on the landscape – although I had been accepted to begin a PhD, I had once again been refused funding from the Student Awards Agency, so my participation was looking a bit doubtful. I contacted my MSPs, both local and regional – I thought perhaps with our new Scottish Parliament, they might be able to achieve something. Margaret Smith battled bravely on with Henry MacLeish, the minister for life-long learning, but to no avail. Meantime, Lord James Douglas-Hamilton put me in touch with the Scottish International Education Trust. One of its founders is the actor Sean Connery, and James always refers to it as the 'Sean Connery Trust', although other founders include the singer Kenneth MacKellar and the rugby player Andy Irvine. I also wrote to around fifty grant-making trusts which I trawled from the directory in the library. All I could do then was wait.

of this, gradually her visits to the Day Unit declined over the next few months.

In July Sam spent a week at the Abernethy Trust outdoor centre at Ardeonaig. This was arranged through school and sponsored by the local Rotary Club. This was a turning point for her, because for the first time she understood what the Christian life is all about, and she committed herself to being a Christian. She also discovered outdoor activities like climbing and paddling, which brought some uncomplicated enjoyment to her life. She returned home to find her exam results: four Standard Grades at grade 1 and four at grade 2. This was excellent work, given how ill she had been over the winter and the tense situation at home.

August brought a few changes. Tamsin's boyfriend Andrew bowed out of her life, telling her by telephone. She was upset for a few minutes and then said she had begun to find him boring anyway. She had one relapse of her mental illness: one day, out of the blue, she said that she would not take any more medication, because Daniel had poisoned it. She was convinced that he had broken into the house overnight and tampered with it. I managed to get an emergency appointment that day with a psychiatrist at the Young People's Unit, and we got a fresh prescription. Her dose was increased and she seemed to settle down again. Towards the end of August, with the Day Unit visits declining, she began attending a class one day a week to do Higher biology. She also began going to a dance class in modern ballroom, which she absolutely loved. There were positive moments: she travelled to and from the dance class by public transport, a big improvement for her. She had also travelled by bus to and from the Day Unit, but only for a few weeks until she stopped going altogether.

Sam returned to school determined to work hard at her Highers, because, having spent a week in August doing work experience at a local veterinary surgery, she wanted to be a vet and understood she would need to get five A grades at one sitting. She also began attending a local Episcopal church (which is the Church of England in Scotland). Once a month they had a Powerpoint concert for young people, in which local bands played while the Christian message was spread. Sam loved these and after a few months became one of the ushers, sporting an official tee shirt. She attended services every Sunday, too, and began working towards confirmation.

Through June, July and August I was working hard on my dissertation, meeting my supervisor most weeks, reading extensively and writing a chapter almost every week. I mostly enjoy writing, but writing philosophy is like tearing off chunks of flesh without anaesthetic. However, I persisted, writing and rewriting until my dissertation began to look a bit more scholarly. Finally, at the end of September, the deadline came. I felt there was nothing more I could do to improve it, and it was submitted. The last day was a tremendous rush, because I hadn't realised how long it would take to print it, and hadn't thought about putting it in a presentation folder. When I arrived at the philosophy office at 4 p.m., clutching a bundle of paper, the secretary took pity on me and found a folder in a cupboard. It was only some weeks later that I realised I had submitted it on single-line spacing instead of double, but it was too late to worry then. I felt quite fatalistic about the whole thing.

Autumn 1999–Spring 2000

We settled into something of a routine over the end of 1999 and beginning of 2000. Sam was busy at school, which she loved, coming home every day still smiling. But unfortunately, she had a lot of illness through the autumn and winter: chest infection after chest infection. This had a serious effect on her studies, and her exam grades at Christmas were not very encouraging. It was decided that she should sit only four Highers the following spring, which meant she almost certainly would not get a place at veterinary school. However, she now confided that she had felt she might be bored as a vet. She was very interested in genetics and achieved high grades at that branch of biology, and began leaning towards doing a science degree.

In the early spring of 2000 Sam joined the Combined Cadet Force (CCF) at her school and tramped off every Wednesday in full combat fatigues. Within the first few weeks she had gained badges for Second Class Indoor and First Class Outdoor rifle shooting. She continued to do well at judo, too, improving with every grading, and began coaching the youngest children at the judo school she attended. By now she was five feet ten inches in height, and a most commanding figure. I thought then that if Daniel were ever misguided enough to appear in front of her, he would have cause immediately to regret it!

Tamsin's mental health seemed to be stabilising: there were no more major crises, but gradually the dose of medication she needed increased, and gradually, so gradual that it was evident only in hindsight, she began withdrawing from life. She stopped going to the biology classes – too stressful – and even her beloved dancing now happened only if I drove her to and from the venue. She began to experience chest pains and palpitations almost every day, and it took us a while to realise that these appeared to be linked to her medication; but we had to wait several weeks to get an appointment to see her psychiatrist.

In January 2000 Tamsin was finally awarded £15,300 in criminal injuries compensation. This had been an ongoing battle, because the Criminal Injuries Board felt that she should have only the standard £3,000 award for 'prolonged and serious abuse'. It was not until I attended an appeal hearing in December that I realised they were of the opinion that her mental health issues were unconnected to the abuse. I found this hard to credit, so hard in fact that I didn't argue very strongly against it at the hearing. On the way back from Glasgow, where the appeal had been heard, arguments began to arise in my mind, and on reaching home I sent an email to the hearing, saying that while there certainly is a genetic basis for schizophrenia, it also requires a triggering event. Dr Calder, who had recently returned from a long bout of illness, also sent some supporting information, and this was enough to sway the appeal panel towards awarding her £15,000 for her mental health injuries, and ten per cent of the £3,000 award for abuse. Most of the money went into an investment account, but Tamsin used some of it to raise an action for damages against Daniel, which she achieved just before the deadline of her nineteenth birthday in April. If her suit for damages should succeed, she would have to repay the criminal injuries compensation, but the fact that it would come out of Daniel's pocket – or his mother's – would be very satisfying.

I heard in October that I had been awarded a one-year fees-only bursary from the university. I was awarded the department of philosophy's Small Scholarship award of £1,000 and the Scottish International Education Trust gave me a renewable grant of £2,000 – which earned me the unofficial title among postgrads as the James Bond Scholar (because Sean Connery is one of the sponsors)! This meant I could continue my studies and begin working for a PhD. Also in October I had one of the most frightening experiences of my life: giving a paper at the department's October conference. This was an annual event at which the previous year's MSc students and other postgrads were invited to give papers so that the new students and any new staff members could get to know each other and everyone in the department. Not so frightening, you might think, and certainly I didn't expect it to be frightening – wrong! One professor asked me the same question in three different ways, and I still couldn't answer it because I didn't understand what he was asking. It took my MSc supervisor to rescue me. That was the only paper I ever gave. I did, however, enjoy my studies tremendously. My only regret was that I could not be an Aristotle scholar, because I do not speak or understand classical Greek. I have huge admiration for Aristotle, especially for his book *De Anima* (On The Mind). His insights into psychology were achieved by arguing from first principles; there were no experiments or findings from neuroanatomy to help him, but he got an awe-inspiring amount right.

I heard in October that I had gained my MSc in philosophy, although unfortunately I didn't achieve a distinction. But given that it was a completely new discipline for me, and that I had spent more time nursing Tamsin than studying, I was pleased to get the degree. The award ceremony again took place in the McEwan Hall, but this time it was in December. I was thrilled to bits to get a cheer from my fellow postgrads when my name was read out.

Summer 2000

Finally we managed to get an appointment with a psychiatrist to discuss Tamsin's medication and the chest pains and palpitations she was experiencing. The doctor was of the opinion that these were being caused by her medication, which by now was above the recommended dosage. She wanted Tamsin to reduce the medication until she was completely off it. Tamsin was worried that this might cause the return of The Doctors and spiders, and indeed that was what happened. We had a pretty horrific week with increasing psychotic signs and symptoms; but because we had an appointment for the Friday, no one wanted to see Tamsin before then. It was only that Friday that we were told that the psychiatrists were now all agreed that Tamsin had a neurotic, rather than a psychotic, illness. Tamsin heard the word 'neurotic' and, understanding it in its common usage as a sign that she was somehow faking her illness, stormed off out of the building. But I felt this was good news: when used in the psychiatric sense, 'neurotic' refers to the less serious group of psychiatric illnesses, like depression and anxiety, which are potentially curable, rather than the more serious psychotic illnesses, which, although they respond to treatment, are chronic. It was not until much later that I realised that Tamsin and I should have been angry that she had been treated with serious psychiatric drugs for an illness which she did not have. However, by that time Tamsin was improving by leaps and bounds, and I felt the best thing to do was to put it behind us.

Sam had a super time that summer. During the summer term, she achieved her Blue Belt in judo. At the beginning of the school holidays, she went off to Bisley, to shoot in the annual CCF and army championships, and helped her school to win an award. A couple of weeks later, she went to CCF camp at Cultybraggan, learning survival skills among others; and all the boys were furious with her because, during a stalking exercise, she was the only person to get within firing range of the sentry. Finally, she went for four weeks in August to Ardeonaig, to be a helper. She absolutely loved her time there and began to think of a career in outdoor education.

The bad news for Sam was that she got caught up in the New Highers scandal, in which many, many students were awarded lower grades than expected or no grades at all. Sam had been expected to achieve at least a C in all four subjects. Instead she got a B for biology and a C for chemistry; she narrowly failed history, being awarded an Intermediate 2, and apparently completely failed English. The school appealed against her English 'fail' and she was eventually awarded a C.

We discussed these results with Sam's head of year: Sam

was still only 16 and could easily stay on for another two years. It was decided that she would take A levels in chemistry, biology and maths. We felt that Highers would lack credibility for some years, and that this would give her the best chance of reaching university entrance requirements.

While Sam was at Ardeonaig, Tamsin and I had a week's holiday in Galloway, in a caravan. This was made possible by my being awarded an academic prize of £700 and a bursary from the university's Hardship Fund of £1,500. We had a lovely time, driving around the wilds of Galloway and getting lost frequently. The weather was nice enough for a day or two at the beach. Tamsin found a riding school where she went for a hack; and she organised a lesson in horse driving for me, which I thoroughly enjoyed.

I had applied for funding again from SAAS, with a little more hope this year, because they had removed the requirement for postgrad students to be under the age of forty. But again I failed. However, I was awarded part of the Shaw Philosophical Fellowship, which paid the next year's fees. I knew I had the SIET's £2,000 grant and I also got a grant of £1,000 from the Crowther Fund, the Open University's postgraduate fund. So another year's study was assured.

The awful events of the past few years were, very slowly, beginning to fade from our memories. We were settled in a house we loved, and where we felt secure. Sam's future for the next two years was more academic work. Tamsin was leading a quiet life, but feeling more secure, although there were still times when she would not go out of the house in case Daniel should go by and see her. She still needed a lot of support, just to get through every day; but there were no more crises, no voices, no self-harming. Life was begin-ning to reach some kind of normality for us. This was by no means the beginning of the end of our story; but perhaps, just perhaps, it was the end of the beginning.

2005

Five years have now passed. The summer of 2000 did, indeed, prove to be the end of the beginning; and, although we have faced many more difficulties, nothing as bad as the first half of 1999 has happened. We have, indeed, had some successes to offset the occasional failure.

I began teaching first year philosophy students in the autumn of 2000, and discovered that I really did love teaching. Then I contacted the Open University and was offered the chance to teach social psychology, starting in February 2001. The good news about this was that I could now see a career path opening. The bad news was that I earned too much to continue receiving severe disablement allowance; but, because I was not paid to work more than sixteen hours per week, I could not access disability working tax credits. This led, the following autumn, to my tutoring six hours a week at the university, in an attempt to earn enough to continue being a student. Six hours a week doesn't sound like much; but, given preparation time and marking essays and exams, it is the same amount of undergraduate teaching which a full time lecturer is expected to undertake. It certainly cut into my study time.

The most momentous event of 2000 was that I heard that I was now to receive the money which Uncle Bob had left me. This meant that our lives would have to change again. If I kept the money I would no longer receive housing benefit, and there was enough money to pay my rent for five years, after which I would be penniless again. I had always intended to buy a property, if I could find something which we could afford in an area where we wanted to live. The only places in Edinburgh where we could get a flat or house for that amount were places where we would not want to live. However, a gardener's cottage came on the market in a village some seventeen miles south of Edinburgh city centre. It had obvious problems with damp, being under ground level at the back, and needed a lot of work. There was around a third of an acre garden, too, which had been – literally! – ploughed before it came on the market. But it was hidden away down a pretty lane, which dead-ended just past the cottage and was lined with silver birch trees, and we fell in love with it.

I was to receive £33,000 from my uncle, and the cottage was valued at £45,000. I applied for a mortgage without much hope, giving as income my teaching money, the money which Daniel paid for Sam while she was still at school, and my disability benefits. Much to my surprise, I was offered a mortgage of up to £45,000. Tamsin offered to put in her investment money too, so we made an offer and waited, gnawing our fingernails. Much as I had expected, we received a phone call saying our offer had not been accepted; I felt we could never be lucky enough to live in a place like that. We began looking elsewhere, and had our sights set on a house in East Calder, west of Edinburgh. Then out of the blue, my solicitor called to say the sale of the cottage had fallen through, and were we still interested? Were we ever!

We got most of the heavy building work done – installing damp protection, rewiring and replumbing – before we moved in. When we did move in, we had a toilet in the bathroom, but no sink or shower, and hot and cold water pipes in the kitchen – and nothing else. Within the first week or two, Sam and I had built and installed the kitchen, and built a stud wall to take a shower cubicle. We had no central heating, but we did, for the first time ever, have a dishwasher, which I loved. I hate washing up. For cooking we had a very early coal-fired Rayburn, which belched huge clouds of smoke every time we lit it, and a microwave. There was no gas supply at the cottage, and I didn't want an electric cooker. In the sitting room we had a wood-burning stove, which I loved, and which rapidly heated the whole sitting room. The bedrooms were cold, but we invested in electric blankets so that we were at least warm in bed. I lost half a stone in weight that first winter, simply from keeping myself warm.

It wasn't a very convenient place to live. For the first time I understood why my mother had dusted and hoovered our house every day when I was a child: log and coal fires make an enormous amount of mess, with ash getting everywhere. But we loved it. We felt safe: it was not the sort of place where anyone would drive idly by; in fact, it was quite hard to find.

Tamsin had bought Sam a small motorcycle, so that she

could drive herself to and from school: there was no way I could have driven her, because of the distances involved, and because of the cost of fuel; and the bus journey would have been pretty long and difficult. Sam loved her motor-cycle, and soon was happily driving herself through Edinburgh. I refused to think about what might happen to her, and actually nothing did. She had one minor accident on a wet day, which brought nothing more serious than bruises. Sam has always been a very well co-ordinated person, and had none of the difficulties with physical activity which Tamsin had as part of her learning difficulties.

That winter we discovered that the local Riding for the Disabled met at a farm just a couple of miles from our cottage, and soon Tamsin was riding regularly on Saturday mornings. Sam could not ride because she did not fit the criteria for being a client, but she was soon spending every Saturday as a helper, getting the horses and ponies ready and leading one of them with a rider. Tamsin had a bit of difficulty at first, because her body was a radically different shape than it had been the last time she rode, because of having gained several stones in weight while on the anti-psychotic drugs. But she still had the mental connection with horses that she had had before, and soon was riding happily and confidently.

After Christmas I was able to start riding again, too. My chiropractor had always said there was no reason for me not to ride, and so I had a try with RDA. I was surprised to find how easily my body arranged itself in the saddle, and to find that most of my skills, although rusty, were still there. I enjoyed this immensely.

In December 2001 I took part in the first protest march

of my life: against the proposed fox-hunting ban in Scotland. On the march we met some people from the so-called Rural Rebels, the 'militant' arm of the Countryside Alliance. I soon discovered that these were mostly very nice ordinary people who were somewhat astonished to find themselves labelled as public enemies, but who had great fun in living up to this while never actually breaking any laws. We soon became closely involved with this movement, and had lots of fun doorstopping Bute House, where the Scottish Cabinet met every Wednesday morning.

Friends in the Rural Rebels, having discovered that Tamsin's birthday was in April, put on a lunch for her at Brown's, a very posh restaurant in George Street. We had a super day there. The most exciting aspect of Tamsin's birthday was that Daniel's mother was finally forced to relinquish the money she had been putting into National Savings for her. It amounted to just over £3,000. I was sad to see that the final payment into this account was in December 1996. I felt that this expressed her feeling towards Tamsin, and thought it a pity that her grandchild was being punished for her son's offences. Tamsin had no doubts about what to do with it: she was going to buy a horse. She had worked out that she could pay for its keep, at the same stables that RDA used, out of her benefits. Just as well, really, because I was reaching the sad conclusion that if we were to stay at the cottage, I would have to give up my studies and get a full-time job. My health had improved so much from several years of regular chiropractic treatments that I felt I could cope with full-time work. After all, between my thesis work and my teaching, I had very little free time. A full-time job should be a breeze after this.

We soon found a horse for Tamsin. I had assumed that

she would want a nice bay horse of around 15.2 hands, with thoroughbred breeding, but no – she wanted a coloured cob. Off we went to a local dealer's yard, where we found a super black-and-white cob, well schooled, doing show-jumping and cross-country. One of the dealer's staff showed him off, and then Tamsin and Sam both tried riding him. Tamsin wasn't sure, so we made no commitment there, but went home to talk it through. To her credit, Tamsin spent a couple of days thinking about it, and then concluded that he was too good for her, and that she would not be able to do him justice. On our first visit to the dealer, she had noticed a brown-and-white cob going out for a hack as we arrived, and she asked to try this horse. He was at a much earlier stage in his schooling, and she obviously felt more at home with him. He didn't yet have a name, and we decided to call him Peter Piper, Peter for short – the name he is still known by today. Yes, she bought him!

When we started riding him at the RDA yard, it soon became apparent that Peter had had very little schooling. His balance was so bad that he could not trot a small circle carrying a rider, and he was very stiff on his left side. We went back to basics then, lungeing him to help improve his balance. Soon we were adding small jumps into the circle he worked on, and immediately we could see that he loved jumping. Within a few weeks he was jumping small jumps under saddle, full of enthusiasm.

The biggest problem about keeping Peter there was that the people who ran the RDA constantly interfered with how we looked after him and how we rode him. They had wanted Tamsin to buy an old slug, and felt that she would not be able to cope with a six-year-old cob full of life. They began to hide the materials which we used to make jumps, because they said he was too young and we would damage him. After a couple of months we moved him to a different yard on the other side of the village, which was a really good decision, because we were mostly left in peace to do what we wanted. The new yard had around forty acres set aside for a cross-country course, which could also be used for hacking out, and two schools, one of which had floodlights.

I might add that Tamsin's and my combined experience was probably more than the combined experience of any two of these people. We knew exactly what we were doing, and were very careful not to take things too quickly.

Peter proved to be the turning point for Tamsin. Now she had a reason to get out of bed every day. Some days it was still a struggle to get her up, but she knew she had to go and see to her horse. It wasn't easy for her. In the first two weeks at the new yard, Peter threw her three times. Because his left side was so stiff, he could turn on a sixpence and throw the rider out over his shoulder. She didn't ride him at all through that first winter, but we did go to the yard every day to turn him out into the fields in the morning, and fetch him in at night. His stable had to be cleaned every day, too.

Sam was also having new experiences. She left school in the summer of 2002 with A levels in Chemistry and Biology, an AS level in maths, and an unconditional offer to do a degree in Outdoor Leadership in Cumbria. All through the summer her solicitor waged war on Daniel to get him to provide a reasonable level of support for her. It was at this time that I discovered that he believed I was receiving £13,000 per year in disability benefits. I wish! The true figure was £5,000, but he would not accept this.

Finally, just before she was due to start in September, he caved in and agreed to pay for her uni accommodation (first-year students were expected to live on campus) and to provide a reasonable amount for equipment and living expenses. Off we trotted to the local outdoor shop, where Sam had a whale of a time, spending more than £1,000 on equipment and clothing.

A few days later, I drove her down to Cumbria for the start of her course. She was soon settled into the accommodation, which is arranged like a small village, with sixteen students in each building. It wasn't long before she was sure that this was, indeed, what she wanted to do. Her speciality was paddling, in canoes rather than kayaks, and she had paddling for two days every fortnight. She was in heaven.

All through the spring, summer and autumn of 2002, I had been searching fruitlessly for work. I was still teaching for the OU, and that brought in just about enough money to pay the mortgage and the bills, but it was a real struggle. Finally, in November I was offered a job working as an independent advocate for older people. Advocates in this sense are not legally trained. Their purpose is to discover what an older person is having trouble with and then help to find a solution, either by helping them to speak up or by speaking up for them if that is what they want. Advocates work by putting forward the older person's view, loudly and clearly, about their preferred solution, to everyone involved with the older person. Advocates are the only professionals who do not work in the person's 'best interests', but speak directly for them. Within a couple of weeks, I absolutely loved the job. I didn't much like the boss, and we had several clashes over the coming year or so, but I never stopped loving the work.

During the summer of 2003, Sam went to the USA with Camp America, working in a small Christian camp for girls only. She seemed to enjoy the work, although it was long hours: camp counsellors were on duty for twenty-three hours out of every twenty-four. They had one day off every week, and visited some of the small towns around the camp, which was in upstate New York and a long way from any city.

All that summer, Tamsin and I were visiting small horse shows around Edinburgh, of which there seemed to be at least one every weekend. There was a horse lorry at the yard which anyone could hire for £10 a day plus diesel, and we had friends who were happy to drive (I can only drive an automatic). Tamsin and Peter didn't have much success at show-jumping, largely I think because Tamsin was still lacking confidence in jumping, but we never left a show empty-handed, always having some success in the showing classes. All that seemed to be holding them back was Peter's manners, again because of Tamsin's lack of confidence. For example, she had a lot of trouble getting Peter to canter on the correct leg, but would only canter him in the school once or twice a day, so that neither of them was getting the work they needed to progress.

I was having some fun that summer, riding Peter round the cross-country course at the yard and jumping some tiny fences. We were at one show where there was a Clear Round course: you paid about £2 to jump round the course, and if you went clear, you got a rosette. Tamsin had been unable to get Peter past the first couple of jumps, and friends from the yard egged me on, so I had a go myself. I went flying through the air at the third jump, and managed to get concussed. No fool like an old fool!

Autumn came and brought sadness with it. All summer, Sam's dog, Lucy, had been showing signs of neck problems: her front legs began to knuckle over and she yelped if her head moved too quickly. We were back and forward to the local vets, but they seemed to be getting nowhere fast. Just after Sam returned from America, we contacted our Edinburgh vet, who arranged to see her that day. By this time, she couldn't really walk at all on her front legs. The vet arranged for an MRI scan the following Monday, but she died on Saturday morning. It came as a huge shock to us, because we had felt that she could get over this, and she was only eight years old.

Sam felt she had to have another dog immediately, that day — she couldn't bear the thought of not being a dog owner. We tried all the local rescue centres without success, and eventually found ourselves in Ayrshire, looking at a collie pup. We brought her home; Sam named her Meg. She was a complete bundle of mischief, not at all like Fly; in fact, she was almost a reincarnation of my first collie, Penny.

Sam's owning a pup required a rearrangement of her digs for the following year at uni. She had passed her driving test just after returning from America, and had bought my mother's little car. She had already booked a room at a farm near the campus, but the farmer was adamant that she was not allowed to take Meg with her. We found a static caravan with central heating down near Appleby, just in time for the start of term; however, it proved to be too big a distance for Sam to commute. Then she found a room in a house closer to campus, and that worked out very well for the first term. However, the house owner, who lived there with her collies, decreed after Christmas that Meg would not be allowed in the house (her collies lived in the garage). Sam pretty much had to stay there because it was so hard to find anywhere to rent which would allow pets; but she ended up most evenings working on her laptop, sitting out in the garage with Meg. In the meantime, Meg was having a lovely time chewing the inside of the car to ribbons! By the time the summer term began, Sam had decided to leave Meg at home with Tamsin and me, and to come home whenever she could. Meg seemed to settle down better.

In October Tamsin suddenly decided that she wanted to move Peter. She felt that some of the people at the yard had been unpleasant to her—it may have been the case, but equally it could be that she had misinterpreted what they had said or done. We found another, much smaller yard, where most of the horses were on full livery (all the care for the horse was provided, at a cost to the owner). Not only could Tamsin have Peter on DIY livery (where she provided all the care), the owner also said that Tamsin could stay at the yard all day and help out with the other horses in exchange for some riding lessons. This seemed to work out very well.

One Monday in November 2003, Sam called from uni to tell me she was sick. Her GP thought she might have appendicitis. I offered to drive down immediately to collect her, but she wanted to sleep overnight and see if it got better. The following day there was to be a meeting with other advocates from all over Scotland, where we could get to know each other and share practices and experiences. I called Sam before leaving home, and she thought she was no worse. I called again after reaching the meeting, which was being held in central Scotland. This time she felt she was quite a lot worse. My boss hadn't yet arrived, but I felt I needed to fetch Sam home. I arranged with a colleague that she would explain where I had gone, and shot off down the M74. When I arrived, Sam was obviously unwell. I helped her to pack some clothes and drove her home, arriving in time for her to see the emergency GP. He, too, felt she might have appendicitis. Tamsin was at the yard, as usual, and we drove round to ask if we could leave Meg there while I took Sam to the hospital. There she was admitted and kept under observation for two days, before being discharged. I returned to work on Friday, to find that I was in deep trouble, because I had not asked permission to go and fetch Sam.

A few weeks later, it was Tamsin's turn to be ill – out of the blue she started having what looked very much like epileptic seizures! She was rushed off to the new Royal Infirmary and then transferred to the Western General Hospital, which was the centre for neurology. Sam came home in a rush, and we waited anxiously to see what would happen next. Tamsin was put into the High Dependency Unit to begin with, but over the next few days the seizures declined and eventually stopped. She had some scans and an EEG, and the neurologist said that these were 'non-epileptic seizures', which were almost certainly connected to her mental health issues and the trauma she had experienced. Apparently these are quite common among kids who have been abused. There was no treatment for these – it seemed people just had to get used to them. This was, for Tamsin, quite unacceptable, but there was nothing we could do about it. Fortunately, these appear to have run their course, because she hasn't had any for many months now.

I don't remember much about the first two weeks I was in the hospital, but eventually I was diagnosed with colitis. After a week on steroids, I began to improve and was allowed home. It took eight months until I was able to work again, and then only part-time. I resigned from the advocacy project, because they needed an advocate who could actually work. I was extremely fortunate in that a part-time job came up at the uni where Sam was still studying. Although it was part-time, it was paid at lecturer's rates, which gave us just enough to live on and pay the mortgage.

Sam finished her degree and was awarded second-class honours, brilliant considering that she had been running the household as well as studying. Tamsin had a hard time while I was in hospital; I don't think she really understood what was happening. All she could see was that I was away from her, and Sam was telling her what to do. But the benefit of my being in hospital was that Tamsin was put in touch with a community psychiatric nurse as a matter of urgency. She enrolled in a course which was supposed to prepare her for work, or to live alone, and actually managed to get herself out of bed in time for the bus every day for the four weeks of the course. The mere fact of being out of Scotland, and away from where all the bad things had happened, seemed to be enough for her to forget a lot of her previous fears and anxieties.

My intuition, that first night when Tamsin disclosed the abuse, that my world had shifted, has proved to be correct. For a lot of the time I had been living from day to day, waiting for things to get back to normal. It has taken a long time to understand fully that things will never be 'normal' again. Our definition of normality has changed for ever, and with it our scale of values. We have learnt to live without enough money; we have learnt to live with uncertainty, and anxiety, and terror, and illness. Material goods no longer hold the charms they once did; we have enough clothes to cover our bodies, although they might be a bit worn; we manage to pay the mortgage and bills every month; we manage to eat every day, although not what you'd call a healthy diet. And we have enough to keep Tamsin's horse. Above all, we value each other and pull together as a team.

Many times when she was ill, I would sit and stroke Tamsin's hair to calm her while she fell asleep. I would look at her and remember holding her in my arms when she was a baby: I used to trace the clean, elegant sweep of her eyebrows with my finger; I used to look at her beautiful big blue eyes in their sockets, and marvel at her existence. I remember her as a toddler: determined to take on the whole world on her terms; struggling to make herself understood; throwing grass mowings in the air with gleeful giggles. I remember her as a child: long plaits swinging as she trotted around on ponies; utterly fearless over jumps, yet terrified of riding bicycles; learning to use words, to make outrageous puns, to tell silly jokes. I remember her as a teenager at boarding school: suddenly discovering that she was not the only child with specific learning difficulties; growing in confidence in her abilities; larking about with her friends. Throughout it all, she has fought against difficulties and frustrations with humour and courage, and has never allowed herself to be defeated.

Sam has been – well, it's hard to praise her highly enough. She has dealt with impossible situations with a wisdom and courage far beyond her years. She has her moments, but so do I and so does Tamsin, and it's by no means always me that calms things down when arguments become heated. No one could have blamed Sam if she had held a grudge against Tamsin for losing her dad, but to her credit she never has. She has always been quite clear that he carried the responsibility for his behaviour, and that Tamsin was not to blame.

In many ways I will never again be 'like most people'. When a cataclysm like this strikes, it changes the whole of your world – there isn't a part left untouched. Your system of values undergoes a radical revision, and you find out what is really important to you. For me, what matters most is my kids – helping them to recover, making sure we have a safe, secure place to live and enough food to eat, and that we can keep all our animals. Anything more than that is a luxury – it can be jettisoned at the slightest threat, with no regrets.

we belonged. Surely, some friends appear to have reasoned, he can't be a paedophile. Surely it must all have been an isolated incident, a misunderstanding, and he admitted to it without realising what the consequences might be. He was convicted, *only* because he admitted the abuse; Tamsin was too unwell to testify, and that's probably still the case. He admitted it, partly I think because he thought, and still thinks, that he didn't do anything really bad. And by their behaviour, some of our friends, particularly those in the church, agree that he didn't do anything really bad.

What is my evidence for this claim? While he was in prison, as described in the book, some of our friends wrote him supportive letters. One said that when he wrote to her, she thought about what she would want in his situation, and that was contact with friends. It seems to have been quite easy for the church people to deal with him. He's a sinner, and they know what to do with sinners: you forgive them and welcome them back into the fold, and pray for them. I went to a church service once where the address was given by a prison visitor. She made a point of saying that she prayed for abusers, and asked prayers for them during the service: a sort of 'Look at how caring I am!' After the service I challenged her on this: why pray for abusers, but not their victims? Of course we should also pray for victims, she replied; but I have yet to hear anyone, in any church service, even mention victims, never mind pray for them.

This attitude seems to be inherent in all branches of the Christian church. Andrew Greeley is a Catholic priest in Chicago whose novels I have greatly enjoyed over the years. This year I found a new novel which purported to deal with the Catholic church and child abuse. But the novel was written in such a way as to ask pardon for the erring priest; there was virtually no mention of the damaged children. He put his email address at the end of the book, and so I emailed him and attached a copy of my manuscript, and asked him what he thought of it. He never replied.

George, the minister at the church I used to belong to, seemed to be of this mind also. When I challenged him on the question of people writing to Daniel, he said categoric-ally that neither he nor anyone else in the church could be asked to take sides in our divorce. Fair enough; I never actu-ally expected people to take sides. What I did *not* expect, what hurt me almost more than anything else, was that in effect, they *did* take sides: they took Daniel's side. They supported him while he was in prison, and if he had ever turned up at the church, I bet they would have been pleased to see him. But when Tamsin had such an awful time, from December 1998 until the following autumn, they vanished. Nobody wrote to us; nobody phoned; nobody visited. Actually that's not quite true: George phoned three times in nine months, always about something else, and each time enquired how things were: just the same, I replied, and he rang off. It was only much later that I heard that George had told the people in the church that he was in constant touch with me, and that they should not contact us directly. If these rumours were true, then I'm surprised because I only got three calls in nine months. I'm not saying George lied; I'm just saying it's not my idea of being in constant touch. In any case, the people who I thought were my friends did not have to abide by what George said; they could have kept in touch anyway.

I met some of these people a few years later, when I attended a church service to celebrate my father's achievement in having been a lay preacher for more than forty years. Many of them ignored me, could not look at me, turned their backs when I came near. Those who did greet me were excessively cheerful and bright, and obviously were having a hard time interacting with me. That hurt, too, even though I should by then have known better. Needless to say, for the first time in my life I now no longer belong to a church.

At the heart of this betrayal is denial: denial of the harm that the abuser has caused. As I said above, it's easy for the church to deal with sinners, because they are told by the Bible how to deal with them. But to open yourself to the full knowledge of what the abuser has done is much too hard. Much easier to think of it as a mistake for which no one should suffer. Much easier to believe that the survivors made a big deal out of what wasn't really much of a sin. Much easier to live in denial. It almost seems that, to the church members, abusing your child is forgivable, but having a nervous breakdown is not.

I don't think people have a clear understanding of the harm that is caused by child sex abuse. Before Tamsin's disclosure, I thought I was a pretty clued-up parent, but I had not the slightest understanding of what lay in store for us. It's probably just as well. Tamsin has had the most horrendous time anyone could imagine – probably worse than it is possible to imagine. She was misdiagnosed as having schizophrenia, and inappropriately medicated as a result. She has self-harmed – and been blamed for attention-seeking because of it. Anyone who understands anything about self-harming knows that physical pain is easier to cope with than mental pain, and also removes one's attention from mental pain. It's a kind of safety valve. Unfortunately, apart from those who practise it, not many people – not even many mental health professionals – understand anything about self-harm. Tamsin is extremely anxious all the time, to the extent that she cannot tell what is important and what doesn't matter; she needs to have someone with her most of the time to give her a sense of proportion. Like most abused kids, she has been through a period of promiscuity. Yes, you'd think that abused kids would want nothing more to do with sex; but the fact is, they do not know, have not experienced, any other way of relating to men. If she ever has children – she'd like about five – she will have enormous issues about trust with any partner. The experience of having a child makes all of us examine our childhood with fresh eyes – how traumatic that will be for her! She will never get over the abuse by her father; it will taint the whole of her life. In this she is not unusual. In a survey carried out in the psychiatric hospital which treated her, seventy-six per cent of first admissions were due to abuse, physical, emotional and sexual. This makes child abuse the main cause of psychiatric illness.

I suspect that the damage runs less deep when a child is abused only once by someone who is not a relative or close friend; but the child is still damaged. Any child who has been abused is damaged by it. One abused child is one too many. The cost to society is huge, both in terms of lost potential and in cash terms. Tamsin, now 24 (in 2005), has never worked since leaving school. Only now, nine years after disclosing the abuse, is she well enough to attend college. Daniel has finally agreed to pay damages to Tamsin. The

Compensation Recovery Unit, which claws back state bene-fits when someone receives compensation, calculated that Tamsin has had £34,000 paid to her in DLA and incapacity benefit. On top of that are the costs of multiple admissions to hospital, medication, psychotherapy and other medical interventions. All because Daniel could not keep his hands to himself.

People don't understand that child sex abusers live in a constant state of deep denial. My first indication of this came after Daniel had been charged and bailed. I expected him to feel ashamed and contrite. Far from it — what he felt was anger, pure and simple. This anger appears also to have been fuelled by his family's attitude. In a letter which he sent me shortly after being charged (brought to me by the minister and against his bail conditions, I might add!), he said that his mother was 'rather bitter that the whole thing had not been dealt with within the family'. Throughout, he and his family have taken the attitude that this was an unfortunate mishap which I have blown out of all proportion. (This atti-tude is not dissimilar to that taken by our church friends.) It is true that in court he pleaded guilty to one charge of lewd and libidinous behaviour. However, Tamsin has always maintainted that what he did was not a one-off and I believe my daughter. She claims she was abused before she was ten years old and that it had gone on for at least five years, and possibly more. Daniel has always denied this and ultimately it is his word against his daughter's. What I do know is that he is capable of abusing his daughter.

Child sex abusers do not believe that what they do is wrong. They convince themselves that the child wants it to happen as much as they do; indeed, it is not uncommon for them to blame the child for leading them on. They tell each other that children are damaged only because of the fuss their parents make when they disclose the abuse. Daniel and his family still appear to believe that I divorced him for adultery. Before Sam started university, Daniel visited the campus to talk to those who would be her tutors. When I told the university that he was a sex offender, they were horrified, and said that if he turned up on campus again, he would be detained and handed over to the police. As he was on the Sex Offenders List, he was absolutely not allowed to visit a campus with 130 youngsters under the age of eighteen. But when our solicitor told him that the university knew of his status, he was absolutely livid. He said that that was all in the past and no longer relevant, again betraying the fact that he still denies causing Tamsin any harm.

In Daniel's case, nobody has tried to penetrate this denial. In his first contacts with the police, none of them would tell him how ill Tamsin was, for fear that he might harm himself. When the sheriff adjourned his hearing for background reports, nobody contacted Tamsin or me to find out the effects of his behaviour. While in prison, he was segregated with other sex offenders, for his own safety; nobody tried to make him face up to the consequences of his actions. When he was released on parole, with restrictions on contacting us, it didn't stop him from making strenuous efforts to contact Tamsin (which thankfully were unsuccessful). Because I did not learn of these attempts until two months later, he was not subject to any sanctions, because his actions had not been reported at the time they occurred, and at the time they were reported, he was no longer subject to restrictions. And I have no reason to believe that Daniel is any different from any other child sex offender.

It is in this denial that the danger to other children lies. If an abuser does not believe that what he does is harmful, he has no reason not to do it again. Daniel has been assessed as low risk; that is to say, he is not believed to be predatory. But in my mind I am absolutely certain that, if the circumstances arose where he had prolonged access to a child or children, he would offend again. He has no reason not to. He has learnt that if he is questioned about abuse and denies it, nothing will happen.

I have no doubt that if Tamsin's friend, Grace, had not rebuffed him sharply, he would have groomed her to the point where he could have abused her, too. He had certainly begun grooming Sam. And if he had access to other children, he would do this again. And who is going to deny him access to children? He is certainly not going to admit his conviction, because he feels he was unfairly pursued by a jealous wife. If he began another relationship where he had access to children, he's not going to confess that it's illegal for him to share a house with children.

What doesn't seem to be clearly understood is that child sex abuse is not just, or even mainly, about sex. As with other sex offences, it's about power, domination and control. So to allow a convicted sex offender to work in a girls' school, because he's only ever been convicted of abusing boys, is missing the point. The vast majority of child sex abuse never reaches the stage where charges are brought; and of those cases where the abuser is charged, very few convictions result. Thus, if a man — for they are overwhelmingly men — has a conviction for child sex abuse, it is unlikely to be for a first offence, and this person is, without a shadow of doubt, a danger to any child who comes within his sphere of influence. No one who has a conviction for child abuse should ever again be allowed anywhere near children.

There seems also to be a good deal of confusion over the difference between someone who is placed on the Sex Offenders Register for a conviction, and someone who is on the register for a caution. For someone to receive a police caution, they have to admit that they have committed an offence. So someone who has been cautioned for accessing child pornography, for example, should be barred from having contact with children, just as if they had been convicted of abusing a child. It might be thought that down-loading porn from the Internet is not the same thing as abusing a child. But don't forget, *every single picture of child-adult sex represents an abused child*: a child who has suffered like Tamsin. If there were no market, there would be no porn. In addition, it seems that men who enjoy looking at child pornography tend to move towards getting involved in abuse; the porn acts as a sort of appetiser.

We shouldn't be in any doubt about this. We're not talking here about members of the public at large; we're talking about men who have admitted a child sex offence, or who have been found guilty of committing a child sex offence. By their actions, they have marked themselves out as people who cannot be trusted around children. And don't forget, they chose this course of action. Nobody made them abuse a child. Nobody held a gun to their head. This was a free decision, freely taken. So their access to children should be denied for the rest of their lives.

The problem with having separate lists and rights of

appeal is that it sends out mixed messages: on the one hand, we want to mark out these men, but on the other, should they really lose their whole career? Who knows: maybe if the consequences to the offender were clearly and unequivocally stated, it might even act as a deterrent. If you know that you will lose your job or career if you abuse a child, it might make you think twice.

Of course, we as a society are also in denial. We become hysterical about so-called paedophiles; we hunt them down and drive them out of our communities. We warn our children about stranger-danger, about talking to or going off with men they don't know. We exercise ourselves about offenders who might be working in our schools. But the real source of danger to children is much closer to home than their school or playground. *The vast majority of abused children are abused by relatives or close friends.* This is the truth; but it's a truth we don't want to admit, never mind examine. We would much rather objectify offenders as paedophiles, and think of them as strange, shadowy figures, totally unlike the people we know.

Until we stop burying our heads in the sand, until we stop sending out mixed messages about child sex abuse, nothing will change. Men will continue to abuse children without penalty, and we will continue to believe myths about stranger-danger. And children will continue to be harmed. This is the bottom line. Children are precious, the most valuable resource in our society, and one abused child is one too many.

I had to write this book. I wrote most of it in a two-week period over the Easter holidays in 1999. I had meant to study, but the book kept getting in the way of everything else. I couldn't think of anything else until I had written it. It became an obsession. I sat at my computer all day and far into the night, until I couldn't lift my arms to the keyboard, only to begin again the next morning.

In many ways we three have been victimised. We have been made to feel like victims by the police, by social workers, by the church, by the civil and criminal law systems. But we're not victims. We have been savagely hurt, yes, and some of these hurts may never heal. But, as Tamsin pointed out: we're not victims – we're survivors!